OREGON

IDAHO

NEVADA

CALIF[ORNIA]

AGENCY VALLEY RIVER
Malheur
VALE

SILVIES VALLEY
HARNEY VALLEY
Silvies River

IRON MT.
STEENS MT.

FT. McDERMITT

Quin River

WINNEMUCCA

BLACK ROCK DESERT

LAKEVIEW

Sacramento Riv[er]

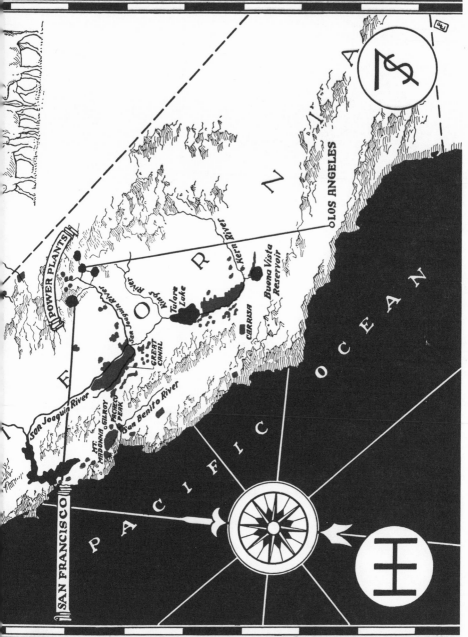

THE CATTLE KING

THE
CATTLE
KING

A DRAMATIZED
BIOGRAPHY

BY

EDWARD F. TREADWELL

WESTERN TANAGER PRESS
Santa Cruz

ISBN 0-934136-10-6

Library of Congress Card Number: 81-50165

Printed in the United States of America

Western Tanager Press
1111 Pacific Ave.
Santa Cruz, CA 95060

HENRY MILLER AT EIGHTY

ABOUT THE AUTHOR

EDWARD F. TREADWELL was born May 19, 1875, in Woodland, California. In 1897 he was graduated from Hastings Law College and shortly thereafter admitted to the State Bar. For fifteen years, beginning in 1907, Treadwell was general counsel for the firm of Miller & Lux, Inc. From 1901 to 1906 he served in the California Legislative Assembly; from 1908 to 1911 he was Mayor of Burlingame, California. Treadwell's practice was concentrated in the area of riparian and water rights, and he was involved in many important court cases in this field. He was married to Eulila Ayres and had three sons. Mr. Treadwell died in 1955 at the age of eighty.

The Cattle King was first published in 1931. A revised edition appeared in 1950 and was reprinted in 1966. This edition of *The Cattle King* is the third printing of that revision.

FOREWORD

AS THE writer starts upon this work, there are before him many shelves containing volumes of writings largely by himself. They contain many thousands of pages. Still he realizes that they are but the transitory work of a lawyer, written for occasions which have passed, and of little permanent value to his fellow men. The life of a lawyer is indeed "writ in water." The author has long had the ambition to write something of more permanent value, but has always recognized that he lacked sufficient imagination. That is the reason he selected the subject of this work, for it is a living demonstration of the saying that truth is stranger than fiction. No imagination could conjure up a story more replete with color, character, courage, perseverance, power, wealth and romance than the story of the real life sketched herein.

The west has produced many men who have reached the top of the ladder in many walks of life, but, when measured by actual achievement in connection with the development of the material resources of the west, Henry Miller holds a preëminent place. To own over one million acres of land situated in five states, fully stocked, two banks and their branches, reservoirs, and other properties, all operated as a unit, appraised at fifty million dollars, and acquired, developed, protected, reclaimed and irrigated by the sole efforts of one man starting in life with nothing but his natural endowments, is an achievement which cannot but attract attention and wonder.

It is the purpose of this book to show the character of the man who accomplished this task, and the manner in which it was brought about. It is unnecessary to add any word in his praise, for the story itself is the best evidence of the just appraisement of him as a unique and outstanding character of western life.

THE AUTHOR.

CONTENTS

x CONTENTS

LIST OF ILLUSTRATIONS

Written in appreciation of Henry Miller, the outstanding figure in western life and development, whose achievements are therein portrayed.

I. THE VISION

A TRAVELER in the extreme northern part of Wurttemberg, Germany, going along the placid River Neckar from Heidelberg to Heilbronn, will find a road sign informing him that the town of Brackenheim lies fifteen kilometers to the southwest of the latter city. If his curiosity tempts him to see that hamlet, he will pass through a country slightly rolling, mostly devoted to hay and grain, but having a few apple trees and some vines. He will pass through several villages with narrow streets, primarily devoted to chickens, ducks and geese. Finally he will drop into a little valley, cross a narrow bridge, and find himself in the main street of the town. The street is short and if not careful he may pass through the town before realizing its presence. The street is irregular and runs up hill, and the houses, with high steep roofs, likewise rise from it on both sides. About half way up the street is a rectangular indentation with no signs of being a city square, except a building facing it with the word "Rathaus," indicating that it is the town hall.

That the town has a civic consciousness will also be seen from the memorial of the World War given by a native of the town residing in New York. This is also shown by the sole manufacture of the town, Brackenheim Bock Beer, advertised as "B.B.B." and which the inhabitants will assure you is "sehr gut." This is further shown by the town hospital on a slight eminence just outside the town. Across the road, also on a slight eminence, is a cemetery, where those lie whom medical science could no longer save. This is a delightful spot on a sloping hillside with a church in the center. The church was originally Roman Catholic, but at the time of the Reformation passed to the control of the Reformed Church. The graves are neatly kept by a woman caretaker.

The monuments over the graves are simple, generally only a crude white cross, but near the gate the attention is directed to one which, while simple, is more pretentious than its neighbors. A tall, tapering, brown stone monument in a well kept plot commands the attention of the curious. On three sides inscriptions are cut, which indicate that Johanne Christine Buchwald was born July 19, 1768, and married a man named Fischer. She died February 5, 1847, at the age of seventy-nine years. She had a daughter Christine Doroth Fischer, born August 7, 1796, who married Christian Johann Kreiser, and died March 25, 1842, at the age of forty-six. Her husband, Christian Johann Kreiser, was born December 14, 1780, and died March 9, 1854. In other words, he was born sixteen years before his wife and lived twelve years after her death. There is nothing in these simple inscriptions to excite our curiosity, but beneath that of Christine Doroth Kreiser is this inscription:

"Gewidmet vom Sohn
HENRY in San Francisco 1876"

indicating that it was erected by their son living in San Francisco, California.

If we now enter the church and examine the records, we find that the son Henry was born to this couple on July 21, 1827, and christened Heinrich Alfred Kreiser. His mother died at the early age of forty-six, when Henry was but fifteen, but his father lived to the ripe age of seventy-four, and his grandmother on his mother's side to the age of seventy-nine. The same records show that this couple also had three daughters. The father came from a family of stock raisers and the mother's family were vintners.

Let us now turn to a hot summer day when Henry was but eight years of age. He had left the village to drive a few head of calves to a small piece of land on which his father, who was the town butcher, had the right of pasture. The day was hot and the road dusty. He was big of head and shoulders, but short, and his little legs had to move rapidly to keep the calves from the adjoining fields. His feet were small and incased in crude canvas shoes, but his legs were bare and he wore no hat. As he guided the unruly calves he saw out in the field the forms of three women slowly progressing with bent backs clearing the weeds from the growing grain. The task was so tedious that they seemed hardly to move. He saw another laboriously cutting hay with a sickle and tying it in small bundles to carry home for the cattle. He saw an old man herding five pigs.

On his way he passed his grandmother pushing a crude cart stacked with bundles of wood, or rather small twigs, which she had gathered far away in the forest and was taking to the town for fuel. She was struggling in the hot sun with the weight of the load and Henry stopped and laughingly said, "Granny, won't you ever learn how to load a cart?" and deftly readjusted the load so that the weight was more evenly balanced. She went on her weary way, gladdened, as she saw her little grandson scamper away to gather the calves which had taken the opportunity to enter the tempting clover on the adjoining land. Well he knew the scolding he would get for this from the man who owned it.

Later he met his mother pushing a cart loaded with bundles of hay which she had cut with the sickle and was taking to the village for the stock being fattened nearby. On top of the load was perched the youngest of her children, and by her side one slightly older was walking. She had left early in the morning, while Henry was milking the cows, which were kept under the house, so he had not seen her. He stopped and gave her a morning kiss and gave the child at her side a drink from the little water barrel which was swung on his back, and told his mother where she would find a cool place to stop for the noon-day rest, and then skillfully rescued his calves from another bunch which were passing and trudged along.

He finally reached the little strip of land which he was entitled to pasture. The whole country was in little strips of grain, clover and other crops. Each seemed so small, and there being no fences, he had some difficulty in keeping his little herd from trespassing on the adjoining strips. One, more venturesome than the rest, got away, and though Henry ran as fast as his little legs could carry him and skillfully herded it back, he did not succeed in doing so without being soundly abused by the owner. This he took good-naturedly until the owner called him the "son of a pig," and then he grew so angry that for lack of a better way of relieving his feelings he beat the offending calf with the stick he carried. When he had about cooled down and got his little herd feeding properly, he heard a laugh and turning around saw a little girl herding pigs on the opposite strip of land. Her laugh again aroused his anger, for her name was Linda and he liked the little girl and hated to have her hear a disrespectful word spoken of his mother. He first pretended not to see her, but gradually herded the calves so that by noon he was under the only shade near her strip of land, and she had as skillfully maneuvered her charges, so that she was at the same point.

Linda teasingly asked why he had not beaten the old man instead of the calf, but she got no answer, except that he hoped some day to be big enough to do so. By this time he was about tired out and sank down on the ground under a tree and produced his crust of bread and barrel of water. Linda still lingered and he finally raised his eyes, now wreathed in smiles, and said he was strong enough to break the bread into two pieces (which by the way was no small task), and the girl sat by his side and shared his simple fare. He held the barrel while she drank and managed to spill some of the water down her neck, causing a remark from her that she did not blame the old man for scolding him. Although the meal was light, it was sufficient to cause drowsiness to fast overcome the tired boy, but every time he would fall asleep the girl reminded him that his calves would run away. Finally she had pity on him and told him to sleep and she would watch both calves and pigs, and instantly he fell into a deep sleep. Ability to sleep was one of the special accomplishments of this growing and active boy, but to-day the heat and the excitement of the encounter with the old man filled his sleep with dreams.

The scenes he saw were first confused and vague,

but gradually became distinct. He first saw the little strips of land, the women slowly moving through the fields, the patient oxen pulling the plows, and the old men laboriously cutting hay with sickles. Then these strips of land widened and lengthened, and extended far over plains and hills, and the little strips of grain became boundless seas of golden wheat, and the few calves grew into the hundreds, yea the thousands, and the herds extended as far as the eye could see. The few women and old men grew into an army of men and machines driving the stock, cutting and threshing the grain, and cutting and stacking the hay, the few sheep became immense droves covering the tops of the distant hills, and the pigs in Linda's charge became black masses rooting up the ground under every tree and in every gully. He heard the low bellow of the bulls, the mournful cry of the calves separated from the cows, and saw the wild stampede of frightened steers. And then he saw on the left hip of every animal the letter H, and this seemed to dance in the sun and seemed to become two or double. He understood that the H was for Henry, but the double H puzzled him, and he could not figure out why there should be two. Then the herd seemed to be coming toward him and he felt its hot breath upon his face, and this woke him with a start, to find one of the calves calmly licking his face and Linda sitting by laughing at the queer picture.

As he trudged gamely home that evening, now driving his calves against the setting sun, he thought of his dream and in his mind multiplied his band far into the rays of the western sky and hoped that he might find that land without boundaries and without cross neighbors, where the herds might roam at will, all marked with the letter H on the left hip. Still he was somewhat worried about the double H, but soon attributed it to the fact that there were so many that he confused them; and from that day the vision of the far away land to the west never left him.

II. WESTWARD, HO!

SEVEN years had passed. Little Linda had gone with her family to the "States" and never been heard from. Henry was now fifteen. He had received the little schooling the village afforded, had been trained by his father in the art of raising, slaughtering, and marketing livestock, and had completed the seven years of his apprenticeship, during which he received, in addition to his food and clothing, ten Prussian dollars a year.

It was early morning and the sun was rising and casting its rays into the home of man and beast belonging to the Kreiser family.

The wife and mother, still young, but pale and worn, might be seen moving about the kitchen fire, preparing the breakfast porridge. As the sun rose she struck a triangular gong hanging by the door, and soon the whole house seemed to become alive. From the garret above, the eldest daughter, Frederike, descended to aid her mother; from another door appeared Elizabeth partly dressed, and from another appeared Karoline, the youngest, carrying her clothes so that she might dress by the stove. The husband and father came in, ready to take down the shutters of his shop to catch the early trade. The

house seemed to fairly burst with life and its smallness became pathetic as all this life attempted to
crowd around the table, or board, by the kitchen
wall. The sound of the cows below munching the
hay, the click of the milk pails, and the musical
sound of the milk flowing from udder to pail could
be heard. This rhythmic sound finally died out, the
stool was hung upon the wall, the pail was put
upon the shelf, and a young man appeared on the
outside porch. A few vigorous strokes of the long
handled pump filled the basin with water. He
pulled over his head a loose gunny sack garment
which covered the clothes he would wear behind
the meat block, methodically hung it on its accustomed hook, and splashed the water over his hands,
arms, face, neck and head, rubbing vigorously with
homemade soap, and then with the coarse towel
which hung by the pump.

As he faced about he showed a big head, set
down closely on his shoulders, a large frame, but
short legs, and unusually small feet. His eyes were
very small, but shone like the buttons on a new
pair of shoes. His head was bent slightly forward
and downward.

He entered the kitchen as the family had finally
managed to crowd around the board, which was
much too small for this fast growing family. He
smiled at his mother and gently kissed her fore-
head, and then took his accustomed place at the
middle of the board. The family was not slow to

see a merry twinkle in his eye. He was full of life and appeared to be particularly happy.

"Why so happy, Henry," ventured his father, "did the cows let down nicely this morning?"

"Oh, tolerable," answered the son.

"Maybe he's in love," said his eldest sister with a giggle.

"Maybe he's been dreaming again about those lands and herds out west," volunteered his youngest sister, who had often made him talk her to sleep by telling her his dreams. This seemed to be a singular breach of confidence, so he dropped his eyes to his plate and struggled manfully with the resisting food.

His mother came to the rescue and said, "If you will all stop teasing him, he will tell us all about it."

He seemed to take this almost as a command, for he immediately raised his face, now lit up by a peculiar smile, and said, "I have finished my apprenticeship and am going to America." This announcement almost caused a riot.

"What will I do in the shop?" moaned the father. "There isn't a man in Germany who can cut up a steer better or quicker than you."

"What will I do for wood?" cried his mother.

"Then I will have no one to tell me dreams," lisped the baby.

"And the Kaiser will have no soldier to fight his wars," said the eldest sister, who wished to see her brother in his military uniform, and hoped herself to marry a soldier. This remark fully aroused the young man and he said:

"I hate the military. The officers are insufferable and consider us but swine. There is no room in this country. The land is all owned by the nobles. There is not room to breathe. This little house is bursting with our family and there are too many mouths to feed. The cattle cannot move without trespassing. I want a country where I will have room to move and do something."

As the son gave vent to this explosive tirade, the father's memory went back to the Napoleonic wars, to Austerlitz, Jena and Waterloo; he saw the broad shadow of Otto Eduard Leopold von Bismarck-Schönhausen lengthening across the country; he saw Prussianism, Militarism, and, in prophetic vision, the Empire, Verdun and the Marne, and realized that the most certain future of a young man born in 1827 was to be cannon-fodder.

In these words the boy broke one of the ties that bound him and stood in the way of his cherished desire, the tie of the Fatherland. The tense strain that followed was relieved by the voice of his sister, remarking that Linda had been in America several years and no one had heard of her becoming the wife of a banker. The laugh that followed this sally emboldened his baby sister to remark, "Maybe he wants to go to America to see Linda." This again sent his eyes to his plate, and the wrinkles around his eyes showed that the shaft had gone home, although the charge was unfounded.

"Maybe," ventured the baby sister, who still had her mind on wonderful dreams, "he wants to have all those lands and cattle marked H."

Much to the surprise of all, he gave the child a hug and said, "Yes, that is what I want and what I shall have."

He looked down at his father, now aging, and his mother, now plainly failing. He was touched by their affection, which he shared, and by the love of his sisters, and he continued: "Think of all the money I can make and all the fine things I can send you, and pretty soon I can send for you and you can all come to America."

"Wouldn't that be wonderful!" shouted the children in unison, but the poor mother began to cry.

He rose, and, as he passed out to go to the shop, he put his arms around her and said, "I will not go till you say I may," but he secretly knew that he could win her over to his plan.

*   *   *   *   *   *

When he came home that night, there was a strange stillness about the house. His mother had suffered a stroke and had been put to bed. The village doctor was alarmed, for it was clear she was sinking rapidly. The struggle of bringing up a family under such conditions had proved too much for her strength, and she gradually failed.

She said good-by to each of the children, and to Henry she said, "Go to the land of your dreams and God bless you," and soon after passed away in her husband's arms. And thus another tie which held the boy from his purpose was broken.

The old grandmother and Henry's sisters took over the household duties, and then began two unhappy years for Henry. His sisters tried to force him to conform to the narrow life of the locality in which they lived. While his apprenticeship had been completed and he had earned his own living since he was eight years of age, parental control was still over him. He traveled from hamlet to hamlet buying livestock. He learned everything from slaughtering a steer to making a fiddle string from the guts. Finally he was made to herd a flock of geese, and this so infuriated and humiliated him that he came home and told his sisters he was through. He packed a rude bundle of clothes, put a stick through it, swung it over his shoulder, and made his way to Holland and then to England. History has left no record of how he spent two years in those countries, but finally he made his way to the sea coast and shipped for the new world of his dreams.

III. THE NEW WORLD

THE trip by steerage from Europe to America
in the sailing vessels of the middle of the
Nineteenth Century has often been described, and
that description need not be here repeated. Henry
spent his time in an endeavor to learn whatever
he could of the new world toward which he was
heading. He got acquainted with anyone who knew
anything of it and tried in every way to learn the
language of the country. He had obtained a book
which aimed to teach the language, and with this
he struggled for hours. Whenever he could find
anyone who spoke English who would talk to him,
he tried to speak some of the words he learned
from the book, but the result was far from satisfactory. His German accent, inherited from a long
line of ancestors, seemed to be a fixed quantity and
he simply could not twist his tongue to the pro-
nunciation of English words. While the people
were friendly and tried to help him, they could
not refrain from laughing at his efforts.

When, on a bright day in 1847, Henry Kreiser,
now nineteen years old, finally walked down the
gangplank, and emerged on the streets of New
York, he had the poor remains of the bundle he

took from Brackenheim and about five dollars in American money. He found himself not in the open country with plenty of space, but in a busy city in which all were struggling for position. He recognized that he would have to struggle for existence. On the boat he had obtained the name of a place where he might lodge, which was run by a German with whom he could converse, and this place he sought and finally found, and then began the search for work. The one thing he knew, which could be of any use in a city, was meat and how to cut it. He went from shop to shop, but could hardly make himself understood, and they had plenty of workers anyhow. The search for employment continued for several days, and his supply of money was about gone. He finally got a job working in a garden at four dollars a month and board. He then worked for a pork butcher, working sixteen hours a day for eight dollars a month. He tended a stall in Washington Market during the morning and dressed hogs in the afternoon. In addition to his wages he got the intestines, which he sold as sausage cases for about one dollar a day.

In his wanderings he had passed a dark and uninviting shop run by an old man. The chance of employment was so slight that he had passed without seeking it; but one morning as he went by he noticed the old man trying to take down a side of beef, but he seemed too weak to handle it. Henry walked in, removed his cap, and with a word to the old man, which was not understood, seized the side of beef and laid it on the block. He then asked for employment, but the old man only groaned and said his customers had left him and he could hardly pay his rent and could not afford a helper. But the young man would not take "No" for an answer, and said, "Let me show you how I can cut meat," and in a moment he was sharpening a knife. The skill with which he carved that side of beef made the eyes of the old man almost pop out of his head, and he said, "I would like to have you, son, but I can't afford it."

Henry said, "If you will let me sleep in the back of the shop, I will work for half price."

This finally won the old man and in a few minutes Henry had a white apron over his clothes, and was serving the customers. But business was none too good and when the shutters were put up at night the old man went home none too happy.

When he returned the next morning he hardly knew the place. The young man had washed the sidewalk and the entire front of the shop, spread sawdust over the floor, hung a carefully dressed lamb in the window, exhibited some sausage in a clean dish, set out two new cans of lard, and protected the whole by a new piece of netting which he had found in the back of the shop, and when the old man came he was engaged in painting the front of the shop with white paint, which he had likewise found back of the shop. By the time this was finished, he washed himself and slipped on his white apron none too soon, for the improvement in the shop already began to attract more customers. They laughed when he tried to talk, but they all liked to see him cut meat, and soon the servant girls seemed to become aware of his existence, and rather liked the German boy who cut meat so skillfully.

The place also had a slovenly boy who delivered the meat in a basket, but he was slow and unreliable and would frequently stop on his way to play marbles, and would deliver the meat at the wrong address. So one day the old man in anger kicked him out of the place and put up a sign "Boy Wanted." Henry saw his chance and said, "Why not let me deliver the meat? We will have two regular deliveries, and I can make them during the slack hours." This was finally agreed to and the boy's pay was added to the wages of Henry.

The trips with the meat basket were a delight, because they took the young man to the great homes, and he talked to the servants and learned what kind of meat they wanted, and often took their orders for the next day, and then sometimes he would be introduced to a servant of a neighboring house who liked him and soon he got that trade too. In fact everything was soon going in the normal way, which would in time place his name along with his employer's on the front of the shop and he would become a prosperous retail meat

dealer, like hundreds of others in that big city, and
be able on Sunday to take his family to the Turn
Verein picnic. But one day he called at a house
and the Irish girl was in a fighting mood and announced, "I'm lavin' and nary a bit do I care what
you fetch tomorrow." But he knew what the mistress needed, so next day he prepared it and proceeded to deliver it at the back door. When the
door was opened he was just about to speak to
the new girl, but the words were never spoken. He
dropped his basket and she dropped her broom,
they both stared as if they had seen ghosts, and
finally she cried, "Henry!" and he cried, "Linda!"

She saw before her a strong young man, and he
saw a flaxen-haired girl blooming into womanhood.
Then explanations followed, and questions flew
thick and fast, until they were brought back to life
by the voice of the girl's mistress. Henry had to
move his short legs rapidly to get back to relieve
the old man for the noon-day meal, and all the
afternoon that flaxen hair seemed to be ever before
him, and he was glad when the last shutter was
finally on the shop and he was free.

His visit that night to the back porch of Linda's
house was but one out of many. It resulted in noc-
turnal strolls, in which he told of all the happen-
ings at Brackenheim since Linda had left, and she
told of the vicissitudes of herself and her parents.
Her father had a good job, but she wanted to work
too so that they could get enough money to buy a

little farm up the Hudson River. He tried to tell her what he had been doing, but she laughed at his English, for his tongue still refused to respond to the new language. The upshot of the matter was that she volunteered to teach him English. For hours she would sit with him on the back porch, or in the kitchen, or on hot days on some park bench, and give him words to pronounce. Some he never could master, and, try as he might, he could not use the proper tenses. His mistakes caused many a laugh, but he took it all in good part, and with certain limitations, which he never overcame, made very good progress.

We do not know why every language book begins with the conjugation of the word "love," or its equivalent, "I love," "I loved," et cetera. Linda's methods of teaching were not according to the book, and probably began with things with which Henry was more familiar, but every aid to romance was present. The time, it was night; the place, it was the park; the girl, she was certainly charming; and the boy was one hundred per cent normal and human. She talked of home, of his mother, of their youth, she patiently sat by his side and held the book, and in the dim glow it had to be brought close to the eyes, and her flaxen hair often fluttered against the side of his face, and so almost unconsciously their hearts were bound together.

And then on Sundays when Linda had a day off, they would go into the country, and one day they lingered after the sun had set and until the stars had come out. They sat on the ground under the trees and near the river. The beautiful warm evening added fuel to the fast rising fire of their affection.

When Henry arrived home that night and reached the little room, if it could be called such, in which he slept, a reaction seized him. He felt that marriage meant slavery and the giving up of that freedom which was necessary to accomplish what he had set out to do. He thought of his vision, yet unfulfilled; he thought of the promises he had made his family in Brackenheim, still unperformed. Thus troubled in mind he finally threw himself on his bed and was soon sleeping like a child.

IV. HENRY MILLER

SOON after Henry Kreiser had been employed by the meat dealer he met in a neighboring shoe store a young man about his own age, but a native of America. He was a salesman in the store and wore nice clothes. His name was Henry Miller. Our Henry cultivated his acquaintance, because he himself had a small foot for a big boy and was particular as to the boots he should wear. In fact he had a weakness to show the smallness of his foot by getting a boot which fitted as snugly as possible. He even suffered from standing and walking all day in a boot somewhat too tight for his foot. He would, therefore, get his friend, Henry Miller, the shoe salesman, to fit him, and would take him out to have beer and pretzels and get the benefit of his ability to speak English.

It was about this time that the country was electrified by the report of the discovery of gold in California. Both boys eagerly sought every bit of news as to that far away land. Henry, the meat boy, soon pictured it as the land of his dreams and his desire. To get there also fired the imagination of Henry, the shoe salesman. The most important difference between them was that the shoe

24

salesman had saved enough money to make the trip, but Henry, the meat boy, had scarcely saved enough from his meager wages. Since his employment the business had prospered and his wages had several times been increased, but he constantly sent money to his family in Brackenheim, so that, economize as he might, saving money was a slow process.

Finally Henry, the shoe salesman, purchased a ticket for passage from New York to San Francisco, and many talks they had, and Henry, the meat boy, promised to follow as soon as he had a few more dollars. The boat was to sail the day after that fateful Sunday spent by Henry, the meat boy, on the banks of the Hudson. He was awakened that Monday morning by a knocking on the little window that admitted light to his room, and on opening the side door he found his friend Henry, the shoe salesman. He was clearly excited and explained that he had decided that he did not want to go to California, and suggested that Henry, the meat boy, take his ticket. Whether this was due to cowardice, or whether he too had passed his Sunday on the banks of the Hudson, Henry, the meat boy, never learned, for the events of the day flashed through his mind and this presented itself as a way out of his difficulty. His shrewdness, however, told him that here was something to be sold and he had better barter a bit, so he objected that he had barely enough money for the trip, and would be without means when he reached California. Finally a price was agreed upon, and the ticket changed hands. In a short time he informed his employer that he was going, took his wages, gathered together his few belongings, and departed.

He debated as to what he should say or write to Linda, but finally decided that he had made a fool of himself and had better say nothing, so he went without a word. He argued to himself that he could be of no use to her as a husband and that she would be better off without him. He argued that when he had made his fortune, he could come back to her, and with this poor solace he silenced his conscience and went on his way, and thus another tie, that of youthful love, was sacrificed, that the promise to his mother might not go unfulfilled.

Several years later, when his success in California had become assured, he wrote to her, but found that she had married, so his early romance was ended.

When he looked at the ticket he saw it was in the name of "Henry Miller" and was marked "Not Transferable." He was anxious to go and was unfamiliar with business affairs, and feared that if he told that he had bought the ticket he could not go, so he decided to go as "Henry Miller." As Henry Miller he did go, and under that name he continued till the time of his death. Thus one other tie, the family name of Kreiser, was broken asunder in aid of his ambition.

Several years later he had enough influence to get the Legislature of the State of California to pass a special act formally authorizing this change of name from "Henri Alfred Kreicer" to "Henri Miller." While the statute said "Henri," it was always thereafter in fact written "Henry." The act also misspelled the name Kreiser.

CHAP. CXXXVI.—*An Act to change the Name of Henry Alfred Kreicer to Henri Miller.*

[Became a Law by operation of the Constitution, March 30, 1858.]

The People of the State of California, represented in Senate and Assembly, do enact as follows:

SECTION 1. That the name of Henri Alfred Kreicer be and it is hereby changed to Henrí Miller.

[This bill having remained with the Governor ten days, (Sundays excepted,) and the Senate and Assembly being in session, it has become a law this thirtieth day of March, one thousand eight hundred and fifty-eight.

FERRIS FORMAN, Secretary of State.]

V. CALIFORNIA

WHEN Henry Miller went upon the boat he was well and neatly clothed in the dress of the period. He was scrupulously clean and neat in his appearance at all times. No one knew how much, or rather how little, money he had in his purse. He found himself in a strange company, mostly of men. The great majority were fired with the ambition of making immediate fortunes in the mines. In fact they hardly visualized the mines, but thought that gold was almost picked up. These men were mostly of good character and had those friendly and reliable characteristics so often found in the venturesome young man of ambition.

There were others who had no other object than to prey on those who, by hardship and energy, wrung the gold from the earth. Gamblers, saloon keepers, criminals fleeing to safer climes, and women of loose morals, made up a goodly part of the human cargo. Then there was a certain proportion of substantial business men, who hoped to take advantage of the business opportunity which would be presented by the necessity of feeding, clothing, and housing this growing population of the west. Some of them were bringing a non-

28

descript stock in trade and others expected goods
to follow them in sailing vessels. It was to this
class that our hero naturally turned.

He knew nothing of mining and cared nothing
for easy money. All he knew was the raising,
slaughtering and sale of livestock, and he knew
that the demand for meat would be intense, so he
spent his time learning whatever he could of the
geography of the country to which he was going,
its climate, size, and population. He listened to
every word he could hear and continued to improve his ability to speak, read, and write the
language of Henry Miller.

One of the things he learned was that there were
large herds of cattle in California, and that
thousands of them were slaughtered every year for
the hides and tallow, the balance of the animal
being left for the wild beasts that infested the
region. When he compared this with the manner
in which he had been accustomed to utilize every
scrap of meat, he could hardly believe his inform-
ant was serious.

The trip was by the Isthmus of Panama and was
a slow one. He saw the necessity of keeping in the
good regard of the men he met and counted every
penny so that he might not find himself without
sufficient funds to complete the trip with honor and
independence.

He might have succeeded better, except for an
unexpected thing which happened upon his arrival

at the Isthmus of Panama. After an arduous journey on foot across the Isthmus, it was found that there was no boat to take the party to California, and it was quite uncertain when any would be available. The Panama fever was raging, and there was a poor supply of accommodations for the travelers. Among other things, it was found that the only butcher in the locality had been stricken with fever. Henry Miller was not slow to grasp the opportunity. He used pretty much of all his remaining money to buy the few implements which the native butcher had used in carrying on his trade. He obtained the assistance of another passenger and together they managed to rustle up some native cattle. In this manner he first came into contact with the type of cattle that prevailed in that territory, longhorned, poor color, wild and skinny. He was destined later in life to become better acquainted with the type.

With this equipment, he proceeded to supply the demand of the stranded passengers. His partner soon suggested that they were the only butchers in the locality and prices should be raised, but Henry Miller was more far-sighted and well knew that his conduct would be watched and remembered for many a day, and he, therefore, fixed a price which seemed to him to assure them an ample profit, but, at the same time, did not gouge their fellow passengers. All went well for some time, and the passengers came to know him and to enjoy seeing him cut the beef which they came to buy. But very soon the Panama fever got him too, so he had to give up his work and leave things in the hands of his inexperienced partner. When he recovered, he found the business wrecked and very little salvage, as he could not get much, if anything, for the implements he had purchased. Consequently when the boat finally came he went aboard poor in purse, weak in body, and greatly emaciated, but with a wealth of friends and admirers who had observed his plucky efforts. As a result, he succeeded in walking down the gangplank at San Francisco with about the same Five Dollars with which he had arrived in New York. To be exact he had Six Dollars in his pocket.

During the trip he became intensely interested in conversations carried on between a returning Spanish priest and a Yankee from Massachusetts. One was extolling the works of the Spanish régime in California, the other was contemptuously maintaining that a few dilapidated Missions were poor marks of progress, and that the education and reformation of the Indians were a waste of time. He saw clearly the conflict between material advancement and religious idealism. Being himself a Protestant, he was not particularly attracted by the religious view of the matter, and the Yankee point of view that farms, houses, cattle and cities were more important than Missions strongly appealed to him.

The discussion was started by the Yankee remarking to the Padre:

"California must be an awful place."

"What makes you think so, my son?" asked the priest.

The Yankee replied, "I see that in 1844 Daniel Webster inquired in the United States Senate: 'What do we want of this vast worthless area, this region of savages and wild beasts, of deserts of shifting sands and whirlwinds of dust, cactus and prairie dogs? To what use could we ever hope to put these deserts or these endless mountain ranges, impenetrable and covered to their bases with eternal snow? What can we ever hope to do with the Western Coast of three thousand miles, rock-bound, cheerless and uninviting, with not a harbor in it? What use have we for such a country? Mr. President, I will never vote one cent from the public treasury to place the Pacific Coast one inch nearer Boston than it is to-day.' "

"Your Mr. Webster," said the priest, "is a great orator, but he knows nothing of California. California has the finest harbor in the world and the most hospitable climate. It will grow anything, and it has a history as interesting as Massachusetts."

"A history!" exclaimed the youth, "I thought it had just been discovered."

"That is the view shared by many in the New England states who boast of a long history," said the good father, and then patiently continued:

"Many people think of California as starting with the discovery of gold in 1848. This is a most erroneous view of the situation. Before that time, California had a long religious, political and agricultural history.

"In the Sixteenth Century a romancer, Ordoñez de Montalvo, wrote a romantic tale called Las Sergas de Esplandián, containing a description of a delightful land abounding in wealth of gold and pearls. It was pictured as an island near the Terrestrial Paradise surrounded by a sea whose waters were turquoise blue as they gently rolled along its coral sands. Its fruits, foliage and climate made it a land of delight. This wholly fanciful land was ruled by Queen Calafia and the author called it California.

"It is no wonder, when explorers braved the waters of the Pacific and explored the country along its shores, and it became necessary to map this theretofore unknown country, that this name 'California,' thus coined in the realm of romance, should be applied to this peaceful and delightful land which bordered on the ocean they named 'Pacific.'

"Cabrillo landed in San Diego in 1542. The first religious service by the Church of England in California was held within a few miles of San Francisco by Sir Francis Drake in 1579. Sebástian Vizcaino landed in Monterey in December, 1602. The first of the Missions was established in 1769, and those Mission settlements continued to move north until they stretched along the Coast from San Diego to San Francisco. Between 1769 and 1797 Missions were established at San Diego, San Luis Rey, San Juan Capistrano, Santa Barbara, San Gabriel, San Buena Ventura, La Purísima Concepción, San Luis Obispo, San Miguel, San Antonio, San Carlos, San Juan Bautista, Santa Cruz, Santa Clara, and San Francisco de Asís.

"San Francisco Bay was first discovered by an adventurous band of Spaniards led by Don Gaspar de Portolá, on November first, 1769, and its Mission was established in 1776.

"Until 1846 California was under Spanish and Mexican rule, and there was a continuous line of Spanish governors of California from 1770 to 1822. The Spanish rulers were expelled from Mexican countries in 1829. There was a continuous line of Mexican governors in California from 1825 to 1846. On June 14, 1846, the Americans raised the 'Bear Flag' at Sonoma, and on July 7, 1846, Commodore Sloat raised the American flag at Monterey. From that time the country was under a United States military government, until the people in 1849 adopted a constitution and organized a state government.

"During the Spanish and Mexican régime local civil government under Alcaldes prevailed in pueblos throughout the territory."

This sketch of the history of California aroused

the curiosity of the youth for more knowledge, and he continued to ply the Padre with questions. In brief, this is what he might have learned of the land toward which he was headed if he had attempted to catalogue the information that passed in those countless debates:

The Spanish and Mexican governments were most generous with California land, and made extensive grants of land in California. Frequently a single grant comprised thirty to forty thousand acres.

Any one desiring to obtain title to land might make application to the Governor for not more than eleven square leagues, a square league containing 4428.4 acres. The Governor then issued an *expediente,* or official title. Possession was obtained through the local Alcalde, who, with two witnesses and a riata, fifty *varas* or one hundred and thirty-seven and a half feet in length, measured the land on horseback without a compass. Piles of stones marked the corners. The land was unsurveyed and necessarily the boundaries of the grants were extremely general, not to say vague and uncertain. They were usually measured by leagues rather than by feet, yards, rods, or miles, and bounded by natural objects, such as the ocean, rivers and mountain ranges.

The owners were verily monarchs of all they surveyed. They had all the luxurious tastes of the Spanish nobility, and maintained *haciendas* of no mean style. They lived in comparative luxury, making both Indian and Peon slaves to their wants. They were fond of fine horses, and engaged principally in raising horses and cattle. These were raised in the easiest manner, which was to permit them to range on the natural grasses which were plentiful on the vast *ranchos*. Riding, racing and cock fighting were their principal amusements. They knew little of the agricultural wealth of the soil, and nothing of the mineral wealth under it.

The Missions continued their growth, furnishing the religious life of the time, and gathering together the Indians into villages, teaching them the habits of civilization, trade, agriculture, and the Christian religion. It was a great undertaking, and was carried on according to a fixed plan. The Mission bell was the center of every settlement, and the Missions were but a few days' journey apart. They furnished protection against the wild tribes of Indians which still roamed over the country, but, as the Missions grew, they aroused the envy of the military and political government, and finally their power was completely destroyed. On February 27, 1767, Don Carlos issued his proclamation expelling the Jesuits, and their Missions were turned over to the Franciscans by Don Gaspar de Portolá. The Secularization Act, which practically destroyed the Missions, was passed on August 17, 1833. Their Indian converts were scattered, their priests were driven out, their churches largely destroyed and abandoned.

The Spanish and Mexican rule was of a people coming from Spain and Central America, and gradually working their way north. Politically, the government was largely military, and, of course, distinctively Spanish in character. Religiously, the population came entirely from Catholic countries, and was loyal to the Church of Rome.

And then the "Gringo" came. This was a hateful term applied in Spanish American countries to foreigners, principally Americans, but is now a term of which Californians are proud. These Gringos were the children of those who had pushed out from the Atlantic States into the Middle West and gradually passed on through Missouri, Kansas and Utah and finally broken through the mountains to the Pacific Coast. They brought with them the principles of American government. They were racially, politically and religiously a different people. They were few in number. They came with the first immigrant train in 1841. They came with General Frémont. They came with the Donner Party in 1846. They came from the War with Mexico. They came with the Gold Rush in 1849. They brought the English language, the common law of England, and the spirit of American institutions.

Three notable things occurred when the State

was admitted to the Union on September 9, 1850. The English language was established as the official language. Slavery was made impossible, and the common law of England was adopted as the rule of decision in the State. This last had an important bearing on the fortunes of Henry Miller. Two other measures likewise had an important effect on his career. The Act of Congress admitting the State to the Union extended to California the so-called Swamp Land Act, which had the effect of granting the State all of the swamp and overflow land therein. It finally developed that there were over two million acres of such land in California.

Congress also passed an act providing for the settlement of claims to land under Spanish and Mexican grants, and thus means were provided for fixing the boundaries and settling the titles to the numerous *ranchos* which had been granted by the Spanish and Mexican governments. The State was also granted every sixteenth and thirty-sixth section, or two sections in every township in the State, and five hundred thousand acres of land, for school purposes, forty-six thousand acres for a Seminary of Learning, and sixty-four hundred acres for State buildings. These acts were important, because the State proceeded to dispose of its land on a commercial basis, which made it possible for one person directly or indirectly to acquire large tracts of land.

During the Gold Rush, attention was directed

CALIFORNIA 39

to the mining region. *Ranchos* were abandoned, and their owners became involved in mining ventures, often resulting in financial ruin.

It was into this State, vast, undeveloped, agriculturally undiscovered, swamped in parts, and semi-arid in others, that Henry Miller set foot in 1850, with Six Dollars in his pocket, and it was into its principal city, San Francisco, teeming with excitement, growing by leaps and bounds, thinking gold, talking gold, and seeing gold, that he started the third chapter of his eventful life.

VI. SMALL BEGINNINGS

TO REMAIN in San Francisco after coming
six thousand miles with men answering the
call of gold is conclusive evidence either of a low,
base, cowardly mind, or of a monumental strength
of character and determination to continue on a
straight course in the attainment of a fixed goal.
Obviously Henry Miller may be acquitted of the
first, and only an uncanny ability to read the future
and a willingness to sacrifice all present advantages
in order to attain his ultimate object of conquering
the agricultural possibilities of the region, can account for his choice. He remained in San Francisco. The golden harvest of his dreams was more
alluring to him than the golden harvest of the
mines. He almost jumped from the boat into a
meat shop. He had none of the difficulties of getting work he met in New York, for laborers of all
kinds were extremely difficult to obtain, and those
who worked did so only until they earned their
"stake" to take them to the mines.

But the plain truth (at a later date so bluntly
spoken by a United States Senator from California)
that "a man must eat" was in operation. Food
was scarce and expensive, fresh meat was a luxury,

and when the "poke" was opened much "dust" was dropped on the scale before a beef steak passed from butcher to customer. Livestock was being raised, butchered and sold in San Francisco. The only reason that one of the lawyers of San Francisco did not buy the site of the Palace Hotel for a few dollars was that his wife objected to it because hogs were being raised on the adjoining lot. This same lawyer later became the confidential adviser of Henry Miller, but that is another story. In a few days Henry Miller was feeding cattle, slaughtering cattle, and cutting meat, but only for a short time did he work for wages.

Years after he told of his experiences on the first day in San Francisco. "I asks a man, 'Where is a putcher shop,' He points to a shack on a hill near Kearny and California Streets. I goes up the hill and finds a man sitting on a box in front of a lean-to. Flies were buzzing around him. He was reading a newspaper which had come on the boat. He took no notice of me, so I coughed. When he looked over the top of the paper, I says, 'I just come on the poat. I'm a putcher, and wants a job.' He went on with his reading and said, 'Can't you see I'm busy? I don't want no putcher.' I knew he was making fun of my English, so I went on. Years later I sees this man carrying his blankets in Idaho. That's what comes of a lazy bum who lets the flies run away with his putcher shop. I then goes down the street and sees a sign 'Dishwasher Wanted.' I takes the job."

He did not wash dishes long. In a few days he approached an Irishman named Edward Barron, who was running a butcher shop at the head of Dupont Street, and was immediately employed. His big opportunity did not come until the next year, 1851, when the city was almost destroyed by fire. He then found himself on an equality with the other inhabitants, and took possession of a lot on Jackson Street between Dupont and Kearny Streets and opened a shop of his own. Here he slaughtered calves and carried them on his back to North Beach and other parts of the city.

During the early years of the gold rush the animals which were brought to San Francisco for slaughter were largely inferior in character, but Henry Miller soon got a reputation for selling good meat. The secret was that he went early to bed and got up early in the morning and was first at the stockyards and had the pick of the stock. He would frequent the saloons where the cattle men gathered and pick up all possible information about available cattle and prices, but he never drank, and the cigars which he took in lieu of a drink he passed on to the next cattle man he met.

One of the pioneers of the city was John Center, who lived to the age of ninety-three. He also stayed in the city and laid claim to a large area of land in the Potrero and Mission districts, and went into the contracting business, making a fortune in the laying out of streets, building wharves, and filling in the lower part of the city. He had a large gang of workmen, mostly Chinese. He had sixteen head of steers and wanted them slaughtered. Someone who had become acquainted with Henry Miller on the Isthmus told him that he was the man he wanted. Center employed him to do the job. Long before the sun was up Henry Miller rode out to the Willows in the Mission region, slaughtered and dressed all those steers, left them hanging, got back to the city, donned his white apron, and was on hand to open the shop for his customers. The fame of this exploit spread. With the money he received, added to his earnings, he bought a few hogs, and next thing he was making and peddling sausages, real pork sausages. There is really nothing worse than a poor sausage, and nothing better than a good one. The proverbial "hot dog" of to-day is but a mean descendant of the pure bred sausage of the farm which Henry Miller made famous in early days in California.

Years later Henry Miller might have been found one evening sitting in the combined lobby and bar room of a country hotel, now wealthy and successful, and everyone doing him honor. In came a little dried up, greasy meat jobber. Henry Miller grunted in response to his greeting, which was extremely effusive and ingratiating, not to say distasteful. This was followed by a few jibes from the others around the room who shared Henry Miller's dislike for the jobber. This exasperated the jobber and he finally said to Henry Miller with considerable heat: "I knew you when you was peddling sausages in Frisco." As quick as a flash, Henry Miller stiffened and replied: "If I had no more brains than you, I would still be peddling sausages."

This caused a laugh which silenced the jobber and the story forever clung to him, because he was not much more than a peddler, picking up here and there a few hides, or a few head of veal calves or old cows for the local market.

During these early years of his career, Henry Miller was as strong as an ox. He had a fiery temper. He never carried a gun, but his fists were ever ready to defend him. Once coming upon his men skinning a steer in an unskillful manner he threw himself from his horse, threw his hat on the ground and stamped upon it, grabbed the knife, said, "Do you think you're skinning a rabbit?" and skinned the animal himself, entirely unmindful of the unsuitable clothing he was wearing for such a task.

For the first few years Henry Miller's activity was confined to the sale of such cattle as were brought to San Francisco for sale. They came principally from the *ranchos* of the Spaniards and were of the Mexican type.

After he had been in business two years, his business increased to such an extent that he was able to purchase from Livingston and Kincaid three hundred prime oxen for thirty-three thousand dollars. This is said to be the first band of American cattle ever driven into San Francisco and this was the beginning of the development of native American cattle which were destined to crowd out the Mexican cattle with which up to that time the Spanish *rancheros* had supplied the market.

These early years in San Francisco were the heydays of the Spaniards. Before the discovery of gold, cattle in California were grown principally for their hides, and were worth two to four dollars a head. After the discovery of gold, the price on the range went up to thirty or forty dollars a head.

The *rancheros* were amazed at their good fortune, and immediately took on expensive habits. It is said that during that period a proud Spaniard would not think of giving less than a gold piece to a boy who held his horse.

But their cattle were poor and Henry Miller knew that the way to control the local market was to control the production of cattle, so he turned his attention to the country from which the cattle came.

VII. THE SAN JOAQUIN VALLEY AND THE "DOUBLE H" BRAND (**HH**)

DURING the first few years of the new city the meat consumed came from cattle raised either within the city itself, or from the neighboring counties. At that time San Francisco extended as far south as San Francisquito Creek, which is now the boundary between the counties of San Mateo and Santa Clara. As the demand for meat grew the distance from which cattle were brought to the city gradually increased, and from time to time Henry Miller received fragmentary information about a great cattle country known as the San Joaquin Valley. Men from the mines told him of cattle being driven from that country to the mines. The richness of the valley, with its vast acreage of grass produced by the overflow of the great rivers, was described by these travelers and sent a thrill through his veins, but it was far distant and he had never been there, and the cattle from that region were mostly sent directly to the mines.

One day he was sorting some hides which had been dried and were ready for tanning. His eye

was quick to see one particularly large and with a
fine reddish color. He picked it up and turned it
over to examine the fleshy side of it, because in
that way any chance cut by the careless handling
of the knife during the process of skinning is revealed. It was a fine specimen, and as the left hip
came into view he saw through the skin the clear
outline of the brand. It gave him quite a shock, for
there was clearly pictured the same brand that he
had seen in his dreams on that day when he was
but eight years old and was herding calves near
Brackenheim, Germany,—the " **HH** " brand. He
had some difficulty in finding where it came from,
but finally remembered that he had received a
bunch of cattle from the San Joaquin Valley belonging to a man named Hildreth, so he prepared
for a trip and a long one to the land of his dreams.

Let us pause here for a brief account of the discovery of the San Joaquin Valley.

In 1774, at the Presidio of Tubac, Mexico, was
stationed a Spanish soldier named Juan Bautista
de Anza. One of his men was named José Joaquín
Moraga, then thirty-three years old. Moraga had a
wife and a son, Gabriel, then nine years old. Anza
conceived a plan of opening up communication
between Sonora, Mexico, and Monterey, California, in order that the Missions might be better
protected by the military, and offered to conduct
an expedition for that purpose, if given the proper
men. The request was not granted at first, but later

it was renewed and was supported by Father Junipero Serra, in charge of the Missions, and was finally approved by the King.

On the eighth of January, 1774, the party, composed of twenty soldiers, with guides and muleteers, making thirty-four in all, left Tubac.

Anza and his party crossed the dreadful Camino del Diablo, which was later strewn with the skulls of hundreds who perished in attempting to cross the dry, sandy wastes of what is now Arizona, and passed through the land of the friendly Yumas at the junction of the Gila and Colorado rivers. Here they faced and crossed the Colorado desert. They traversed the then desert wastes of Imperial Valley; came to the Indios Serranos, a miserable class of Indians, entirely naked, and skillful with the bomerang; scaled the passes of the San Jacinto Mountains and thus finally reached California and San Gabriel. The hardships of this trip may well be left to the imagination of those who know something of the character of the country traversed.

In the following year Anza repeated the journey by a slightly different route. Among the soldiers who accompanied him was Joaquin Moraga, who bade a fond farewell to his wife and little son Gabriel.

During this trip, Moraga distinguished himself in many ways, having been sent back to capture deserters whom he ran down on the desert. At San Gabriel he was made a lieutenant.

The party then continued north, finally reaching Monterey, and thus became a part of the military power of this new country known as California.

San Francisco bay had already been discovered, but Anza with Lieutenant Moraga formed a party and continued north to explore the country on the other shore of the bay (*Contra Costa*). They followed the east side of the bay to Carquinez Straits and continuing up that body of water finally reached the mouth of a river, which Anza named Rió de San Francisco.

They attempted to reach this river at another point in the country which was hidden behind the Mount Hamilton Range of mountains, but missed the Livermore Pass, and became entangled in the rough country at the north end of Mount Hamilton. However, they reached a high pass called Arroyo de Buenos Ayres where they were able to catch a glimpse of the distant valley lying between the range where they stood and the Sierra Nevada, but that was as near as they ever got to the land of the German boy's dream.

Soon the government paid the expense of bringing Moraga's wife and son, Gabriel, to join the husband and father at the Presidio at San Francisco.

This boy, Gabriel, developed into a soldier. He was tall, well built, dark complexioned, brave, gentlemanly, and soon became the foremost soldier of his day in California. He saw thirty-seven years of service and engaged in forty-six Indian expeditions. These expeditions were to quell Indian disturbances, punish depredations, pacify the Indians, and bring them in as neophytes at the Missions.

On one of these expeditions in 1806, Gabriel Moraga, with a party of soldiers and a diarist, penetrated the mountains which Anza and his father had explored, and passed into the land of almost limitless plains which later came to be known as San Joaquin Valley. He crossed and recrossed the river, the mouth of which Anza and his father had discovered and named Rio de San Francisco, and traversed the country from the Tulares to San Francisco Bay. He named the river and valley San Joaquin after the saint whose name his father bore. This valley was the land of the German boy's dream and became the principal scene of his exploits.

Leaving the city on horseback, Henry Miller proceeded out the Mission Road on to El Camino Real. As he reached the top of the hill on the Rancho Laguna de la Merced, he could look down upon the Pacific Ocean and at that point the cattle ranches commenced, and the Coast Range Mountains began to rise between his path and the ocean. He passed along the foothills of what is now San Mateo County, and through the *ranchos* of the Spaniards, beginning with *Buri Buri,* which was destined to become in a large part the property of his future partner, then through the won-

derful oak covered valley of Santa Clara, bounded
on the west by the Coast Range Mountains and on
the east by the Mount Hamilton Range. At the
lower end he passed through *Las Animas Rancho,*
which was to become his property and summer
home, and then on to old Gilroy. Here a road
turned to the east over the Mount Hamilton Range
through Pacheco Pass, connecting the Santa Clara
Valley with the San Joaquin Valley. It was narrow, rocky and tortuous, and passed through the
San Luis Rancho belonging then and for many
years thereafter to the Spanish family of Pacheco.

As he gradually rose out of the Santa Clara
Valley, he turned his horse to the west and a wonderful panorama spread before him. In front was
the Santa Clara Valley, stretching north as far as
the eyes could see and covered with giant oaks. At
his feet was Lake San Felipe, with the Tesques-
quite, Pajaro and San Benito rivers winding their
way westward toward the Pacific Ocean. To the
west rose the Coast Range Mountains and most
prominently and immediately in front of him was
the peak know as Mount Madonna. Like senti-
nels along the mountain ridge he could see a few
redwood trees, *Sequoia Sempervirens,* the most
southerly of those trees, which begin in Del Norte
County in the north of California and stretch in-
termittently all the way to Santa Cruz. These redwoods are found in no other place in the world,

and are excelled in size only by the *Sequoia Gigantea* found higher in the Sierra Nevada.

The lower reaches of the hills were almost bare of trees but were covered with a luxurious growth of grass, and the great valley was in spots carpeted with golden grain. The beauty of the entire scene was appalling, and he exclaimed, "It is a beautiful valley. I must own it." Little did he realize that from the place where he stood to and over the top of the mountain, he would own all of that strip of land, approximately twenty-five miles square,— the valley, the hills, the mountain top. He but little realized that he was looking on his future summer home, where his wife and children would live, and even upon the little piece of flat land on the hill side where a square of cypress trees would be planted, and where his wife, daughter, and first born son would lie buried beneath the California sunshine.

The outlook from this point made a profound impression upon Henry Miller, and it was destined to play an important part in his life. Many times he climbed the same hill, and whenever he came to the turn in the road where it rises above the *Rancho San Felipe* he rested his horse and again looked out over this view of the valley.

Turning his horse to the east he gradually climbed the mountain. He passed Pacheco Peak and finally reached the summit and looked down for the first time upon the San Joaquin Valley. The scene that lay before him was quite different from the one he had viewed from the western end of the road, but not the less wonderful. There opened before him one of the most extensive panoramas in the world, a valley fifty miles wide and two hundred miles long. Through the middle the San Joaquin River, the second largest river in the State, wound its way to the Bay of San Francisco, and beyond rose the ranges of the Sierra Nevada with their snow clad tops and saw-like pinnacles. Along the course of the river could be seen green foliage, but the balance of the valley was one great plain; dry, parched, hot, without any growth but short grass, without habitation except the jackrabbit and the coyote, but it was the land of his dreams. He knew that yonder mountains held the snow and ice which fed the river, but he little realized then that before he died he would even take a prominent part in regulating and determining the time that the snow and ice would flow as water down upon the parched plain. He knew that the rich valley land was fertile beyond words, and he knew that there was room enough for the herds that must supply the wants of man in the fast growing metropolis.

As he descended the mountain into the plain the heat became intense, the dust blinded his eyes and large spots of alkali, which had been left by evaporation on the surface of the soil, added to his discomfort. There was no water, but there was ever before him the illusive mirage which made it appear that he was at all times approaching a lake. He headed for a clump of willows in the far distance and finally came to a creek, which he later learned was called Los Baños. At the headwaters of this creek, years before, a band of Padres from San Juan Bautista venturing into this country had bathed and named the creek Los Baños, or "The Baths."

Having refreshed himself at the creek, he continued toward the river. Still there was no sign of human habitation, except that he could see that cattle had ranged the country. Finally, down near the river he saw the first cattle, and, getting closer to them, again saw the "**H·H**" brand on the left hip. Continuing on he saw a hut and some small corrals, and finally came to the ranch house of the *Rancho Sanjón de Santa Rita,* or the patron saint of women about to become mothers. Little did he realize, with all his ambition, that he was about to create the greatest livestock business in the world.

He was met by a coarse cattle man, booted and spurred and riding a fine horse, but otherwise everything was poverty-stricken and forlorn. This was one of the Hildreth brothers who came from Minnesota where they were engaged in floating logs down the river. When he came to the San Joaquin Valley he used the same brand for his cattle that he had used to mark his logs. When he

learned that Henry Miller came from San Francisco, his hospitable heart was opened, and for
several days they exchanged views and explored
the country. Henry Miller learned that the man
was the proud possessor of a quarter of a Spanish
grant of some forty-eight thousand acres of land
along the west side of the San Joaquin River, known
as *Rancho Sanjón de Santa Rita.* It was traversed
by several channels of the river, and where the
water had overflowed the grass was luxurious and
the soil obviously rich.

Hildreth had no enthusiasm for the country and
wanted to get away to the mines. He had been
sending his cattle to the mines and learned much
of them. Henry Miller told him the purpose of his
trip was to make arrangements to get cattle for
San Francisco. Hildreth said that this was not
feasible as the drive was too long. Finally he said
he wished he could sell the place, and when Henry
Miller mounted his horse for the return trip he
had an option to buy 8835 acres of the *Rancho
Sanjón de Santa Rita,* at one dollar and fifteen
cents an acre, and seventy-five hundred head of
cattle at five dollars a head, together with the
"Double H" brand.

As he rode back to San Francisco, he did some
deep thinking. From the San Joaquin River to the
mountains he passed through property for twenty-
five miles which he was destined to own, and when
he again looked down into the Santa Clara Valley

and on to the Coast Range he viewed land which in time would all fall under his dominion. The possibility of this could hardly be anticipated, but he observed every topographical feature. He figured how the cattle could be moved and where they could be kept in summer and in winter, and, before he finally reached San Francisco, he had a fully developed plan for controlling the livestock market of that metropolis.

On the way he visited all the *ranchos* and became acquainted with the cattle men of the region. Generally before he left, he had an option in his pocket for their fat cattle. As he stopped at Baden Creek to slack his horse's thirst, a tall Alsatian named Charles Lux greeted him. They had already met in the city where they were competitors. A short distance away he could see the house of Charles Lux in the willows, and to this they went and laid the foundation for a lifelong association.

Upon his return he went to his banker, William C. Ralston, and showed him his contract with Hildreth, gave him a glowing account of the country, and by a few figures showed the profit he could make on the cattle. Ralston was impressed and agreed that the bank would advance the money necessary to carry out the contract. As he was leaving, Ralston said: "You are covering a big territory, Mr. Miller, and will need some one to help you here while you are looking after the cattle in the country."

"I have thought of that, Mr. Ralston, and think I know the man I need."

In the next few days he moved among the cattle dealers of the city and they were greatly interested in his trip and what he had seen. But he was close-mouthed about his option on the cattle.

Soon the situation became clear to his competitors, who awoke to the fact that he had the market cornered.

His leading competitor at that time was Charles Lux, and with this advantage Henry Miller had no difficulty in arranging for the joint purchase of a large number of the cattle he had under option. The venture was so successful that the next year, 1858, he formed a partnership with Charles Lux under the name of Miller and Lux, and thus he got a man to attend to the city business while he was in the country.

When the partnership was first formed it was a loose affair. Charles Lux had preceded Henry Miller to California, and felt the superiority of his position, so the firm was often called Lux and Miller. It was not long before Henry Miller demonstrated that he was the dynamic force in the firm, and he was soon recognized as the senior partner of Miller and Lux. No greater honor could have been done him than that shown by the action of this proud Alsatian in thus subordinating himself to the later arrival.

Then began a veritable orgy of land and cattle

buying which continued without abatement for thirty years.

His cattle were constantly moving from Santa Rita in the San Joaquin Valley, through the Pacheco Pass to Gilroy, and along El Camino Real to San Francisco.

First small properties were rented or bought at convenient intervals to rest, feed and fatten the cattle on the way.

To these other lands would be added until all or large parts of *Ranchos Santa Rita, Buri Buri, Salispuedes, Juristac, La Laguna, Bolsa de San Felipe, San Justo, Las Lomarías, Muertas, Aromitas y Agua Caliente, San Antonio, San Lorenzo, Orestimba, Las Animas,* and *Tesquesquito* speedily fell under his dominion.

One of his favorite methods was to buy out one or more of the heirs of the Spaniard who formerly owned the grant. This gave him as a tenant in common the right to range his cattle on the land. Often the other heirs had no cattle, so he would soon be practically in sole possession, but he would be careful in no way to exclude the others so as to make it necessary to account to them for the profits or use of the land. Gradually he would buy them all out, or if any of them became troublesome, he would compel a partition.

His dusty figure on horseback became a familiar sight for miles around. Rain or shine, day or night, he might be seen guiding the cattle on their long drive to market. Buying hay, getting water, employing vaqueros and moving supplies, was a continuous process. But above all the buying of land became an obsession.

Henry Miller has been called the "man who knew dirt." Early in his career a real estate agent came to him and said, "Mr. Miller, you don't need that lot on Jackson Street any more, why not sell it?" Henry Miller replied, "Land in California is cheap now, it will be valuable. Wise men buy land, fools sell. I will keep it." And thus he established the ruling principle of his life, to buy and not to sell.

To do this required that the land be made to produce. He was never "land poor" but always land rich. He had no illusions about land. It might be in tules and cattails, but if the soil was fine deep silt, he knew he could reclaim it by drainage, levees and fire.

If it only had a little spring feed, and was dry the balance of the year, he knew water would make it blossom if it had deep sediment built up from the overflow of the creeks.

If it had hardpan or yellow maul near the surface, he knew the most he could do with it was a crop of grain.

If the land had black alkali he knew it was worthless. If by reason of years of non-use white alkali had accumulated on the surface, he would flood it and thus wash the alkali out, and by keeping the water fresh he would get water grasses started which were strong enough to withstand the alkali in the soil. Abundant crops of wild hay were thus produced. After several years of treatment the land might be made to grow grain or other crops.

By merely looking at a piece of land at different seasons of the year, he could tell from the nature of the weeds and grasses which grew on it the extent of the alkali, and just what it could be made to grow.

Soon the United States surveyors were running lines all over the state. Much of the surveying was done by contract, and even before the plats were filed favored ones were tipped off, so that they might pick out the choice lands to file upon.

In the wake of the surveyors came the settlers and in the wake of the settlers came the land speculators. It was often charged by the Government that fraud was committed in obtaining title to land and many were prosecuted. No such charge was ever made against Henry Miller. In one case he had franchised some land and the Government later found that the person acquiring the land had committed a fraud on the Government. But it was held that Henry Miller purchased it in good faith, so he reclaimed it. He was always ready to buy from those who left the land for the mines or from those who were unable to utilize the land profitably, but at his own price.

School land, swamp land, homesteads and pre-emptions were bought up. Along the rivers and creeks, across the plains, up into the mountains his holdings grew, and as the land was acquired it was stocked until the "Double H" brand was seen in every valley, on every plain, and in every ravine.

VIII. THE GREAT CANAL

A S FAST as land was acquired along the San Joaquin River, dams were thrown in the sloughs, levees were thrown up, and the water spread over large tracts for the production of grasses. The economy and effectiveness of this method of wild irrigation were remarkable. A few levees across low places would often spread the water over large areas of land, and the eye of Henry Miller was as acute and keen as a surveyor's instrument to determine where the levees should be placed. To prevent perpetual inundation, the low places along the banks of the river were likewise filled. Crude but substantial boxes were placed in the head of branch channels to regulate the flow of the water. He became the wizard of the west in making green grass grow.

The basic principle was that water-loving grasses were desired. These were best produced by water reasonably deep on the surface, but kept fresh. This was best done by allowing the water to fill the land behind one levee and then flow over and into the next check. By using almost unlimited amounts of water, which was plentiful, this was accomplished with a minimum of labor. One *zanjero* could cover thousands of acres of land. By these means a small outlay of money gave immediate results. The grass would stand well up on the sides of the feeding animal. It could readily be cut for hay, but as a general rule, he was as economical in harvesting as in the growing of the crops. The cattle were not ordinarily supplied with waiters to hand them their food, but the cafeteria style was in vogue. The cattle did the harvesting; they cut and ate the grass where it grew. They transported it on the hoof in the form of fat. A piece of land would be bought and instantly it would be made to produce; this produce was automatically fed into the cattle, and they were automatically fed into the slaughter house and carried to the meat block. The land was thus made to pay for itself and a profit besides.

It is an old saying that a ranch house must have two things on it, a roof and a mortgage, but Henry Miller never had a mortgage on any of his land. He did not buy land merely to own it, or as a speculation, but he bought it principally to produce his annual stock in trade. His turn-over was rapid and produced a constant flow of gold, which was used to expand as the demand for meat grew.

In order to control the water he acquired land on both sides of the river for a distance of over a hundred and twenty miles, and he actually constructed levees along both sides of the river, so as to control entirely the flow of water, for a distance of fifty miles. This work was done largely with his own horses, mules and scrapers during the non-harvest period and was done at an astonishingly low unit of cost.

It is interesting to compare the work that he did in the San Joaquin Valley with the work done by public control in Sacramento Valley. There the reclamation of land from the overflow of the Sacramento River resulted in a charge on the land of several hundred dollars per acre which it was impossible for the landowners to pay. Practically no genuine attempt was made to pay it, but the landowners appealed to the State for assistance and received it; appealed to the Government for help and got it; and still the people who bought the securities of the district, and whose money was used to construct the works, were unable to collect their money for years and finally were compelled to sell their warrants to the State at fifty cents on the dollar.

But these accomplishments did not satisfy his ambition. His holdings extended far back from the river toward the foothills of the Mount Hamilton Range. They comprised a wide plain producing a little winter browse, but parched and dry in the summer. The erosion of ages from the mountains had deposited over this land a fine deep sediment and his practical eye knew it was the finest of his land if the water could be but led to it. He had determined where the water could be diverted near the confluence of the San Joaquin

River and Kings River and placed over this entire area, but he knew the cost would be large. It was part of his future program, but he felt that the country had not yet been sufficiently developed to justify such an enormous undertaking.

But then the speculator came on the scene. One day he found posted on the bank of the river at that point a notice that one John Bensley had "appropriated" a large amount of water to be used through a canal to be constructed for irrigation, transportation and mechanical purposes.

Henry Miller hied to his lawyer, who gave him an opinion that he thought the common law of riparian rights, which made the water belong to the land, was in force in the State, and not the law of "appropriation," by which the first comer might acquire rights therein; but the attorney was not sure.

A little later he was one day riding along the river and met an engineer named Brereton, an interesting character who had had experience with irrigation projects on the Nile and in India. They sat on the river bank and Brereton unfolded his scheme. It was indeed colossal. It contemplated a canal large enough to float boats running from Tulare Lake to San Francisco Bay, a distance of over one hundred and fifty miles. This was to be used to carry freight, and to supply water for the irrigation of land. A branch canal was to be taken out at the site already selected by Henry Miller to connect with this main canal. Brereton enlarged upon the project. He said that the people were already aroused against the railroad and would welcome anything that would give relief to the people, and particularly means of cheaply carrying farm products from the San Joaquin Valley to San Francisco Bay. He pointed out that for that reason the project would have public confidence and support.

Henry Miller was a good listener. He did not discourage the enthusiastic engineer, but he knew at once that under conditions then prevailing canal boats could not compete with railroads in that country, and his land did not extend south of the point which he had selected for the head of the canal, so he said, "It is a fine plan, but you will have to go slow. Build the branch canal first and it can be enlarged later. The country is not developed enough yet to warrant the cost."

The next thing Henry Miller heard was that Bensley was trying to interest San Francisco capital in his scheme. Soon the names of Alvinzo Hayward, A. H. Rose, Charles Webb Howard, O. Simmons, L. B. Benchley, J. Mora Moss, Isaac Friedlander, W. S. Chapman, W. H. Talbot, and other influential and public spirited men were mentioned in connection with the matter, and in 1871 the San Joaquin and Kings River Canal and Irrigation Company was organized with a capital of one million dollars. Public calls for subscriptions to the stock were made. The point that not only would land be irrigated, but that transportation facilities would be afforded, was stressed. The growing hostility of the farmers to the railroad was played upon, and the project was thus pictured as one of great public benefit. Chapman, who was himself a large owner of land in the San Joaquin Valley, invested heavily in the project, and from all over the country money was raised for the great work.

Then it was that Henry Miller let it be known that this enterprise could not go on until some understanding was had with him as to his riparian rights, and as a result contracts were signed by which he granted the canal company rights of way, gave it a subsidy, and in return the company agreed to furnish him water at a very low rate indeed, only one-half of the rate to be charged others. He received other advantages by the agreement as to free stock water and water to overflow his grass land when the water was not needed by other persons. Being thus protected he was able to sit back and see what these men might in fact be able to do.

He soon found that the enterprise was controlled by the promoters rather than by the financiers. They paid over one hundred thousand dollars for the alleged rights of Bensley, which consisted of the aforesaid notice posted upon a sycamore tree. They quarreled among themselves and spent large sums of money on the survey of the absurd ship

canal from Tulare Lake. He did not try to control
the matter, but merely guided things so that the
canal in which he was interested was dug. He held
before them the prospects of immediate income
from his land under his contract. He showed them
how to build the canal and where to build it and
it was his horses, men and tools that actually constructed it.

There was no railroad reaching the territory, so
the supplies were brought up the San Joaquin
River by barge, a distance of over a hundred and
fifty miles. This, however, owing to the tortuous
condition of the channel, could only be done during the short period of high water, so, at other
periods in the year, supplies were carried over the
Pacheco Pass, a distance of fifty miles from the
railroad which then ran from San Francisco to
Gilroy.

The people who had charge of the enterprise
refused to follow the lead of the railroad company,
which had employed Chinese labor, and advertised that this canal was to be the people's canal,
and was to be constructed by white labor, so no
Chinese were employed in its construction. For
implements all they had were plows and the old
style slip scraper, (this was before the so-called
Fresno Scraper, which got its name from that vicinity) and horses and mules. Henry Miller let them
handle the finances and control the general policy
of the company, or at least let them think they

were controlling it, but he was on the ground seeing that the men and animals were well fed and
that construction work progressed. The engineer
and superintendent worshiped him, and, although
he only held a nominal position with the company,
he practically superintended the construction work.

As a result in one year's time this canal was dug
a distance of fifty-eight miles, and a dam, three
hundred and fifty feet long, made of brush and
sand, was put across the river, which often carried
upwards of thirty thousand cubic feet of water per
second. Nothing like it had ever been built in the
West. Many scoffed and laughed at the idea that
such a river could be controlled in this manner,
but Henry Miller insisted that it could and it was.

While this work was going forward, Henry
Miller was getting his own land into shape to receive the water. Miles of lateral canals were constructed; thousands of acres were plowed; levees
were thrown up. A continuous line of freight
wagons traveled the road from Gilroy to Los Baños.
His figure on horseback, covered with dust, could
be seen any time of day or night, directing the
drivers and encouraging the workmen. Machinery,
foodstuffs, and lumber made up freight for trains
of wagons, drawn by horses and mules. They cut
deep into the soil and formed great ruts. The
heat was intense and the dust rose from each passing team and settled like a pall over the outfit.
Temporary camps were set up along the road

where the men might eat; water wagons carried water to troughs along the route. The jingling of bells on the horses—sometimes as many as sixteen horses to a wagon or string of wagons—could be heard, and passing on the narrow road became a problem. Drivers swore and cursed at the animals and at each other when they failed to wait at a turn-out. Down in the valley the line of the canal was indicated by a long cloud of dust raised by horses, mules and scrapers.

As the work proceeded an added obstacle was met. The legislature had declared the San Joaquin River navigable to a point above the location of this dam, so that they had to construct it in such a way that if perchance a boat did come up to the dam, it could get through and the dam would not act as an obstruction to navigation and be subject to abatement. This obstacle, however, was also overcome by constructing a collapsible wooden weir on one end of the dam.

As soon as the river dropped in the fall, scrapers were placed in the bed of the river and sand was piled up, and alternating layers of sand and brush were put in the channel, allowing the water in the meantime to run through the collapsible weir. There was a small island in the middle of the stream, and this was used as an anchor for the structure. Thousands upon thousands of yards of sand, and acres upon acres of willow trees were hauled into place and cunningly interlaced so as to finally form a dam over three hundred and fifty feet in length. The first year after it was constructed there was one of the biggest floods ever experienced, but the dam held. It remained in the river over twenty-five years, when it was replaced by a wooden weir, and that again remained in the river for twenty-five years and was replaced by a concrete weir,—the three structures well illustrating the advances in engineering during the period. The original cost of the canal and dam was over one and a quarter million dollars. Considering the unfavorable conditions, the construction was a marvel. A few years later the canal was extended to its present length of seventy-one miles.

No sooner had the canal been completed than the trouble of the promoters began. In the first place so far as getting water of Kings River from Tulare Lake was concerned, it was found that other and prior rights to that water prevented this, so that part of the project had to be abandoned. This was in line with Henry Miller's views. Then an intense opposition to a privately owned canal developed. This was but a repetition of the history of the railroad; all hailed its construction with delight, but, when completed, its owners were considered public enemies.

The charge of two dollars and fifty cents per acre for water was called an "outrageous exaction." The company was called a "monopoly." The so-called "granger movement" was at its height, and the political campaign was enlivened by picturing this giant monopolization of water. Everyone connected with the project was abused. The successful candidate for Governor, Newton Booth, had expressed the view that the enterprise should be publicly owned. Those interested in it were so disgusted that, under date of December 9, 1873, they sent a memorial to the Governor offering to sell the enterprise at a price to be fixed by commissioners to be appointed by the Governor. The Governor showed the sincerity of his expression by taking no notice of the memorial, and the canal is still in private ownership.

But this was not all. They say you can take a horse to water, but you can not make him drink. So when the canal was completed, Henry Miller, instead of taking water for all of the land covered by his contract, took it for such as he desired. The promoters argued and the contract was examined but was found to be singularly unilateral. He was entitled to the water, but was not required to take it. Opinions were sought, suit was filed and general dissatisfaction prevailed. Settlers were few, and their grain, grown by irrigation, could not compete with the grain grown by the dry farmers. There was no railroad transportation. The canal company had to establish an experimental farm to demonstrate that the country could be made to grow anything. This caused more loss of money.

Finally, in disgust, the promoters threw up

their hands and sold the controlling interest to Henry Miller for less than one-third of its cost. The promoters beat a sad and sorry retreat, the San Francisco financiers gladly assumed the rôle of minority stockholders, and Henry Miller not only had a canal system to irrigate his land, but to sell water to the entire community. Chapman, the leading spirit in the enterprise, lost his vast east side lands to the Scotch capitalists who had advanced him money, and all of his west side lands fell under the control of Henry Miller. The canal was immediately put in condition and under economical management. Alfalfa was introduced into the territory and it became a prolific dairy and cattle country. The water supply was the cheapest and best in the State.

During these hectic years of contest between Henry Miller and the canal speculators, a peculiar situation developed. Under his contract, he was entitled to spread over his grass land any water which was wasted by the canal company, because not demanded by its customers. As settlers were few, the water had to be wasted, and it developed that it could not be wasted in any way except to send it down channels which inevitably led it to Henry Miller's land. Even as settlers did increase, many of them would not irrigate at night, and many of them had religious scruples and would not irrigate on Sunday, and the result was that the water had to be turned out of the canal and ran down the channels to be used to grow grass for Henry Miller without compensation. Years later this resulted in an amusing incident in a case in court involving waste from this canal. It was contended that the non-use of water on Sunday was a necessary and legitimate loss. The opposing attorney, one of the leading jury lawyers of the period, tall and impressive, and with a peculiar ability to talk through his nose, turned with withering scorn and said, "I can visualize this German squatting on the top of Camp Thirteen Waste, seeing this water flowing out on Sunday to enrich his grasses, fatten his steers and increase his bank account, holding his hands over his expansive stomach, turning his eyes devoutly toward Heaven, and singing:

" 'Day of all the days the best,
Emblem of eternal rest'. "

As this canal was the first occasion in the State to test the conflict between public and private ownership, it also played a conspicuous part in various other economic questions. Until the extremely lean years in the nineties, the company collected its own rates, but then public bodies attempted to fix rates. The company contested their validity in the Federal Courts. The public bodies claimed that the rate base should be the reproduction cost less depreciation, at the greatly depreciated cost of that period. The company claimed

HENRY MILLER AT TWENTY

HENRY MILLER AT FORTY

that the original cost should be the basis. Both judges and economists still differ on this subject. In those years people generally opposed to public utilities strongly urged present value as against original cost. The company prevailed in the lower court, but the Supreme Court of the United States decided against it and established the rule of present value.

Later the matter was again litigated on the basis of present value and the company then claimed that it owned a "water right," and that although it may not have cost the company anything, it was worth one million dollars and the company should have a return on it. It lost its contention in the trial court, but established it in the Supreme Court of the United States. Thus the doctrine was established and the contention of the rate payers was turned against them, and the capitalization of the "unearned increment" made possible. The *O'Fallon* case, which has recently attracted national attention, is but an echo of this decision.

One day Henry Miller was going over the great canal and saw some men working on a stop gate. "What are you building that for, when we have Camp Thirteen Gate?" he asked. The foreman deferentially answered, "This biga canal gota too mucha grade. She runa too fast. Him gate stop her." As Henry Miller went on down the canal, he saw the green fields below the canal and on the higher ground above the canal the country was parched and dry. He owned many thousands of acres of fine land above the canal and as he jogged along the words of the foreman kept coming into his mind. He noticed that the water flowed quite swiftly in the canal, and it finally dawned on him that if the canal had been built with less grade it would have covered more land and that, if the original canal could have been built higher, a branch canal could be taken out on the high side of the canal and run at a less grade. When he got to town he hurried into the engineer's room and said, "Mr. McCray, I wants a canal out of the main canal for the land above the main canal." "That would run uphill, Mr. Miller," said McCray. "You builds me a canal," Henry Miller said, and stamped out of the room.

The survey was made and fully justified his surmise, and a canal thirty-five miles in length was dug during the hard times in the nineties when men worked for a dollar a day. The cheapness with which the canal was dug bothered the company in fixing its value for rate fixing purposes. When he saw how cheaply it was dug, he determined to build a new river weir and get the advantage of cheap prices on labor and material. Men were tramping the country almost in armies looking for work, and he employed as many as possible and did all the work possible during the period of low prices.

Thus it came about that Henry Miller became

the owner of the best canal system in the west, finally supplying water to over one hundred and fifty thousand acres of land, and he thus became a purveyor of water to the public. This was his one great public undertaking. That he discharged the public duty satisfactorily is more than proved by the fact that while many other communities formed irrigation districts and took over the private systems, the people of this area steadfastly refused to disturb the private ownership of this canal.

IX. THE SWAMP OF THE KERN

IN ORDER to aid in the reclamation of swamp
and overflowed land, Congress passed the
Swamp Land Act, September 28, 1850, nineteen
days after California was admitted to the Union.
The act provided that "to enable the several states
. . . to construct the necessary levees and drains,
to reclaim the swamp and over-flow land therein"
there should be granted to the several states "the
whole of the swamp and overflowed land, made
unfit thereby for cultivation. . . . The proceeds of
said lands, whether by sale or by direct appropriation in kind, shall be applied exclusively, as far
as necessary, to the reclamation of said lands, by
means of levees and drains."

By this bountiful act California received over
two million acres of land. Her observance of the
obligations of the act were largely formal and
perfunctory. She first provided for the sale of the
land for one dollar and a quarter per acre, and
then provided that the owner of a body of swamp
land might make proof before the Board of Super-
visors of the county of the expenditure of a dollar
and a quarter per acre in the reclamation of the
land and obtain repayment of the purchase price.

This presented a grand opportunity to acquire large tracts of such land, and as it was just the kind of land needed for cattle, Henry Miller availed himself generously of the opportunity. The swamp land bordered the rivers, and along the San Joaquin he acquired a continuous strip for over one hundred miles.

But even this comparatively easy method of obtaining land did not satisfy the cupidity of others. A man named Montgomery conceived the scheme of reclaiming a large body of the swamp land in the southern portion of the San Joaquin Valley, amounting to about ninety thousand acres. He and his associates prevailed upon the Legislature of the State to grant them this entire acreage on certain conditions as to reclamation. Not being able to carry out the huge project, they sold large tracts to others, and Henry Miller and his associates acquired from them many acres along the lower end of Kern River. From this and other sources they obtained a tract of land fifty miles in length and containing over one hundred thousand acres.

When Montgomery failed to carry out the provisions of the act, the Attorney-General of the State brought a suit to cancel the patent. This was quite distasteful to Henry Miller and his associates, so they prepared an act providing that when Montgomery had sold part of the land and it had been reclaimed, such fact might be established in the suit and the land allotted to such purchaser.

This act was rushed through the legislature and became law.

This land was in what might be called the overflow basin of Kern River. Through it the river flowed in various channels or sloughs, the principal one being known as Buena Vista Slough, but in flood time the lands were entirely inundated, because the sloughs were inadequate to carry the water, which flowed over the land and finally drained into Tulare Lake.

In order to comply with the terms of the act Henry Miller conceived a huge reclamation project, consisting of a new river channel along one side of the property. For this purpose a right of way for a "canal" was obtained from the United States over the adjoining land, and the new channel was put on government land, which was dry and worthless. Horses, mules, plows and scrapers were collected, and the dust was made to fly. The canal was one hundred feet wide and fifty miles in length. Gates were constructed to control the flow of the river into this new channel, and soon one hundred thousand acres of land were reclaimed.

No sooner was this accomplished than the news came that others had their eyes on the waters of Kern River. From Kentucky had come a picturesque character named J. B. Haggin. He had spent considerable time in Arabia and was a lover of fine horses. He had joined forces with Lloyd Tevis, already a strong man in financial circles in San

Francisco. Under the name of Haggin & Tevis, they had acquired land further up the river near Bakersfield, and conceived the idea of spreading the water of the river over the extensive plains of the valley. But the land which they proposed to irrigate had been patented by the Government in small parcels and only a small part was riparian to the river.

There thus arose the contest between this claim of Haggin & Tevis to "appropriate" the water and sell it to settlers on the broad plains of the valley and the claim of Henry Miller that the water was part and parcel of the land touching the bank of the stream,—a battle between the law of appropriation and the law of riparian rights, and a battle between giants.

In the early stages of this contest the most bitter feelings were engendered. Stop-gates were torn out and armed forces guarded the canals. At one time two sets of armed men faced each other from the opposite sides of the levee, each watching the other for the first hostile move. Bloodshed was only averted by the arrival of the sheriff with an injunction. This transferred the contest to the courts.

In this fight the best legal talent was procured. The case of Henry Miller was put into the hands of Hall McAllister, considered to be the most brilliant member of the bar of the State. In proof of this and the wisdom of his selection by Henry Miller, the fact may be pointed to that his statue now stands before the City Hall of San Francisco, the greatest honor ever accorded a lawyer of California. He was backed up by T. I. Bergin, R. E. Houghton and others.

The case of Haggin & Tevis was put in the hands of John Garber, the leader of the bar in appellate court work, a man with the face of the idealized type of the American Indian, wrinkled and bronzed, with long, coarse hair and with one of the keenest analytical minds possessed by the great lawyers of California. He had around him Thornton, Bishop, Flournoy, Mhoon, Stanley, Stoney, Hayes and others. Those interests also later obtained the friendly assistance of the Crockers, who were attempting to appropriate the waters of the Merced River. They were represented by William F. Herrin, then a young man, but later destined to become Chief Counsel of the Southern Pacific Railroad Company, and for many years the most powerful political factor in the State.

On the side of Henry Miller the contention was made that the river flowed in defined channels through his land, and that as such riparian owner he was entitled to the full flow of the stream. This claim was predicated on the fact that such was the common law of England, and that the Legislature of California, when it met in San Jose in 1850, had adopted the common law of England as the law of the State and the rule of decision therein. As a matter of interest it might be stated that this action of the Legislature was taken even before the State had been admitted to the Union.

On the other hand Haggin & Tevis claimed that California was a semi-arid State, that irrigation was essential, that the common law rule of riparian right was not applicable to her conditions, and that it was, therefore, not the law of the State.

Those claiming the right of appropriation were fortified by the fact that during mining days, when no one owned the land, the right of appropriation was recognized. In other words, neither having any real title, priority or possession of land or water was equivalent to right. Then the United States Government had expressly recognized such right of appropriation, as against the Government as the owner of the public domain.

In the vicinity where this dispute arose there were hundreds of persons to be benefited by the right of appropriation and only a few by riparian rights. Public sentiment was, therefore, strongly against the Miller claim in the place where the question must be tried. In other parts of the State the sentiment was divided, but the great mass were against the "monopolistic" claim of the riparian owners. Thus Henry Miller was drawn into one of the greatest judicial contests of the West.

At the trial Henry Miller was a commanding figure. He had passed the years of his impetuous youth and developed into a striking mature figure. His active life, spent mostly in the saddle, had preserved his spare figure. He wore a dark pointed beard, with the upper lip shaved. His nose was prominent and his eyes were dreamy. His clothes were dark and simple.

Around him was gathered an army of pioneers, rough, rugged, and tanned by the dust and heat of the range.

When Henry Miller took the witness stand, people leaned forward to catch every word. His pronounced German accent and his idiomatic language tended to add flavor to his words, and his ability to see every trap set for him by the able counsel who examined him was uncanny.

His knowledge of the country was phenomenal. Every turn in the river, every slough, every watering place, every ford was indelibly fixed on his mind; and every flood, how long it lasted, and what land it covered, were matters of contemporary history to which he could testify.

If the other side would try to have a channel disappear at a certain point, he could testify to swimming at that very point.

He and his pioneer witnesses reproduced a picture of the country more vivid than any map.

He recounted how he had controlled the stream, allowing enough water to flow through the channels to produce grass for his cattle, and explained how worthless his land would be if the water were taken away.

He was backed up by his neighboring landowners who were themselves important figures: Frederick Cox, a politician and member of the Legislature; Crawford Clark, a picturesque character who was driven by a desire to own land quite as strong as the motive that drove Henry Miller; John Center, who had given Henry Miller his first worthwhile job in the State; George N. Cornwall, who in later years lost his land and committed suicide; John H. Redington, the leading wholesale drug dealer in the State; Horatio Stebbins, a leading clergyman of San Francisco; L. H. Bonestell, a leading paper dealer in the State; and Horatio B. Livermore, whose career is one of the most picturesque in the West.

Opposed to this aggregation were Haggin and Tevis, surrounded by the new-comers in the country, men who had no money with which to buy swamp land, so had taken up homesteads and pre-emptions. They had endured the discomforts of "proving up" on the dry plains with the hope that water would be brought to them. Individually they presented pathetic figures, but in the aggregate they were a power. They represented the voting strength of the country.

Long before the trial was over, it was clear that the judge was strongly in their favor, and the trial became only the making of a record of his errors.

Shortly after the trial Henry Miller had a nervous breakdown, and was practically compelled to quit for a time and was induced to take a trip to Europe. There he found his native town, Brackenheim, proud of his achievements, and his native country, Germany, glorying in the crowning of the Emperor at the Palace of Versailles and firmly in the control of Bismarck, now at the height of his power. Brackenheim named one of its streets "Henry Miller Strasse." He met Bismarck, with whom he has frequently been compared, and returned to the United States and California renewed and revived and ready to conquer the world.

When he again jumped into the saddle the first thing he found was that the great case had been decided against him, and the waters of the Kern River had by the judgment of the trial court been taken away from him and given to the populace of Kern County. He was quick to charge this loss to the mismanagement of his partner, and when the papers were shown him his indignation was brought to the boiling point when he saw that in his absence the papers had been manipulated by one of his minor attorneys in such a way that his partner's name appeared before his; and in the abbreviated title of the case (*Lux* v. *Haggin*, 69 Cal. 255) his name did not appear at all.

It did not take him long to show his partner who was the head of the firm and he immediately grabbed the reins, as it were, and took personal charge of the case. He listened to the antiquated jargon of the attorneys, their Latin phrases, and their statement that the water belonged where it had flowed from time immemorial. He clearly saw the point, but strange to say this was one of the words he was never able to master, although it was one which he loved to use, and no one had the heart to correct him when he referred, as he did, to "time immemortal."

He readily recognized that there was something more involved than the question of law. He had gone through the "granger movement," he had seen the populace aroused to the cry "The Chinese must go"; he had seen the sand-lotter, Dennis Kearney, leading the voters of the great metropolitan center as so many sheep to the slaughter. He had seen Dennis Kearney grow in power and even force the adoption of a new Constitution for the State, which Bryce later dubbed a specimen of the worst Constitution in the United States. He knew that the cry of the multitude was against him; he knew that his opponents were fanning their hatred; he knew that they were buying newspapers, and that petty politicians were being brought under their control.

Realizing the situation he proceeded to plan his campaign like a general. He saw that the question would finally be determined according to whether the law or the mere demands of the greatest number would prevail. He said, "We must have judges who believe in law and property, and we must fight the 'sand-lotters' who are trying to get control of the judges."

Both sides invoked the aid of the press. One side pleaded for the rights of the pioneers who had settled along the rivers relying on the English law of riparian rights. The other relied upon the practice of the miners to appropriate water without owning any land. One side extolled the common law and the other pleaded for the law of the West.

Both sides went into politics. The bosses of the State were ranged on the opposite sides of the conflict. They attempted to control conventions and elections. Money flowed like water in the fight.

Henry Miller watched every move of his opponents and matched every effort they put forth.

Suddenly a real difficulty came into the picture. The Crocker interests, at a belated date, found that they were vitally interested in the contest. They employed a young lawyer, named William F. Herrin and soon Henry Miller began to see his fine Italian hand working in the right direction, and where his efforts would count. This made him much trouble. But Herrin was too late.

As an illustration of the extent to which the parties went in this historic litigation, this incident might be recited: One of the vital questions was whether or not the sloughs through the Miller land in fact existed as continuous watercourses or channels. The United States had never mapped the territory, because it is the custom of the United

States simply to segregate the swamp land from the upland and not to survey or subdivide the swamp itself. Therefore the early maps of the country showed none of the channels through his land. However, about the time of this litigation the State Engineer was engaged in making maps of the entire State, and the sheet that involved this particular area was being prepared by the State Engineer. His maps were not being made entirely from individual surveys, but he was using all available material that he could collect, and the engineers of Henry Miller saw to it that a survey of the land delineating and locating all of these channels reached the State Engineer's office. They were nursing the State Engineer and watching every move. They took him over the land and helped point out and locate the channels and he agreed to put the channels upon the map when it was prepared. What took place in the meantime will never be known, except that it may be assumed that the Haggin & Tevis interests were not asleep, and finally the State Engineer's map came out, and true to his promise all of the channels were delineated on the map, but across the face of the map was a rubber stamp which stated, "These channels are not located by the personal surveys of the State Engineer, but are from data supplied by other parties and are not guaranteed." Consequently the entire benefit of the map was lost, and thus the promise of the State Engineer was kept in form only.

The argument in the case covered a wide range, and, of course, the Miller interests played up the fact that this country was not any longer a Spanish or Mexican country, but had been conquered by English speaking people; and the first act of its people was to carry to it the laws of England, which had been brought to almost all of the States of the Union and were considered as a sacred heritage of English speaking people. This argument, of course, immediately appealed to judges who had come from various states where the common law of England was the rule of decision and from colleges where Blackstone was the Bible of the lawyer, who were nurtured in the law of England and considered it as a law that automatically accommodated itself to every clime and every people, a law that was capable of ruling people in the cold climate of Massachusetts, the torrid climate of Arizona, or the semi-arid climate of California.

The Haggin & Tevis interests, on the other hand, argued that the boast of the common law was the fact that when the reason of the rule ceased, the rule itself no longer prevailed. They pointed to the comparatively few acres of land that would be irrigated under the riparian doctrine and to the millions of acres of land in the arid plains of the great valleys of California, which under the riparian doctrine would be doomed to aridity. They argued that the rule of law which existed in the British Isles, where it rained every month in the year, and where irrigation was entirely unnecessary for the production of crops, could not possibly have been intended to prevail in a State where the rainfall was slight and of short duration and the land was incapable of growing the usual crops without artificial moisture.

The minor issue as to whether the channels existed was lost in the overwhelming importance of the main legal question involved, and was finally practically thrown into the discard, when one of the attorneys was arguing that the channels disappeared, and one of the justices leaned toward his neighbor and said, "If the channel disappeared, where did all of that water go to?" His fellow justice replied in an audible whisper, "I guess it must have run into a gopher hole."

When the case was first decided it was decided in favor of the riparian doctrine and in favor of the Miller interests. Immediately there was a public clamor, and one of the justices in particular was picked out for most virulent attack and open vilification through the press of the State. The attack was so scandalous that it defeated its own end, and the people of the State began to sympathize with the justice of high standing who had courage to make an unpopular decision, and instead of defeating him the attack resulted in his overwhelming reëlection.

However, the assault made on the decision was sufficient to cause a rehearing of the case, and the whole matter had to be gone through again. Finally the case came to decision and it fell to the lot of Justice McKinstry to write the opinion of the court. A man of higher standing, morally and intellectually, could not well have been found, but if the whole world had been sought for a man of unimpeachable character, who was still the best suited to uphold the riparian doctrine for which the Miller interests contended, no one could have done better than to have selected Justice McKinstry for that part. He was an old man already and lived to be much older. He was born and bred in the common law, and knew his Blackstone forwards and backwards. He believed honestly and sincerely in the omnipotence of the law and the infallibility of the common law of England to solve every human dispute.

His decision was most erudite and covered, with copious citations and translations, the laws of Mexico, Spain, France, England, the United States and California. It is one of the longest opinions in judicial history, and occupies two hundred pages in the California Reports. It was a victory for the common law, for the riparian doctrine, and for Henry Miller, and through all the assaults that have been made upon it, it still stands as the recognized law of the State, although it was only a four to three decision.

The floodgates of abuse again opened. The Governor of the State was prevailed upon to declare that a public calamity had been occasioned by the decision, and he hastily called the Legislature of the State together to undo the supposed wrong. Again all of the political powers of the State began to pull and haul, but Henry Miller and his legal advisers sat complacently by, knowing full well that nothing the Legislature might do could override the decision of a court determining a right of property.

The Legislature met, the newspapers carried scare headlines, and there was much resoluting, but it only resulted in the passage of one act of the legislature repealing one section of the Civil Code, but the riparian owners introduced into the act a proviso of two lines to the effect that the repeal should not affect vested rights. So the Legislature adjourned, conscious of having performed a great public service, but leaving Miller interests secure in their vested rights as determined by the courts of the State.

Did Henry Miller rest satisfied with the decision which gave him and his associates all of the water of Kern River? Not at all. He immediately said, "There is more water than we can use, and it does not come at the right time of the year. It comes in a great flood early in the spring, and in the hot months of summer the river is dry." So he said to his late antagonists, "You builds me a reservoir, and I gives you two-thirds of the water," and the difficulty was solved. Buena Vista Lake was turned into a reservoir, and a most remarkable reservoir, because it contained twenty-three thousand acres of land, probably the biggest reservoir in the United States. That did not make it a good reservoir, because it had too much surface for evaporation, but it was the best that the topography of the country offered at the time.

The two great interests, now brought close together by the great fight, joined forces. Levees were hastily constructed and a reservoir built to impound one third of the water for Henry Miller and his associates, and the other two-thirds was permitted to be taken out and distributed over the arid land of Kern County. The reservoir has continued to serve its purpose until the present day, but is shortly to be replaced by a more compact reservoir, where this great loss from evaporation will not occur. In this settlement Henry Miller showed that he was not only a great general, but also a great statesman at the peace table.

X. NEVADA AND THE
"SEVEN S" BRAND (𝔍)

IT WAS a tired caravan that halted from exhaustion on the banks of the Walker River in
Nevada. It had traveled from Salt Lake and followed the trail of Walker through the burning sands
of the desert. Horses had died on the way, oxen
had fallen from exhaustion, and the few remaining
wagons had their covers torn to shreds. Indians
and wild animals had pursued and harassed them,
sickness and death stalked their line of march.
Now dirty, grimy, exhausted, hungry, thirsty, discouraged, the remnant of the band found itself at
"Pisen Switch."

Here one trail continued on to California and
one turned to Fort Churchill and the Oregon country. To add to the discomfort of the party dissension had arisen. Gradually this had divided the
party into two groups; on one side was tall, lanky
Jim Mills, "Ang" McLeod, "Hog" Bermingham,
Merritt, Snyder, Spragg, Bewley, Alcorn and Knox,
the latter of whom had never been just right since
going over the sandy desert around Great Salt Lake.
The other side was led by a promising young man

95

named Mallett, about whom we shall hear more in Oregon. When the first group had seen in the far distance the desert contracting into Walker River Canyon and the green foliage along the river like a distant mirage, they vowed that when they reached it they would go no further.

That night about the camp fire this determination was again announced. They said here was land and water and beyond the Sierra Nevada. They were not miners, but farmers. Mallett declared that the country was generally "ornery" and full of alkali and wanted the party to go north into Oregon. Indeed it did appear to be alkaline, and it is uncertain whether the name "Pisen Switch" grew out of the character of liquor that was served at the little saloon at the cross-roads or came from the poisonous alkali that blew in from the desert. The discussion continued far into the night and finally the party split, Mills and his party remaining in what became Mason Valley and Mallett and his adherents going on in to Oregon.

All up and down the Walker River they took up land. While the first appearances had been uninviting, the land proved to be fertile when irrigated. Nevada had received a large land grant from the United States, and this land was sold on long term contracts. After exhausting homesteads and pre-emption rights, they contracted for large bodies of this land in the names of friends, relatives and employees.

Time went on. The Central Pacific Railroad soon constructed its line across Nevada and joined that State with California and San Francisco Bay. Henry Miller had long been aware of the wonderful cattle that they were raising in Nevada. One of the great difficulties of the cattle industry in California was that the hot climate of the San Joaquin Valley was conducive to disease, and various diseases prevailed among the cattle in that region, but in Nevada, where the climate was generally cold, the cattle were extremely healthy and entirely free from disease of any kind. As soon as the railroad came through, it gave a means of transportation for cattle, and he immediately saw the possibility and advantage of breeding cattle in Nevada, where land was cheap and range plentiful, and shipping them by rail to California.

He planted this idea in the mind of a young man named N. H. A. Mason, later popularly called "Hoc" Mason, and promised to finance him in establishing cattle ranches in Nevada, and assuring him of support and promising to give him the preference in the purchase of cattle raised in that country.

Mason went to Nevada and finally landed at "Pisen Switch" in what is now called Mason Valley. The town itself has since changed its name to Yerington, in honor of the man who built a branch railroad from the Southern Pacific line to Churchill. Mason began his operations by buying out

Spragg, Bewley, Alcorn and other settlers in the vicinity. This was followed gradually by the purchase of additional areas until at last he had stretching down the Walker River a holding of twenty thousand acres of land, all of which was paid for by drafts drawn on Henry Miller.

Soon Mason began to grow cattle on those properties and ship them to California as a credit against his expenditures.

He gradually extended his activities further north and up in the neighborhood of the Oregon line, first acquiring a little property known as Quin River Crossing, and from that gradually reaching out, buying from the settlers their small ranches and putting them into one holding. His lands were north of the Black Rock Desert, and were scattered along the streams that came down from Jackson Mountains and Pine Forest Range: Bilk Creek, Leonard Creek, Battle Creek, Craine Creek, Thousand Creek, High Rock Creek, Bartlett Creek, Soldiers Creek, Alder Creek, Virgin Creek, Massacre Creek and many others, to say nothing of numerous springs. On the south was a narrow strip of land along High Rock Creek, which flows in the narrow gorge known as High Rock Canyon. Through this the covered wagons of the pioneers passed to escape the snow which blocked the central Overland Trail. Eagles' nests can be seen on the sides of the canyon and parts of wagons can be found where they were abandoned by the travelers.

On the east rises Disaster Peak, where the Indians massacred an entire party of emigrants.

On the north the chalklike hills have been washed into rounded hillocks giving the appearance in the distance of Arabian mosques.

In the center of the holdings is Summit Lake Piute and Shoshone Indian Reservation, and one of the ranches named Massacre reminds us of some of the most recent of Indian atrocities. Near this place the last hopeless Indian uprising in the West was terminated by the extermination of the band of Indians involved.

One of the ranches carries the legend of a brave woman who was left alone with her eight year old boy and a Chinese cook. The cook suddenly went insane and attacked the woman. She managed to throw him and by almost superhuman power held him while the boy got an ax and with one blow cut off the man's head.

Through the hills were abandoned cabins of miners and prospectors. These became the hiding places of cattle rustlers.

Mason adopted as his brand the "Seven S" brand and it soon was seen on every range in northwestern Nevada.

The ownership of these ranches, each comprising possibly a few hundred acres, along some stream, gave control to thousands of acres of pasture lands on the public domain, where the cattle could freely range during the summer period. The steers were then shipped to California and during the winter months the cows and calves were brought in and fed on the hay raised on the ranches. The success of this method depended upon the balancing of the number of cattle with the amount of hay that was available on the ranches, because the winters were so severe that it was impossible for cattle to survive on the ranges.

In California, Henry Miller for years had looked forward to the time when there would be a drought, and all over his ranches could be found large stacks of hay, carried over from year to year. He would rent additional land, although he had on his own land thousands of tons of hay carried over from previous years. When asked why he was doing this, he said, "There have been dry years in California, and they will come again, and when they do come I wants to be able and ready to meet them."

The cattle business in Nevada was extremely profitable. Mason was buying land like a drunken sailor and was anxious to turn off all the cattle possible in order to meet the expense. He, therefore, carried every head of cattle that could possibly be fed during the winter, making no provision whatever for the future. Then came a series of dry years; 1887 was dry, 1888 was drier, and 1889 was

the driest year in the history of the West. Gradually the number of cattle had to be reduced. Every
expedient was resorted to to keep them alive, many
perished, and the small remnant that was left at
the end of the dry season of 1889 was brought to
the ranches, now poorly, if at all, supplied with
hay. Every possible ton of hay available was procured. The cattle were cut down to a minimum
number, and then came the longest and most severe
winter that the country had ever experienced—the
winter of 1889-90.

For months snow and rain fell. The winter extended without the usual breakup until late in the
spring. The hay was exhausted. The ground was
so covered with snow that it was impossible for
the cattle to feed and the result was that hundreds,
yea, thousands of cattle miserably perished, and
when the winter was over not only Mason but a
great majority of other cattle men in the vicinity
were broke. Mortgages on their places were foreclosed, and in order to protect himself, Henry
Miller invariably became the purchaser and soon
found himself in possession of a vast domain extending from Walker River to the Oregon line.

He immediately visited his new holdings and
became familiar with every acre of the land as he
was with his California holdings. He saw what
land was good and what was bad and what land
should still be acquired. He had great admiration
as well as sympathy for Mason, and took him into

his employ to handle the property. He had the property located and surveyed, abandoned the contracts for land which he deemed worthless, and decided what additional land should be acquired in order to round out the property. He found that the key to the entire situation was water. All over the vast range there were little springs, and one of those springs would control a very large area of range land. If some homesteader took up one hundred sixty acres on which one of those springs was located, it would make the land useless for cattle for many miles around it. He, therefore, had all of the springs in the country located and proceeded to obtain title to them. This he was able to do by the use of various kinds of scrip: railroad scrip, soldier's scrip and Indian scrip. The ranches comprised about ninety thousand acres of land and his cattle could range over two thousand square miles of range.

"Mr. Mason," he said, "I wants you to make the people friendly. Help them in gathering their cattle out of the ranges. Be careful that your men do not brand any of their calves. When you make your drives, see that your men are careful not to drive away the stock of other people so far that they will be unable to return home.

"Do not fence any of the springs on the range, but let anybody's cattle water at them. Sheep men own no land and sheep destroy the range for cattle. You can keep them away from the waterholes, but let everybody that has ranches use the waterholes for their cattle. It will make them friendly and help you in the long run.

"Be friendly with public officials and also with the newspapers. If they speak well of us, everyone will think well of us. Help to elect good men to office and they will keep the taxes down. It is better to pay taxes than to pay a lot of crooks.

"This is a rough country, has lots of mountains in it, and it is too rough for the big Durham cattle. We must get some good mountain climbers, and I will send up some Devon and Hereford bulls to use with the Durham cows. It takes the Hereford to climb over rocky mountains and find the feed. In California we have used the Devon and the Hereford bulls with the Durham cows, till we have produced an animal with red color and white face, so that anybody can tell our stock without looking at the brand. We will do the same thing up here.

"We can't raise any more steers in this country than we have cows. We have to keep the cows here in the winter. We can't winter any more than we have hay for. Get more water out on the land and raise more hay. Whenever you see a good bunch of cattle, buy it, together with the farmer's hay. Whenever you buy hay, get the right to feed it on the ground, then ship the cattle to California and keep the hay for a bad winter.

"You haven't been irrigating right on this ranch.

There is too much alkali in the land to permit the water to stand very deep or very long. Level the land up a little, get the water over quick, drain it off, then the alkali won't come up. Don't try to develop poor land for alfalfa, it is better for native grasses. Stop developing such land and put in a thirty-five dollar a month man to take care of it. When you develop land, develop good land.

"Don't buy hay just by the measure, it depends on the weight and quality whether it is good for anything. This big swamp hay measures fine, but it is no good for cattle, it has no nutriment.

"My attorneys tell me the law is different up here, you can only hold the water by appropriating and using it. Use all of it, use it all the time, get it over the land, never mind little fancy ditches, put dams in the streams and flood it over the land; it is cheaper and gives better results.

"As soon as possible build up and hold over on each ranch an amount of hay equal to a good year's crop, so as to be ready for another dry year; it will come again about ten years from now; we wants to be ready for it. A lot of men want to show profit and eat up all of their hay to do it. It is like eating up your capital to show a profit; you don't fool yourself or anybody else.

"There is only a little good land in this country and we want to get all of it that we can, but don't get yourself mixed up with the Government by getting people to file on land. The homesteaders know that we are in the market, and they know what our price is; whenever they want to sell at our price, buy. Never discuss the price with them. If they want to meet our price, you buy, if not, let them keep their land.

"Don't hurry the cattle when you make a drive. The fat on the cattle is worth more than the wages of a few men who are driving them. Let the cattle go slow, don't get them nervous and tired out. Always keep friendly with the neighbors along the line of your drive to the railroad, so that they will let you water and sell you hay.

"I see that your fences have run down, it pays to keep them up all of the time; always have your men carry a hammer in their overalls when they are riding around, so they can keep the fences in shape. It is cheaper than to rebuild them after they have broken down. Your barns needs whitewash, your houses needs paint. Your hay stacks are too close together. If one of them got on fire you are likely to lose them all. You should have a high tank to protect the houses from fire.

"These old family orchards around the houses should be taken care of. It's a long way to ship anything up here and the men needs lots of apple sauce. Give your men plenty of good food, it keeps them good natured and you gets more work out of them. The bunk houses are in bad condition; they should be kept clean. You won't get the best men to work for you unless you have a good place for them to sleep. It don't make any difference how plain the place is, but it should be kept clean.

"Don't let the men go around the barns with loose matches in their pockets, they are likely to set fire to the hay. Give every man a little metal match box and make him carry it. Never leave cattle very long in a field with a water trough without going to the field and seeing that the water is running. Once we lost twelve horses in a field because the water became shut off and the horses perished. Very bad.

"Don't keep fancy stallions that have to be kept in the stable all the time; let them run with the mares. It saves a lot of work for the men and will get eighty-five per cent of colts."

As they traveled from ranch to ranch there was a continuous run of suggestions as to how these rundown ranches could be brought back into proper shape. Finally Henry Miller broke out and said, "Mr. Mason, how are your water rights up here?"

Mr. Mason said, "They are fine, Mr. Miller, our water rights on the Mason Ranch are very early, way back in the early sixties."

"We are going to have a lot of trouble over this water some day," said Henry Miller. "I hear that Tom Rickey is getting a lot of land up in the mountains in California and taking the water of Walker River out above us. Pretty soon we won't have any water and then there will be a lot of trouble. Many

of these old men are dying and we won't be able
to prove our rights, will we?"

"Well, I hadn't thought of that," said Mr.
Mason.

"Get hold of a good lawyer at once," said Henry
Miller, "and get the testimony of all of these old-
timers, so when trouble comes we will be ready for
it."

So proceedings were had for the perpetuation of
testimony of the old men who staggered across the
plains and into "Pisen Switch" in the early sixties,
and this was transcribed and filed away in the courthouse, to become moldy and covered with dust and
to be almost forgotten.

Years went on. Tom Rickey continued to buy
out the settlers in Antelope Valley and Bridgeport
Valley on the upper reaches of the Walker River
in California. He continued to increase his holdings and to take out more and more water to irrigate his land. Finally he conceived an ambitious
project of diverting a large part of the river into a
natural reservoir in the mountains and then taking
it out by a tunnel for the irrigation of large acre-
ages of land above the ranches belonging to Henry
Miller. Water began getting short in Mason Valley
on the Miller Ranch. When protest was made
Rickey said, "This river rises in California. My
land is in California. My land is riparian to the river,
and I have a right to use all the water. California
does not have to take any notice of Nevada, all

that Nevada gets is what we in California don't use."

"But," said Henry Miller, "we have appropriated the water in Nevada, under the law of Nevada."

"Yes," said Mr. Rickey, "but under the law of California, as decided in *Lux* v. *Haggin*, the riparian owner above doesn't have to take notice of an appropriator below."

Henry Miller had to admit the adroitness of this turning of his great legal victory in California against him in Nevada, but he soon got his bearings and said, "It's true this stream rises in California, but it is also true that it flows into Nevada, and we think that the court will find some way to protect the people who have acquired rights in it under the laws of Nevada. Good day, Mr. Rickey," and the fight was on.

The Miller interests filed suit in the Federal Court in Nevada, and, in order to get all rights finally settled, as well as to try and organize all of the water users in Nevada against Rickey in California, all of the Nevada users above the Miller Ranch were made parties to the suit. In order to prevent them from joining forces with Miller, Rickey sent people up and down the river in Nevada to convince the people that Henry Miller was going to take all of their water away from them, and it was a hard fight to convince them to the contrary. But finally they were all pre-

vailed upon by Henry Miller to enter into a stipu-
lation for a friendly determination of their rights
by a special master or referee selected by the parties
and approved by the court. The rights were determined, but it was thought they were determined
too favorably to Henry Miller and a contest was
raised. Great opposition to the Miller interests resulted, but finally the matter was amicably adjusted
and the rights satisfactorily settled with the people in
Nevada.

Then all parties in Nevada turned to see what
they could do to prevent Rickey from taking all
of the water in California, and the question finally
arose on the jurisdiction of a court in Nevada to
attempt to determine the rights of Rickey in California. The case went through the United States
Circuit Court, the United States Circuit Court of
Appeals and the United States Supreme Court,
and was finally decided in favor of the Miller
interests, holding that on an interstate stream a
court in the lower State, as well as a court in the
upper State, had jurisdiction to determine the rights
of the parties and to protect the parties therein.

The rights themselves had still to be determined,
and thousands upon thousands of pages of testimony were taken, and the musty volumes of "per-
petuated" testimony were brought out to help win
the case for Henry Miller. Before the case was
ever decided, Rickey had acquired all of the land
that was to be acquired in the vicinity and went

out to conquer new fields. The mining excitement at Tonopah was at its height. He took his money over to Tonopah and built a magnificent hotel and started a bank and other enterprises. Suddenly came the panic of 1907 and all of the banks went into liquidation. There was a terrible howl raised by the depositors and stockholders and Rickey was indicted. He left the State under bond and finally succeeded in quashing the indictment, but his losses in the business ventures and the expense of the litigation connected therewith, as well as the expense of the litigation over the water rights, were more than he was able to handle in his old age, so he finally sold out his ranch property. Immediately the purchasers applied for an armistice so far as the water fight was concerned. Again Henry Miller showed his statesmanship; he welcomed a settlement and joined forces with the new owners of the Rickey property, and arranged for the construction of the reservoir which, instead of being used as a speculation, would be used to rateably supply each with his fair share of the water of the stream. The reservoir was built and the great fight was over.

The contest had, nevertheless, left its sting, and many people had become extremely hostile toward Henry Miller as a result of it. The immediate neighbors of the Mason Ranch had felt very much hurt on account of the water rights which were adjudicated to the ranch. "Ang" McLeod and Jim

Mills had themselves been for years carrying on a petty warfare over the waters of the river. Mills had constructed a dam in the river and had attempted to run a lumber mill, and McLeod had contended that this dam flooded his land. The case had gone to the Supreme Court of the State a couple of times and had been tried twice and resulted finally in a decision against Mills, which about broke him.

Then came a great flood and the ranch of "Ang" McLeod was overflowed, his chickens, hogs and calves were washed away, great gullies were cut through his ranch, and large amounts of sand were washed out of the river channel and spread over the land from six inches to a foot and a half in depth. He conceived the idea of blaming this on an old earthen dam constructed in the early days at the upper end of the Mason Ranch by Spragg, Bewley and Alcorn, and sued Miller & Lux for a large sum of money.

When this was brought to the attention of Henry Miller, he said to his attorney, "Well, did we flood him?"

"The engineers say that you did not, and that your dam could not have flooded his ranch," said the attorney.

"We don't want to do any wrong to our neighbors," said Henry Miller, "but if we didn't flood him we'll fight him."

"The feeling is very much against you in that

vicinity, growing out of the water case, and the jury will probably decide against you," said the attorney.

"Then we will appeal," said Henry Miller, and proceeded to the next matter on his desk, and another contest was on.

The jurors and witnesses in the case were the neighbors of "Ang" McLeod. Even Jim Mills was a witness for him. In the case between Mills and McLeod, Mills had been a witness and had attempted to demonstrate to the court that his mill dam did not flood McLeod, and he even testified that he went out into the middle of the raging stream with a hand level and a two foot rule, and that by that means was able to measure the difference in the height of the water above and below his dam. The possibility of such a feat was seriously doubted by the court.

In the new case, in order to make the Miller dam responsible, it was necessary to prove that it not only raised the water up stream for some three miles, but that it raised it clear over and above intervening dams. It was a pretty hard burden, but McLeod was equal to it with a friendly jury and willing witnesses. All farmers were held to be "experts" and permitted to give expert testimony as to what the dam did, and no matter what happened, whether the channel was too small, or too shallow, or had sand in it, or was not able to hold the water, it was all caused by the Miller dam.

The trial went on for weeks and weeks in a little courthouse at Dayton at the foot of Mount Davidson, (which was the scene of the glories of the Comstock). The population had almost all moved from Dayton, whereas the agricultural territory around "Pisen Switch" had been steadily growing in population, and even the name of the town had been changed to Yerington. It had ambitions; it wanted the county seat. Most of the population of Yerington were present at the trial as jurors, witnesses, friends or spectators.

One hot afternoon while the case was in progress the fire bells rang, but the judge never batted an eye, the jurors pretended to be uninterested, the reporter unperturbed continued to take her notes and the attorneys, without even looking around, continued in their endless examination and cross-examination of witnesses. Suddenly thin, tall, lanky sheriff Randall came rushing in, threw up his hands and said, "Your Honor, it is the courthouse, the courthouse is on fire." Immediately the court was adjourned. The jury, under the law of Nevada, was being kept in custody, so the sheriff had to hold them together while the fire was being fought. The jail was emptied and the prisoners were put upon the antiquated fire apparatus to pump water. It was found that the fire had started in the top of the building and was working down.

The inadequacy of the fire apparatus was clearly apparent. The attorneys and witnesses struggled to

take the public records out of the building. As they
cleared the upper floor, the roof fell in. As they
cleared the lower floor, the ceiling fell in. The
jury, witnesses, judge and attorneys stood outside
and finally saw the last of the building go up in
flames. It was never rebuilt, but an election was
immediately held and the glory of the Comstock
was moved to "Pisen Switch." The trial was concluded in an old bar room and in due time resulted in a substantial verdict in favor of "Ang"
McLeod.

As Henry Miller promised, an appeal was taken
and on appeal it was contended that it was physi-
cally impossible that the dam could have raised the
water to the place where the overflow occurred.
This seemed perfectly obvious on its face, but, in
desperation, the attorneys for McLeod began to
study up on engineering principles and they found
that the school books, in giving the algebraic formula to determine how far a dam will affect the
water up-stream, in other words what is known
as the "backwater curve," always expressed it in
terms of the extent to which the water would be
raised at any given point above the dam under certain given conditions. Accepting this formula, they
argued that the effect of the dam was, therefore,
infinite, and the formula would show a raise in the
water at any conceivable point above the dam. Algebraic formulas were copied into the briefs and
learned dissertations indulged in. It was finally

NEVADA   115

found, however, that admitting the infinite effect of the dam, its effect would be infinitely small at the particular point of overflow, and so infinitely small that it had to be expressed with about eight decimals, and, therefore, could not appreciably affect the velocity of the water at that point. The Supreme Court took this view of the case and decided it in favor of the Miller interests.

Thus did the hand of Henry Miller extend from his home State into the neighboring State of Nevada and that became the great breeding ground for his cattle. There the cows were born and remained, fed in the winter on hay in inclosed pastures, and during the summer permitted to graze on the great open ranges, and to come back the next fall with their calves. The calves were kept in the same way until the steers were three years old, and then were shipped to California after a long drive to the railroad and there were "finished" for the market. The process of acquiring land, producing hay, feeding it into animals, and shipping the animals to the market became a monotonous process, ever repeating itself, but ever increasing in size to keep pace with the growing demand for meats.

XI. THE MALHEUR AND THE "L. F." BRAND (⅂)

TO MOST people Oregon probably means green fields, green trees, and much rainfall, such as are seen on the railroad trip from Portland to Ashland. But an entirely different condition prevails to the east of the Cascade Mountains, or in what is known as Eastern Oregon. There the elevation is from four thousand to six thousand feet above sea level and the general condition is one of aridity, such as prevails in Nevada. There are endless plains of sagebrush and rabbitbrush, the only green spots being where the rivers overflow comparatively small tracts of land, or where man has conducted the water from the streams over the valleys. Where the water flows there are luxuriant grasses, and all over the mountain sides there is fine feed for cattle. The summers are hot and dry and the winters intensely cold.

Into this country one day in the early eighties came a man named Overfelt. He was an ambitious man, and began to acquire land and cattle. The first cattle he bought were branded "L. F." (⅂), so that became his brand.

116

He soon found that stretching across the southern end of Eastern Oregon were great tracts of land, consisting of every alternate section for several miles in width, which had been granted to certain persons to compensate them for building military roads across that forbidding territory, and this made it very difficult to locate lands which were subject to entry. But this was not his greatest difficulty, for stretching across the territory were many square miles of land which had been included in an Indian reservation. This forced him into the northern part of the Malheur region where he began picking up small parcels. In gathering his cattle he had gone to the top of the mountain and come into view of Agency Valley on the North Fork of the Malheur, and looking down had seen the small buildings of the Indian Agency.

Here the Government had gathered the remnants of the Indian tribes of the vicinity. The valley consisted of about two thousand acres of flat land traversed by several branches of the river and presented a most alluring picture. The Indian Agent was trying to convert it into farm land for the Indians. He had constructed a blacksmith shop and a flume to carry water from the river for power, and was teaching the Indians blacksmithing and carpenter work. He had surveyed ditches taking out of the various channels of the river to carry the water over the land.

But he was a better engineer than a reader of

Indian character and of their hatred of manual labor. When he sent the Indians to dig ditches along the line of stakes which he had set, there was first grumbling, then much loafing on the job, and soon almost open rebellion. He pleaded, he ordered, he punished, and the ditches continued to extend down the valley, but still the Indians could not understand why he wanted to change the rivers. "Weren't they good enough where they were? Hadn't they always supplied fish for the Indians and water for their horses, and why did white man want to take them away and put them some other place, and why did white man want to make Indians go behind a plow or scraper and dig dirt?"

To intrigue them, he turned water into the ditches as soon as possible, and this helped in loosening up the earth so as to make the work a little easier for them. He attempted to show them ways to work so as to have the horses do most of the heavy pulling, but there was much grumbling and discontent. Still the onward march of the ditches proceeded down the valley, and soon the waters were diverted and carried through these ditches, over the lands, and then back into the river. There was great rejoicing when this was completed and the Indians greatly enjoyed hearing the gurgling of the water washing out the loose dirt at the bottom of the ditches.

But a few days later they saw the Agent again out with his surveying instruments, and soon they saw stakes extending in irregular lines all over the territory between the ditches and the river. He tried to explain to the Indians that levees must be built along these contour lines to hold the water over the land, and showed them the alfalfa seed which he had bought and which would then be planted in the checks.

But hot weather was coming on, and when the Indians were taken back to start on that piece of work, which seemed to them colossal and foolish, they openly revolted and refused to work. Again there were pleadings, commands and punishments, but the more he punished the more stubborn they became. The medicine man became active and induced them into war dances, and they danced until late into the night, and then everything became quiet. The fires were banked, the tepees were closed, and the entire Agency seemed to be in peaceful sleep.

But during the early hours of the morning the Indians, led by their medicine man, emerged from their tepees, and, now daubed with war paint and armed with all kinds of weapons they could gather or steal, left the reservation and took to the mountains.

They went out quietly so as not to arouse the soldiers, but when they got out of the valley and came to other settlements, they started on the warpath, and horses and cattle were driven before them. They raided barns and stole all the horses and saddles they could find, and thus strengthening their band crossed through the country, murdering settlers and burning houses.

Soon they were missed from the reservation, and almost as soon word came of their depredations. The military was hastily put in the saddle and tore through the mountains driving the Indians before them. As the soldiers approached, the Indians scattered, carrying terror in all directions. They refused to surrender and were pursued and hunted down like animals, until the entire tribe was exterminated, and the Indian Agent was left with his hundreds of square miles of Indian Reservation, with his Indian Agency in Agency Valley, and its canals and improvements, but with no Indians.

One day Henry Miller was going through his corrals in California and came across a bunch of steers with the "L. F." (⌐L) upon their hips. He stopped short in amazement and said, "Those are the finest steers I have ever seen. Where did they come from?" he asked. He was told that they came from the Malheur country in Oregon. He said, "I must go to that country. I must have some of those steers. Who does that brand belong to?" "That belongs to a man named Overfelt," said his foreman. "He brought them down himself." "Let me see him," said Henry Miller.

Soon the cattle king of California was face to face with the rough mountaineer of Oregon. "I had heard you knew good cattle when you saw them, Mr. Miller, and I thought you would like

my steers. That is the reason I brought them down.
I've come down to see if I can't get some money
to help me get more cattle and more land in that
country. It is the most wonderful country, Mr.
Miller. The feed stands on the hillsides up to the
belly of the animal, but the winters are very severe
and you must have hay to feed the cows and calves
during the winter. I must buy little ranches along
the river so I can grow hay, and that is going to
take money. The country is entirely free of any
cattle disease and the cattle are not bothered with
anthrax, or any of those troubles, but are all big
and healthy. Do you know, Mr. Miller, where I
can get money to do this?"

Henry Miller's mind was running with the rapidity of a steam engine. He saw a prospective competitor of his California and Nevada ranches, with
a finer product than he could produce in either.
"How much will it take, Mr. Overfelt?" he asked.

"There is no limit to it, Mr. Miller," said Overfelt. "There is a large Indian Reservation that will
shortly be thrown open and a wonderful little valley
that was used as an Indian Agency, and I think
the Government some time will sell that at auction.
As soon as the Indian Reservation is open, hundreds
of settlers will come in and take up the land. They
can't hold it because the drive to market is too long,
and can only be made by a person having a large
number of cattle. They will want to sell and I want
to be there to buy. There will be little ranches on

every stream throughout the Malheur country. They grow wonderful alfalfa hay. I want to be there to get them."

"How do you drive your cattle to market, Mr. Overfelt?" said Henry Miller. Overfelt at once saw his opportunity and said, "I drive them right down by your Quin River Ranch in Nevada."

This was intended to show Henry Miller how the Oregon property could be connected with his Nevada holdings and he was quick to see the significance of it, although he continued to maintain a poker face attitude and said, "I am going to Nevada to-morrow. Why don't you go with me and take me up and show me this Oregon country? If it is as good as you say it is, maybe I can help you."

The next day they were on their way. They went through by way of Fort McDermitt and up to the Town of Vale on the Malheur River. The country they traveled through was for a time forbidding and uninviting. Even the valleys were covered with sagebrush, and, except for the good land along the river, there was considerable alkali. The mountains themselves were largely of chalk, making the road extremely dusty.

But as they went on up into the mountains, they came to valley after valley nestling in the hills and along the streams, in which the bottom land spread out, showing wonderful opportunities for irrigation development.

They went over the ranches Overfelt had already

acquired, irrigated and planted to alfalfa, and the intense green of the alfalfa was made more striking by the extreme aridity of the hills surrounding it. Then finally they arrived at the top of the mountain and looked down on Agency Valley. It nestled like a gem in the setting of the surrounding hills. The Government buildings were in charge of a lone keeper, but an ambitious officer had himself settled on a piece of land in the extreme northern part of the valley, which was outside of the Reservation, and he was keeping the canals up and carrying water through them, and letting it spread over the lands for his cattle. Consequently the floor of the valley was carpeted with verdure in sharp contrast to the dry hills surrounding it. Henry Miller was enraptured with the view but carefully restrained himself from too clearly expressing his opinion.

That night as he sat with Overfelt before the fire he did not hide the fact that he was exhausted from the strenuous activity of the day. He said, "This is a hard, rough country, Mr. Overfelt."

"Yes," said Overfelt, "but I love it just the same."

"I would not want to lend you any money, Mr. Overfelt," said Henry Miller, and Overfelt slunk dejectedly in his chair as if he had been suddenly hit. He had not expected anything so abrupt. He had thought that the great millionaire cattle man would be hospitable and friendly and would return to San Francisco to think the matter over, and, if he decided not to invest, would then diplomatically inform him by letter. But after this long trip of hundreds of miles and while he was still his guest, to say abruptly, "I would not want to lend you any money, Mr. Overfelt" was a little too much for this rough mountaineer.

But Henry Miller continued, "I never loan money to a friend. Whenever you loan money you lose a friend, and I like you, Mr. Overfelt. I will go in partnership with you up here. You put in everything that you have at what it cost you, and I'll advance the money as fast as it is needed to acquire land and cattle. I'll take the cattle at the market as fast as they are produced. You will manage the property up here and receive a salary and we will divide the profits in proportion to the money we put in." With that Henry Miller became the "silent" partner in the firm of "Overfelt & Co."

After the bargain was struck, Henry Miller opened up and gave Overfelt his ideas not only of the country, its possibilities, and how it should be worked, but as to the details of running a cattle business based upon his long experience throughout California and Nevada. Finally as he was about to leave, he said, "Mr. Overfelt, I can never forget Agency Valley. It is beautiful and will make a wonderful headquarters. It is so well protected, it will be fine for cattle. Keep your eyes open and as soon as it is offered for sale, buy it at any price. Do not let anyone else get it. I will never forgive you if you fail to get Agency Valley."

As Overfelt had foreseen, the Government soon threw the Indian Reservation open to entry, with the exception of Agency Valley. Settlers began to come in and settle on every stream and in every valley, and Overfelt & Co. continued to increase their lands and cattle. It soon became apparent that the small man could not exist. Overfelt & Co. advanced the settlers money to build their buildings and sold them cattle during the time it was necessary for them to live on the property in order to acquire title. By the time they had "proved up" they became convinced that it was impossible for a small man to exist, because cattle had to be driven such a long distance to market. They were generally ready to sell as soon as they acquired title. They were probably already indebted to Overfelt & Co. and working for them. They knew that Overfelt & Co. were in the market and, therefore, generally sold to them. There was but little competition and the property was always acquired very cheaply.

Thus in a few years Overfelt & Co. was spoken of in the country simply as "The Company." It owned Silvies Valley up in the timber, Drewsey Field, Warm Springs, Big Stinking Water, Little Stinking Water, Indian Creek, Miller Field, Harper Ranch, Clover Creek, Waldon, Kimball Flat, Kane

Field, Moffat Ranch, Pine Creek, Otis Creek, Lamb Ranch, Hald Ranch and many others.

These were scattered over the numerous tributaries of the Malheur River, which spread out like a great hand over the Blue Mountains. They were anywhere from twenty-five to fifty miles apart and between them there was little or nothing except the natural grass of the mountains. On the ranches were ranch houses, barns, corrals, and above all else ditches to divert water to irrigate the land for alfalfa.

The ownership of these ranches enabled their cattle to graze over an area of the public domain of several thousand square miles.

During the summer the cattle would be turned out from the ranches where they were born and they would wander far away into the hills, and as the grass got short they would go higher and higher in search of good feed. Then at the first chill of winter they would begin to back track and would gradually find their way down through the canyons, and each animal would instinctively come back to the ranch where it was born. There during the long winter the cows and calves would be fed, while the steers would be bunched and the great drive would commence over the plains of Southern Oregon and across the desert of Northern Nevada, until they finally reached the railroad and were shipped to California. Fine big healthy steers, almost ready for slaughter.

One day Overfelt rode on his wonderful roan horse up to the Company's headquarters at Trout Creek in Silvies Valley. He threw the reins carelessly over a post and went into the office. Shortly he heard in the distance the unmistakable sound of the rhythmical tread of a saddle horse. Some one was evidently riding alone and at great speed. He noticed this particularly because the sound came from the south and he knew that the rider was coming upgrade, and he knew that no horse could stand such treatment very long. Rather provoked he rose from the desk and went out to the front gate. Suddenly a rider came in view, pressing his horse, all white with foam, at breakneck speed. As he approached the gate he threw himself from the horse, hardly waiting for it to stop.

He was under great excitement and said, "Mr. Overfelt, I was over to Agency Valley looking for some stray cattle and saw a notice posted which said that the Agency Ranch was to be sold by the Receiver of the United States Land Office at Lakeview to-morrow at twelve o'clock." For a moment Overfelt was stunned. He said, "Lakeview is two hundred miles." He saw the speculators, undoubtedly with advance information of this sale, meeting in the little office of the Receiver of the local Land Office where he had been so many times to hear contests between the Company and adverse claimants, and he saw the picture of Henry Miller saying,

"Mr. Overfelt, I'll never forgive you if you don't get Agency Valley." But he only hesitated for a moment and then threw himself on his great horse and called to the astonished rider, "Lakeview," and in a moment was clattering down the hill, lost in a cloud of dust.

Then began the most gruelling ride that country had ever known. Down through the tortuous canyons of the Silvies River he rode, until his horse was covered with foam and its breath began coming hard. He forced it to the very extreme of its endurance, and whenever he met one of his own riders, or even some other rider whom he knew, he threw himself off of his horse, loosened the saddle and threw it on the other horse, and almost without a word was on his way again. As he approached a ranch he began crying for a horse, and when he arrived if there was a horse ready, he threw himself off and threw his saddle off and put it on the other horse. If one was not ready, he rushed into the corral and lassoed one, changed the saddle and bridle and was off before the astonished occupants could believe their senses.

Thus he went down to the little town of Burns and across Harney Valley, through the springs of the "Double O" Ranch, past the mighty Iron Mountain rising out of the desert, past Skull Springs, where water comes out of a solid rock formed like an immense skull, down into Buzzard Canyon, through the narrow rim rock passes which seemed like ancient waterways, finally into the timber east of Lake Abert, and down the precipitous grade into the little village of Lakeview.

All night he rode. In the dead of night he came to little farm houses and was greeted by barking dogs, but his deep voice could be heard far away calling for a horse, and by the time he arrived the farm house was generally alive and the sleepy occupants were ready to give him a bite to eat and start him again on his way. Through some of the almost interminable dry plains he dared not urge his horse too much, fearing that it would fall under him and he would be compelled to walk. It may not be generally known that an ordinary horse can not do better than twelve miles an hour, so the difficulty of riding in a sparsely settled country a distance of two hundred miles in a few hours can well be realized. He finally began to watch the time. The last few miles were down a very steep decline and it was dangerous to go rapidly because a horse could not keep its feet. He began to worry lest his watch might not correspond with the watch of the Receiver of the Land Office, so he went as fast as he could without risking a broken leg.

The result was that when he finally reached the bottom his horse was in pretty good shape and he put the spurs to it and came down the main street of the little town of Lakeview at a pace which

brought every one out of the saloon doors and
hotels to see him ride, without stopping, on to the
sidewalk in front of the Land Office. He threw
himself off of his horse and dashed through the
door, only to find the astonished Receiver fingering
the notice of sale and smoking a cigar with the
prospective purchasers.

The little party could not have been more surprised if one of the Indian tribes, which was about
to lose its old home, had come in with war paint
and tomahawk. He bellowed out an awful string
of curses and asked the Receiver why he had not
given him notice of this sale, as he had promised.
The Receiver was frightened and could only mur-
mur something about being sorry and that he had
forgotten. By this time the clock had arrived at
twelve and the Receiver went over to the door and
rang a bell, and, as the little group gathered around,
proceeded to read the notice of sale. The two speculators, who were apparently the only persons who
knew of the sale, began to whisper nervously, and
shortly the bidding began.

Overfelt knew the men and he knew about how
much money they could scrape up, and, therefore,
about how much they could bid. Foreseeing no
competition, they no doubt had intended to bid an
amount which would be only sufficient to satisfy
the Land Office. Every bid they made Overfelt
raised by a small amount and that was kept up for

a considerable time, until Overfelt knew that they had about reached their limit. They began nervously to whisper among themselves and to debate whether they would raise his last bid, but finally after consulting for quite a while they raised it a few dollars.

By this time Overfelt had become impatient and said, "You fellows are too cheap for me," and raised the bid at once about three thousand dollars. He did this for two reasons; first, he wanted to bring the thing to an end before they could get reënforcements, and, second, he knew exactly what the property would have been worth, and what the Company would pay for it, if it had been owned by a private individual, and he intended to pay the Government just what he would have paid if a private individual owned it, so that the sale would certainly be approved by the Land Office. He figured correctly. There were no more consultations, no more hesitation, but the bidding ceased. The first, second and last calls were made 'and the land sold to Overfelt & Co.

Overfelt at once reached into his pocket and pulled out his draft book and drew a draft on Miller & Lux for the purchase price and handed it to the Receiver. This draft was a familiar thing in that part of the country, and was made distinctive by the "Bull's Head" pictured on it. It was in "Bull's Head" drafts that all the laborers of the company were paid and all bills for materials were discharged. Money itself was scarce in the community, banks were far distant, and checks were almost unknown, but everybody knew and coveted "Bull's Head" drafts. They were cashed over every bar, accepted in every store, and passed current at every hotel. Time and again the Receiver of the Land Office had accepted them in payment of fees. That Overfelt had authority to draw drafts on the company was known to everyone, and he had drawn thousands of drafts and never had one been dishonored. They were all payable at the Bank of California and every one knew that the company had practically unlimited credit at that institution, to say nothing of a large credit balance.

Imagine then the chagrin and disgust of Overfelt when the Receiver had a whispered consultation with the defeated bidder and handed the draft back to Overfelt and said, "I'm sorry but this is a cash sale and you will have to pay in cash." Overfelt pleaded and protested at this arbitrary action, but the Receiver stood his ground and said, "Unless cash is put up the property will be sold to the next bidder." Overfelt, of course, had no such money with him. The other bidder produced the amount of his last bid, which was accepted by the Receiver, and the land was sold to him.

Immediately Overfelt wired to Henry Miller who directed an appeal to the Commissioner of the

General Land Office at Washington. After a hearing, the Commissioner held that these "Bull's Head" drafts passed as currency in that particular community, under the conditions that there existed, that the draft was no doubt good and should have been accepted by the Receiver, and therefore, the sale to the company was confirmed and a patent for the land issued to it. Thus the Agency Ranch was added to the possession of Henry Miller. Certainly he had reached a proud position in the financial world when the Government of the United States treated his drafts as equivalent to the coin of the realm.

Overfelt was overjoyed because this practically completed his program of acquisition of land, and for years his ride from Silvies to Lakeview was talked of more than the ride of Frémont or of Juan Flaco from Los Angeles to Monterey.

One day Henry Miller was traveling with Overfelt over the ranches. As they approached the Malheur River a little way below the town of Vale they crossed a large ditch, and Henry Miller said, "Whose ditch it that?"

Overfelt said, "That is the Nevada Ditch."

Henry Miller said, "Nevada Ditch? We have been in Oregon for over a hundred miles."

"Yes," said Overfelt, "but it is called the Nevada Ditch just the same. A man named Mallett years ago came out with a party to Nevada and they settled on the Walker River at 'Pisen Switch,' on a place now known as the Mason Ranch. The party finally broke up and Mallett and some of his associates came up here and settled on the Malheur River and took out this ditch and intend to irrigate land clear down to the Snake River. This man Mallett is a great leader, and we must get some of this water out up there in the mountains where we want it before he gets it all away from us."

Years rolled on and as these ranches continued to be developed water began getting short down at the Nevada Ditch. Mallett and his associates had been active in extending their use of water. They had built an extension to their ditch and brought in new settlers, and they brought an action to establish the right to two thousand inches of water superior to the rights of the mountain ranches, and particularly the Agency Ranch. In taking over the property, Henry Miller had inherited two lawyers who had acted as attorneys for Overfelt & Co. They were now quite old and far from well, but, on account of their loyalty, they were put in charge of the case. An engineer testified that the ditch would carry two thousand inches of water and the case was finally decided in favor of the owners of the Nevada Ditch, awarding them that quantity of water. In order to get an earlier priority than the priority of the Agency Ranch, they testified that they had filed notice of appropriation upon a

certain date. As the courthouse with all the public
records had been destroyed by fire, there was no way
to controvert that testimony.

The loss of this case was always a sore spot with
Henry Miller. Years afterward the matter was reopened in a general proceeding for the adjudication
of water rights on the Malheur River and upon
looking for the record of the testimony in the
former case, which should have been in the Supreme
Court of the State, it was found to be missing. It was
finally located, covered with dust, in an attorney's
office. Upon being examined it appeared that the
engineer who had testified that the Nevada Ditch
would carry two thousand inches of water, had, in
making his computation, used the coefficient of
roughness applicable to an iron pipe, instead of
that applicable to an earthen canal, and by that
means had innocently doubled the capacity of
the ditch. So in the new adjudication the right
of the ditch was cut in half and the wrong finally
righted.

But Overfelt did not live to enjoy this happy
conclusion. One day he was riding alone, and was
in a hurry to reach headquarters. He was riding
a wonderfully strong and speedy animal. Suddenly
the saddle slipped and he was found dragged to
death. His death, of course, dissolved the partnership of Overfelt & Co. The accounts were settled
with his widow and the small amount coming to

him was paid to her, and all of this vast domain which he had accumulated was merged with the other holdings of Henry Miller.

XII. HARNEY VALLEY AND THE "S WRENCH" BRAND (⤵)

JOHN DEVINE was seated one day in a hotel lobby in Marysville, California, a young man, strong, tall, alert, overbearing in manner. He would attract attention anywhere. He was joined by a little ferret-like individual who went by the name of "Hen" Owen, and was also called the swamp rat of Oregon. There was a law in Oregon for the sale by the state of swamp land at one dollar and twenty-five cents an acre. By some means Owen had prevailed upon the officials of the State Land Office to construe the law as permitting any one individual to buy any conceivable quantity of swamp land. It was only necessary to make a payment of ten per cent of the purchase price, or twelve and one-half cents an acre, so Owen had gotten together a little money and had purchased from the state one hundred and fifty thousand acres of swamp land.

He had come to California to find people to buy portions of this land and he approached John Devine as a likely customer. He produced his map showing a vast area of swamp land in Harney County, Oregon. It was customary in those days

137

to mark each sub-division which was returned by the Government surveys as swamp land with a red letter "S," and on this map the red letter "S" appeared on thousands of acres of land at the lower end of Silvies River. This land was later called the "Red S Field." It was in the most inaccessible place in the United States at that time and "Hen Owen" had never seen the land, but he knew it was good and gave glowing accounts of the richness of the swamp grasses and how cattle could be grown upon them. Devine was impressed. He took the map and told Owen he was going to look at the land.

When he started on his journey he looked quite different from the men of Eastern Oregon. He had a magnificent prancing horse, with bridle and saddle ornamented with silver mountings. His clothes were more in keeping with the old Spanish régime than with the Oregon country. He followed the stage line running from Marysville to Idaho as far as Wild Horse, Oregon, and then crossed the Alvord Desert, which stretched along the base of Steen's Mountain for more than thirty miles, a flat plain as level as a billiard table, without one single blade of grass. He went on past a little lake called Mann Lake and then turned to the north, passing over Steen's Mountain.

He finally saw in the distance a long piece of table land about five hundred feet in elevation, extending for many miles almost in a straight line and appearing from a distance to be level. It pre-

sented to the imagination the appearance of a colossal railroad grade. A well worn trail passed over
this table land, and he slowly climbed it to the top.
Spread out below him was a great valley of several
hundred thousand acres, marked on the map as
Harney Valley, traversed by two branches of Silvies
River, which came down from Silvies Valley and
flowed to Malheur Lake.

Evidently these rivers had overflowed a large
territory at the lower end and this had produced a
most luxuriant growth of swamp grasses. Standing
at the end of this piece of table land, which was
marked on his map as Wright's Point, he threw out
his arms in one comprehensive gesture and exclaimed, "It's all mine. It's all mine."

He returned at once to California and obtained
the financial assistance of a capitalist of Sacramento
with whom he formed a partnership to exploit this
new and wonderful country.

At this time he married and took his bride with
him into the wild country to which he was going.

His next move was to acquire a cattle brand. In
the early mining days the California Stage Company ran a stage from Marysville, California, across
the northern part of Nevada and through eastern
Oregon into Idaho. Its horses were branded with a
brand constructed of the combination of the first
three letters of "California Stage Company." The
"C's" were placed on the two ends of the letter "S"
reversed. As the California Stage Company had

ceased to exist, Devine appropriated this brand. When he showed it to his uncle, he told his uncle it was a fine brand because it was hard to alter or imitate. The changing or working over of brands in those days was developed to a fine art. It has been said that an enterprising cattle rustler once created the "window sash brand" so that it could easily be put over the Miller " **HH** " brand.

His uncle examined the brand and said, "What are you going to call it, John?" Devine said, "I have not thought of that." His uncle said, "California Stage Company would not do. How would this sound: 'California shall conquer'?" Devine was furious and said, "I will change it by turning the 'C's' into the more angular form of an 'S' wrench, and call it the 'S Wrench' brand," and so it was called and placed on the fat herds the partnership acquired.

His partner was a lover of fine horses, particularly race horses, and they first bought out a settler near the Nevada line at a place called White Horse and here they built wonderful stables and commenced the breeding of fine horses.

Then they went on across the Alvord Desert and bought out the little ranches along the foot of Steen's Mountain, bought out the man who was at Mann Lake, and then went over the mountains and took possession of the swamp which was covered by the certificate of purchase issued to "Hen" Owen.

Here they found all over the property little

cabins which had been built by strangers coming into the country, attracted by the richness of the grass, not knowing that the land had been returned as swamp land and believing it was open to entry. They refused to move. Threats of all kinds were made. Bad blood was stirred up. Some shots were fired. But Devine went over to Portland, waved his certificate of purchase before the Federal Court, obtained a writ of possession, and the United States Marshal came out and bodily removed all of the settlers from the land. Bad blood caused by this did not die out for years to come.

To acquire land became a passion with John Devine. If he saw a piece of land that he wanted, he must have it. It is a well known fact that there has been more or less land of all kinds taken up by means of "dummy" entries. Even the best families indulged in that practice, at least to the extent of having members of their families make a nominal residence on a piece of land. Frequently a family would have a house set on wheels and it would be moved from section to section. A member of the family would make a nominal residence on a piece of land for the requisite length of time, and then the house would be moved on to another piece, and thus the process would go on. Even hired men would obligingly live away from the ranch house and thus get title to land, which in due time would be turned over to the employer. Others went into this line of business on a more extravagant scale and frequently the Government was called upon to set aside patents to timber land and other kinds of land entered by means of dummy entrymen.

But the land agents of Devine conceived even a more remarkable way to acquire land. They would get the name of some person that actually lived in the country and write an application for the purchase of a certain piece of land from the State. This man's name would be signed to the application, which would be certified by Devine as a notary public. The application would then be filed in the State Land Office and a certificate of purchase issued. As soon as that was received, an assignment of the certificate would be drawn, signed in the name of the applicant, and Devine as a notary public would certify to its execution. The assignment would be made to his partner. This would be filed in the State Land Office and when the land was finally paid for, the patent would be issued in the name of his partner. These papers, with the exception of the patent, being all in the Land Office in Salem, men living in the country where the land was located would never suspect that they had applied for and been granted State land, and the county records would simply show the patent to Devine's partner. This process was sometimes apparently modified by using the name of a fictitious person and was carried on until large areas of land were acquired. Devine's partner and financial backer did not appear to have knowledge of the methods employed. Other land was properly acquired by buying out the small settlers.

The holdings at White Horse, Alvord, Mann Lake, Harney Valley, Anderson Valley and other places were added to until Devine and his partner held about a hundred and fifty thousand acres of land and controlled a territory several thousand square miles in extent.

Devine became the cattle baron of Harney County. He was much interested in raising wild hay. He cared nothing about alfalfa, which was expensive to grow, but followed largely the plan of Henry Miller in California of developing grasses which were native to the country. A few levees served to throw the water over vast areas. The low places grew cattails and tules, which afforded the cattle shelter. The higher land grew wire grass, bluejoint, red top, clover and the numerous sedges that were indigenous to the country. The grasses stood up to the backs of the horses and it was no unusual sight to see twenty mowers traveling through the fields, with the precision of an army, laying the grass before their sharp blades. This was raked and then "bucked" on to a great net made of chains. A wooden slide was erected in the field and horses attached to this net pulled the hay up the slide and dropped it, ultimately producing a symmetrical hay stack.

Henry Miller and his partner, Overfelt, often looked at these properties with longing. "This alfalfa farming, Mr. Overfelt," he would say, "is too expensive. It takes too much labor. We'll never make any money raising cattle this way, but we are producing little farms that will be fine when the country builds up. There are too many cheap cattle from Mexico and Arizona to raise them in this expensive manner. Wild hay is the thing in this country."

But Overfelt never ventured into the territory of Devine. The line between them was marked by the Blue Mountains and Steen's Mountain, and Overfelt would no more have dared to encroach upon the territory which Devine said was all his than a doe would encroach upon the lair of a lion.

But still the reign of Devine was destined to be short-lived. His insatiable craving for more land built up a debtor balance with his bankers. The love of his partner for race horses was a tremendous strain on the Company's finances. Then the Oregon legislature came to life and declared the patent to "Hen" Owen illegal and passed an act canceling it, and the land was again thrown open for sale. It was snapped up by speculators and Devine had to buy them all out.

Then came the dry years of 1888 and 1889. His land was stocked to capacity, when suddenly the streams dried up and ceased to flow. The great meadows became parched. The cattle climbed higher and higher into the mountains to find a little grass, and then when the chill of winter came and

they instinctively turned toward home, they were
so weak they could scarcely reach their accustomed
fields, and when they did reach them they found
them barren, no feed, no haystacks. There was no
place to drive the cattle, first, because they were too
weak to drive, second, because the entire country was
in almost the same condition. They died by the
thousands. Devine stormed and cursed, but it was
of no avail, and one day the partners woke up to
the grim fact that they were hopelessly insolvent.
Their bankers took over their property, and when
they came to sell it there was one bidder and that
was Henry Miller, so he added to his already great
domain this property, which he had always viewed
with such longing.

But Henry Miller admired the wonderful activity of John Devine, so he took him into his employ to manage the property, and made some arrangement by which Devine might re-acquire an
interest in the property. But as an employee Devine
did not prove a success. He could not stand dicta-
tion from anyone. He could not understand that
he did not own the property. Notwithstanding his
bankrupt condition, he insisted on continuing his
mania for buying more land. He could not endure
a neighbor. He began drawing "Bull's Head"
drafts like a drunken sailor, and very shortly, instead of getting the property back on its feet and
showing a profit which would enable him to re-
acquire an interest in it, he had it running still fur-

ther in debt. So he and Henry Miller had to part company.

When it came to an accounting, he went down to California and roared like a wounded animal, and threatened Henry Miller's bookkeeper because he had figured out that there was little or nothing coming to him in the settlement. So the matter was finally appealed to Henry Miller himself. He looked over the account, which showed Devine in the red. He said, "I owes him nothing, but he's got together one of the finest pieces of cattle property in the world, and in years to come it will be valuable. He is a great man and I am sorry for him. He has always lived on the Alvord Ranch along there by the desert. I am going to give him that property." And the astonished bookkeeper, who had been upholding the rights of Henry Miller on the accounting, was compelled to hand to Devine a deed to a piece of property lying under Steen's Mountain, comprising some six thousand acres and watered by five streams which came down from the snow top of Steen's Mountain. There Devine sat for the rest of his life looking out from his porch over the Alvord Desert.

In taking over these properties, Henry Miller inherited all of the hatred that Devine had cultivated in that rough country, and years afterwards the State discovered the fraud that had been committed in the acquisition of the property and Henry Miller had to buy it over again from the state. He finally selected a new superintendent and said to him, "Mr. Mason is retiring from Nevada. He has been a fine and faithful man. Mr. Overfelt has been killed. He was a great worker. Mr. Devine has resigned. I never knew a man who could make so many enemies. You take all of these properties under one management and see if you can't make some friends for the Company."

Thus these cattle kingdoms became a part of the cattle empire of Henry Miller.

XIII. PARTNERS

HENRY MILLER'S experience on the Isthmus of Panama had not endeared him to the idea of partners, but as he proceeded to expand and acquire country property he found that he enjoyed more and more the ranches, and was necessarily away from the city the greater part of the time. He had no real competition in San Francisco which he need fear, but there was one dealer who was there a little ahead of him and who was making considerable progress. Like himself, he was a German, but from Alsace, and his name was Charles Lux. Henry Miller was not particularly in need of his knowledge of the livestock business, but was impressed with the easy manner in which he seemed to be able to obtain money and credit and to expand his business. He was preëminently a city man, tall, dignified, impressive, and stood well with the leading financiers of the city, and the Bank of California seemed to be willing to open its doors to him at any time.

As Henry Miller on the other hand disliked city life and enjoyed the rough life of the country, a suggestion by him that they join forces was readily accepted by Charles Lux and, as we have already seen, the firm of Miller & Lux was born in 1857. For thirty years this partnership continued without any serious difference between the partners. Years after, Henry Miller was ungracious enough to say, "I have made three fortunes. One for myself, one for my partner, and one for my lawyers."

The credit of the firm became well established. It carried its account at the Bank of California and during certain seasons it carried large credit balances, and when it came to moving the crops it was able to get almost unlimited credit. Never did the firm put up a dollar's worth of security. As soon as the partnership was formed, Henry Miller went off to the country and began buying livestock and land. The drafts came in so fast they often made Charles Lux almost dizzy, but, on the other hand, fine fat livestock was coming in with equal rapidity and the proceeds from the sale of meat were beyond his wildest expectations.

Henry Miller one day returned to the city and his partner said, "Henry, we have a hundred thousand dollars clear in the bank and don't owe a cent. If we stop now we will have a million. Let's clean up and quit, we've got enough." Henry Miller said, "Charley, we haven't begun yet. What do you mean we've got a hundred thousand dollars in the bank? Why didn't you tell me while I was down the country? I'll attend to that hundred thousand dollars," and he rushed down to the San Joaquin Valley and bought another ranch with all the cattle that were upon it.

Thus the hectic life went on until they owned land in nineteen counties in California and rented hundreds of thousands of acres from the railroad besides. The " **HH** " brand was seen on every plain and on every mountain, and the meat business of the great metropolis was under their complete control.

One day on returning to the city Henry Miller said, "Business can't stand still, it's got to move. San Francisco is growing and needs more meat. We've got to expand to keep up with it. It wouldn't do for us to stop and I've been thinking what would happen if one of us should die. Unless the business went on, there would be a great loss. I think we ought to agree that if either of us dies, the other may continue to carry on the business for at least seven years."

Charles Lux said, "That is a good idea, Henry," and right there Henry Miller pulled out a pad of paper and on one sheet drew a contract by which it was agreed that in case of the death of either of the partners, the survivor might carry on the business for at least seven years. Charles Lux made a copy of it, and each of them signed the two copies, and each took his copy and put it carefully away.

To cement this ideal partnership still further, the two partners married sisters. Henry Miller's hope of an heir was shattered eleven months later by the death of his wife in child-birth. He then married a niece of his partner's wife. This union resulted in a son, Henry Miller, Jr. and two daughters, Nellie Miller and Sarah Alice Miller.

There was apparently about the same difference between the wives of the two partners that there was between the partners themselves. Henry Miller's wife was greatly interested in the multitude of affairs that arose in connection with his business. On the other hand the wife of Charles Lux enjoyed city life and society and appeared to take no particular interest in the affairs of the partnership. At a later date Henry Miller had occasion to express how bitterly he resented this attitude.

In another particular there was a marked difference between the two partners. Both had large families in Germany. Practically all of the surviving sisters, nephews, and nieces of Henry Miller came to California, and in one way or another were worked into the organization, or were otherwise assisted by him. But the Lux family was well situated in Alsace and seemed well content to remain there, with the exception of one brother, who came to California.

When the affairs of the partners were in the most flourishing condition, when the ripe fruits of their endeavors in Nevada and Oregon were about to fall into their laps, one day in 1887 Charles Lux was suddenly stricken with death. When his will was read, it was found that he had given half of his property to his widow and the other half in varying shares to his brothers, sisters, nephews and nieces in Germany. He had appointed his partner, Henry Miller, his widow, and his widow's son by a former marriage, a man named Jesse Sheldon Potter, executors of his will. Then began a series of contests which occupied the courts of California for over twenty years.

If the estate was large in fact, its size was even magnified in Germany. Henry Miller had himself at an earlier date returned to Europe and erected a monument over the graves of his ancestors. He had been received in his native town with almost royal magnificence. The wealth and magnitude of his firm was talked of all over the United States and was much written of in newspapers and periodicals. As is usually the case with true journalism, never satisfied with the bare facts, the extent of the firm's holdings was even exaggerated, and it was seriously stated that the firm could drive their cattle from the Mexican line to Canada and sleep on their own lands every night.

The estate was a tempting morsel for a score of attorneys. One lawyer agreed to pay a friend of the brother who was in California a large commission to "steer" the German heirs to him. As a result, he was employed and was granted a fee equal to two per cent of the estate. Litigation followed between the attorney and the go-between.

Then the attorney had the probate court appoint him attorney for the "absent heirs" and received a thousand dollars a month for several years. He then conveyed his two per cent interest to a cousin in exchange for some worthless mining property, and thus the question arose whether he could keep the cash and his cousin's two per cent. It took years of litigation to unwind this snarl.

The "German Heirs," as they came to be popularly called, sent representatives to America and they rode over the property in California, Oregon and Nevada, looked solemnly upon the great herds of cattle, and went back to Germany and said that they had only seen a few spots of the property and it would take a lifetime really to see it all.

The administration of the estate fell to attorney Edwin B. Mastick, the same lawyer who had failed to purchase the site of the Palace Hotel as a residence because his wife objected to the hogs kept by Charles Lux on a neighboring lot. The widow of Charles Lux was represented by John Garber and his partners. The "German Heirs" had various attorneys, but the outstanding one was the silver-tongued orator, Delphin M. Delmas, who subsequently gained nation-wide fame in his brilliant defense of Harry Thaw, only losing an acquittal by coining the unfortunate phrase *"dementia Americana."* Henry Miller selected as his personal attorney William F. Herrin, the young man who made him so much trouble in the celebrated contest with Haggin & Tevis, and whom he so much admired on account of his work in that case.

It was soon discovered that on account of his adverse position as surviving partner, Henry Miller could not well act as executor of his partner's estate, therefore, he resigned as executor. Shortly after that the widow of Charles Lux died, and this left her son, Jesse Sheldon Potter, sole executor, and he became the storm center of the contest.

The heirs first brought an equity suit to compel an accounting and a liquidation of the affairs of the partnership. Henry Miller pointed to the seven years' contract. Instead of liquidating, he bought hundreds of thousands of acres of land and justified it as being necessary to protect the investments of the firm. He did permit a partition of a relatively small part of the land which was not needed in the business, and this kept the heirs quiet for a time, but not for long.

They pressed the accounting suit. Thousands of pages of testimony were taken. The case was pending before Judge Eugene Garber, a nephew of John Garber, and Henry Miller said, "Judge Garber is one of the finest men I know, but I don't like to have a nephew of John Garber sit in my case." His advisers all said, "We have the greatest confidence in Judge Eugene Garber, and there is no way to get rid of him anyhow."

About this time Herrin was called to a higher

position, and was selected as Chief Counsel of the Southern Pacific Railroad Company, so Henry Miller had to get another attorney. He immediately said, "I would rather have Judge Eugene Garber as my attorney than my judge," so he made a most flattering offer to Judge Garber and as a result he resigned from the bench and became the personal attorney for Henry Miller. As a matter of fact when Judge Garber resigned he probably did not even know that the case was pending before him, because the testimony was being taken entirely out of court and no proceedings in the case had ever come before him during the short time he was on the bench.

So the case dragged on its weary way before another judge. But the seven years' contract, over which a seven years' war was waged, seemed to be such an insurmountable obstacle to success in the case, that the opposing attorneys looked around for some other vulnerable point of attack upon Henry Miller. The vulnerable point which they selected was Jesse Potter. He had been in the employ of the firm for many years and after the death of his stepfather, Charles Lux, he continued in the employ of Henry Miller, although he was executor of the Lux estate. Potter was a young man who enjoyed a gay life. He was a part of the night life of San Francisco. He believed that money was made to spend, not to hoard. He could not wait for the estate to be distributed, but wanted to get his hands on the money at once. Henry Miller accommodated him and advanced him vast sums, which he expended in the gay life of San Francisco in the nineties.

The heirs were demanding that the concern be liquidated and the estate closed, but Henry Miller continued to buy property wherever he deemed it necessary to protect the investments of the firm, and if that could not be justified, he bought it in his own name and rented it to the firm. Finally the heirs thought they saw their opportunity and started a proceeding to remove Potter as executor, on the ground, first, of his alleged incompetency and improvidence, and, second, that he was conspiring with Henry Miller to delay and prolong the distribution of the estate. In that proceeding the entire life history of Henry Miller was at once extolled and condemned.

The trial was indeed impressive. Henry Miller was clearly the principal character in the drama. He had now reached the corpulency which he escaped in middle life, but which came to him with age. His beard was more broad, and had turned to gray. His strong upper lip was still shaven clean. His back was slightly rounded and his head pitched slightly downward, but he was still the embodiment of strength of mind and body.

He had chosen a partner to help him accomplish his ambitious plan. The death of his partner had interfered with that plan, but the plan was by no means abandoned, and he stood ready to defend his every action.

Delmas entered the court-room with his white vest, suède gloves, silk-lined overcoat, and spats, made his ceremonious bow to the court, carefully folded his overcoat, laid his cane and gloves at his side, arranged his Napoleonic lock, and tuned up his sweet voice for the fray.

It was not deemed good policy that the case should be defended by one of the attorneys of Henry Miller, although the attack was really against him as well as against Potter, so a new attorney was injected into the case, a young Irishman named Garret W. McEnerney. In the last few years he had risen from a humble station to a lawyer of the first magnitude. Indomitable industry, a clear analytical mind, and an engaging personality, all flavored with Irish wit, made him a dangerous antagonist. He had not yet gained the full corpulence of body that made him such a striking figure in later years; he had not yet grown the full mane of leonine locks which crowned him in his maturity; he did not yet have the international fame which he acquired in his defense of the Pious Fund, and other notable achievements; but around San Francisco Bay he was already loved and admired.

This is no occasion to review the sordid attacks which were made upon the life of Potter, but it is a proper place to review the attacks that were made upon Henry Miller. He was charged with being grasping, ambitious, and avaricious, and probably those charges were not only not met but were turned to his advantage. If he forgave any wrongdoing in the son of his partner's wife, it was attributed to some ulterior object of acquiring domination and control over him. If he withheld funds from the hungry demands of the "German Heirs," he was charged with starving the heirs of his deceased partner. If he lavishly met the demands of any of them, he was charged with doing so in order to earn interest or to accomplish his object of ingratiating himself and getting them to permit his program of expansion.

He was charged with being illiterate, but the answer came back that it came with ill grace for the "German Heirs" to complain because their country had not given him the education which he would have received in this country, particularly since with such education as he had received he had acquired this vast property for which they were clamoring.

In the appointment by the court of an attorney for absent heirs, who had at one time been an attorney for Henry Miller, was seen evidence of an intent to control the estate. His voluntary resignation as an executor as soon as a contest arose between himself and the heirs was brushed aside as insignificant, whereas his original qualification as executor was pointed to as conclusive evidence of an intent to administer the estate for his own benefit.

It is difficult to imagine anything more beautiful than a legal argument on the facts by Delmas. His preparation was always exhaustive and complete. He would enter an argument with a little pack of cards before him, on each of which he would have a topic, and no one ever wanted him to reach the bottom of that pack of cards. His diction was perfect. No matter how complicated a sentence might be, no matter how many dependent clauses were tucked away in it, no matter what innuendoes might be hidden here and there in parenthetical clauses, no matter what richness of illustration or of imagery it might contain, it was always finally completed, without error in person, tense or mood.

And he had nerves of steel. During the trial of one of his most difficult cases he would daily return to his office and spend two hours studying the German language. On one occasion during the hardest fought battle of his career the press one morning blazed forth with the exposé of an intrigue with a notorious woman, and with innuendoes that when she became troublesome he had arranged for an elopement with her by another man in order to get her out of the country. On the morning that these charges appeared in the press, he was scheduled to argue a motion for a new trial in a complicated will contest. The attorneys expected that he would send a clerk to ask for a continuance. But a few minutes before the opening of court, he came in, garbed as usual in his particular style; coolly and confidently, as was his custom, he laid his overcoat, gloves and hat on a table, arranged his papers, arose, and without a word of preface, started upon one of the most perfect arguments ever delivered in a court of justice, clear cut and unemotional, slow and deliberate, marshaling the facts like a general, and making the mind of the judge anxious to agree with the conclusion contained in a masterly peroration. The motion was granted.

It was this matchless orator that rose at the conclusion of this trial to hold up to every form of obloquy the history, the career, the motives, and the life, of Henry Miller, and these are a few of the high lights in his address:

"When some future moralist, descanting upon the vanity of riches and the emptiness of human ambition, shall seek in the annals of our jurisprudence an example to enforce his homilies he will find none richer in illustration than that afforded by the proceedings before the court, We have here on the one side a man already nearing the limit of human life still restless in the feverish pursuit of wealth . . . wealth which affords him no enjoyment; the increase of appetite growing by what it feeds on; the scope of the horizon expanding the higher the ascent; the means by which the pursuit is followed destroying the possibility of enjoying the reward. On the other hand the sad lesson taught of the rapidity with which the prodigality of descendants may in one lavish hour scatter to the winds the hoarded accumulations of years reaped by the patient toil and labor of the ancestor.

* * * * *

"He fills such a place in the history of the development of this State that your Honor might take judicial cognizance who Henry Miller is.

"We are authorized to infer that he is a German by birth. He came to this State at an early date, still in the prime of manhood. He is evidently a man of slender education, and, if we may judge from his mode of speech and the letters produced here, even lacking in culture, almost, to the degree of illiteracy; still, undoubtedly a man of marked lines of character—character in which the curious explorer might, perhaps, find standing out in bold relief stubbornness, love of success, and, especially, a morbid dread of being outwitted and overreached. Endowed with wonderful energy and great business ability, he is restless in his purpose to supplement by success the deficiencies of his character, and span with a golden bridge the intellectual and social gulf which separates him from more favored individuals.

"It were a curious study of human nature to explore the secret springs of his ambition. These possessions, which, from slender beginnings at an early day, have now expanded until they cover vast areas in three different States and in thirty or forty different counties, the love of which old age cannot abate—do they denote a peasant's love of land, so vividly portrayed by the novelist, Zola, which sometimes carries its victim even into the confines of crime? Is that love the off-spring of that emulation of the nobles of his own country whose power and ancestral pride rest upon their landed possessions?

"In his own sphere Henry Miller boasts that he has

distanced all competitors. It is his special pride that, owing to more perfect organization, the profits of his business are one-fifth larger than those of any other butcher. He aspires at any sacrifice to be the cattle king of the Pacific Coast. The love of rule, a dominant passion in some men, is in him developed to an almost abnormal degree.

"We find him at an early day taking as his partner Charles Lux, a man who, endowed with a more conservative temperament, was well fitted to be a balance wheel to the vaulting ambition of his more daring associate. The death of that partner, in 1887, delayed for a while, but for a while only the accomplishments of Henry Miller's ambition. He paused but for a moment only upon the brink of the grave. He hesitated but for a moment only before the possible legal impediments standing in his way. Then he boldly resolved to plunge and keep on his course, regardless of law, heedless of others' rights, determined to brave down all obstacles. From that time to this, a period now of some nine years, he has never for a minute lost sight of that object.

"What mattered it to him that others had legal rights in this property? They were to be treated as intruders —to be cajoled into subserviency or crushed into submission. His partner's ashes were scarce cold, the tears of the mourners were scarce dry upon their cheeks, when he began to contrive and conspire and to win over and make subservient to his purposes the widow and the stepson of his deceased partner. His signature to the petition for the probate of the will of that partner had scarcely been written when he schemed to subject to his control the whole of the partnership property by himself naming and dictating the appointment of its legal representatives. From that time to this he has managed the property regardless of the rights of others, as if he was its sole and absolute master. By what means he has sought to accomplish and has so far succeeded in accomplishing his purpose the present proceeding and his attitude therein sufficiently attest.

"Who, on the other hand, is Jesse Sheldon Potter?

"Mark, at the outset, how admirably fashioned by accident or nature to subserve the purposes of Henry Miller. He is the stepson of his deceased partner. He is one of the three executors named in that partner's will. He is nearly related to Henry Miller. He is his own pupil, whose character has been molded during his youth, under his own care, in his own house. He is revealed to us as a man fond of pleasure, delighting in the companionship of the depraved and dissolute, having no property of his own and yet needing vast sums of money to minister to his debauched appetites. The only child of a widowed mother, who idolized the son, her wayward boy, to the end; and who, herself, incapacitated by inexperience, the gentleness of her disposition, and the infirmities that bore down upon her, only too gladly surrendered to him the absolute management of her affairs.

"Miller saw at once that through him he could manage the mother, and controlling him control the estate of Charles Lux. Potter's improvidence was early made a lever with which to move him. Mark how completely Henry Miller has ensnared and fettered him—how his very improvidence and dissoluteness have been availed of to bring him into the toils. As early as 1891, when he was being pressed in this court by the 'German Heirs,' it became opportune to Henry Miller to hold over the head of Jesse Potter the terror of his mis-doings. His extravagance was made the means of leading him to borrowing, pledging, mortgaging all he had, until at length, stripped of everything in the world, he stands to-day before his master dependent for the very sustenance of his wife and child upon Miller's bounty.

"These being the characters before us, let us examine into the facts constituting a coöperation toward a given intent by them. Let us first examine whether the purpose of Henry Miller be what I have stated it a moment ago.

"From the very start, after the death of his partner, Miller assumed the attitude that he, and he alone, was the architect of this vast fortune, the creator of these more than princely possessions. To his genius it was due, in his conception, that the landed holdings of Miller & Lux threw into the shade all inferior possessors of the soil in this State; to his management, and to his alone, that their vast herds, numbered by the hundreds of thousands, roamed over every plain and mountain in three States.

"Remember what he told Judge Spencer in 1883, that 'his own individual efforts had produced nearly all the partnership property, and in justice it substantially all belonged to him. Mr. Lux had done little or nothing to produce it, that in justice and right he should have it all; that he had worked for it all and that Mr. Lux had sat down there in San Francisco and had done little or nothing toward earning the property, while he had been delving and exposing himself and working on the outside and amassing this fortune.'

"I quote the Judge's own language as given upon the stand. Miller says himself, in his testimony, that not only he, but his wife 'had slaved and worked to serve the firm, while Mrs. Lux had never added a penny to that property. Mrs Lux had done nothing.' He repeats this further on when he states that by night and by day, in sunshine and in storm, without rest and without enjoyment, he had devoted himself entirely to the expansion of the wealth and possessions of this firm.

"With these ideas in his mind, it was not a difficult task to persuade himself at the outset that, as he had toiled to accumulate these acquisitions, and as the others had not, they in justice at least belonged to him. He was reminded, of course, that the heirs of his partner had some legal claims, but he wholly repudiated any moral or equitable rights on their part, and early resolved to deal with the property in absolute ignorance of such rights.

"This may seem an exaggerated statement, if your Honor please, to be made in a court of justice, and yet I may quote the very words of Mr. Miller. Asked: 'Had you been the absolute owner of this property and intending to enjoy it to its most beneficial extent during your lifetime and transmit it to your own heirs, would you have acted differently in the management from what you have acted since Mr. Lux's death?' he answered: 'I have done it with the impartial expectation to make this property valuable for myself alone.'

"Asked further, 'You carried on your business after Mr. Lux's death just the same as you did before?' he answers, 'Just the same.' Again, 'You did not contract it or take any other steps in carrying it on than you did during Mr. Lux's lifetime?' he answers, 'No, sir, I did not.' And still further: 'You carried on the business just as you did in Mr. Lux's lifetime, without any change?' he answers, 'That was my intention.'

"He claimed, and he ultimately made those who lis-

tened to him acknowledge, that, under some fancied
power granted him in an agreement with his dead partner, he, for seven years, at least, could do just exactly
what he pleased with this vast estate. It mattered not
who gainsaid that proposition, he held on to it with
dogged and characteristic determination in spite of all
obstacles.

"Your Honor might admonish him of his position
as surviving partner and its duties. You did so admonish him with all the authority which belongs to your
exalted office, for you told him here in this very court,
'I never believed that that will conferred upon Mr.
Miller, or that the will could possibly be construed to
vest in Mr. Miller the power to reinvest the income of
that estate in enlarging it. I think it was the duty of
the executors to compel Mr. Miller to cease that work.
I don't think that seven years contemplates an enlarge-
ment of the estate by any means.' He heard, but paid no
attention to the admonition.

*   *   *   *   *

"Now, it favored Miller's position that his dead partner
had in a moment of blind confidence appointed him one
of the executors of his will. His lawyers soon advised
him—as must have been manifest to the dullest understanding of layman or lawyer—that the positions of
surviving partner and of executor of the estate of a
deceased partner were absolutely antagonistic, that their
duties were hostile and conflicting, and that no man
could with honor, however much he might profit, undertake the task of occupying both. Miller paid no attention
to the admonition. The position of executor of his
dead partner's will gave him an advantage, and what
mattered it that a sense of delicacy, of propriety or of
justice would have made a high-minded man spurn the

advantage? It was nothing to Henry Miller. He seized
upon the advantage and made the most of it.

*   *   *   *   *

"Furthermore, the copartnership agreement between
Miller & Lux, which is incorporated into and made a
part of the will of Charles Lux provides (I quote the
exact language):

"'So much of the rents, issues and profits and proceeds of sales which may be necessary for the support of the family of the deceased shall be paid
monthly to such family or its proper representatives.'

"Has Henry Miller ever complied with this wise and
beneficent and humane provision? Never. Receiving
millions of profits, making tens of millions of sales
since the death of his deceased partner, never has he
paid to his widow one cent of such profits or sales. I
speak literally, if your Honor please, and not meta-
phorically. She never has received a cent from this vast
estate to one-fourth of which, amounting to three, four,
five or more millions, she was entitled. She never has
received a cent. She has had to borrow money to live on.
The very family allowance which your Honor and your
Honor's predecessor, in accordance with the humanity
of the law, made for her support to this lady, who was entitled to receive from two to three hundred thousand
dollars of profits per annum, she had to borrow from
Henry Miller, and he has charged her interest on it to
this very day. He tried to hold her exactly where he
held Jesse Potter and his wife and child, making them all
feel that they were dependent upon him. Theoretically
they might be the owners of millions, but they had to beg
their bread from Henry Miller.

"What has become, then of the vast income of this
estate? It has been used and appropriated by Miller to

further his own vain desire to become the autocrat of the cattle market of this Coast. He has gone on regardless of the provisions of the partnership agreement, heedless of your Honor's admonitions, in spite of all dictates of propriety and justice, investing, and expanding, until now he can boast that he has one-third more cattle than when Charles Lux died, twice as many sheep, and he has three times as many horses and four times as many hogs.

"He has invested in land and permanent improvements of land alone the enormous sum of $2,150,000 out of the profits of this business. And this while the brothers and sisters of Charles Lux, the beneficiaries under his will, were going empty-handed to their graves, never having received one penny of the vast fortune which belonged to them. All this while the widow of his dead partner was compelled to borrow the means upon which she lived.

"Of course, for pursuing schemes thus abhorrent to all justice and propriety, some plausible excuse had to be found. It is only when a man becomes absolutely depraved, when conscience is absolutely dead in his bosom, that from the depth of his degradation and despair he exclaims, as did Manfred:

" '. . . I have ceased
To justify my deeds unto myself—
The last infirmity of evil.'

"So Miller found excuses and what were they? First, his dead partner and his wife, it seems, had not been sufficiently appreciative of his vast services in their behalf. 'It seems to me,' he says, with childish petulance, 'I was treated like a beast of burden. The moment the

beast of burden is not serviceable, his good qualities
are forgotten. It appeared to me very strongly that way.
I have spent every day of this time, I haven't had a day
to myself. Through inability I lost about four or five
days during that time, and then I seen the ungrateful
position I was placed under.' I have already read to your
Honor the passage in which he states that his wife had
toiled and slaved while Mrs. Lux had never worked.

* * * * *

"Now, take another topic. Miller was in possession
of the funds. He thoroughly understood the art of using those funds. Philip of Macedon, when scheming to
subject the Athenians to his sway, did not better understand the corrupting power of money than Henry Miller.
Does Miller understand the art of using money? Does
he? He is asked:

" 'Q. You have loaned money to a considerable extent of the firm of Miller & Lux, have you not; you
speak of them as policy loans? A. I have made a policy
loan, necessarily.'

" 'Q. One? A. Several.'

"This plan commenced immediately after Mr. Lux's
death. He says: 'We loaned to the Assessor of Fresno
County, Mr. Hutchinson, some money, something like
$7000 to $8000.'

" 'Q. When? A. It was probably right after Mr. Lux's
death.'

"This loan was made on mortgage of such value that
the borrower finally surrendered the property, and has
never paid the debt. He was the Assessor of Fresno
County, where the bulk of the lands of Miller & Lux lie.
This is classed by Mr. Miller as a policy loan, of course.

" 'We loaned $14,000 to Peter French of Oregon for to keep the man's good will; he is a person, a friend in need, which is a friend indeed.'

"It is idle to say that neither principal nor interest of this loan has ever been paid. It was a policy loan, like the loan to the Assessor of Fresno County.

"One of these loans, to N. H. A. Mason, which he denominates as 'the unfortunate loan,' would reach to-day, with the accumulated interest, to the enormous amount of $250,000 or $300,000. This suffices to show that Miller fully understood the art of making policy loans and the purposes which could be accomplished thereby.

"We find that a loan of $1000 is made by Miller to the attorney whom he had procured to be appointed to represent the absent and minor heirs. Very shortly after his appointment we find that he has loaned right along $200 a month, with certain interruptions, to Henry Lux for his support in accordance with the provisions of the will of his brother, Charles Lux. I note here that Henry Lux was the attorney in fact of the 'German Heirs,' and if Miller's expectations in that direction have been disappointed, it is not because he has not striven to reap the reward, but because the sturdy integrity of the man with whom he was dealing has baffled his hopes.

"To show you the purpose of Miller in making these advances to Henry Lux, under the will of his brother, it is sufficient to call attention to the fact that whenever Henry Lux has shown the slightest opposition to Miller's designs, the supply has at once been cut off. This happened, for the first time, when he undertook to compel Miller to account. As soon as he did so, his allowance was cut off. Mr. Merritt said there were no funds.

*   *   *   *   *

"I now take leave of this case by submitting to your Honor that no cause was ever presented or could ever be presented in court with clearer outlines of justice and right than this. I shall make no fantastic appeal to your Honor, but simply submit that after nine years of waiting it is time that these people should have something of the bounty which their brother and their uncle intended for them. These young ladies and these young gentlemen, now here and in Germany, are entitled to their share of this fortune, they have a right to receive it, and they do, through me, most earnestly demand that at length some one be appointed who shall have the power to wrest what belongs to them from the wrongful grasp of Henry Miller, multi-millionaire though he be. So appealing, so hoping, so believing, they now submit their cause to your Honor."

When McEnerney arose to answer this argument, a striking contrast was presented. With Delmas, clothes were essential and important, but McEnerney was garbed in clothes of the coarsest fabric. He even continued to wear detachable cuffs for twenty years after they ceased to be sold by the haberdashers. The gradually expanding embonpoint of Delmas was so artfully covered by a white waistcoat that the resemblance to the Little Corporal was made the more striking, while the growing girth of McEnerney was simply an evidence of strength and power. He had no weakness to overcome. While his language was eloquent, it was the eloquence of conviction, and did not rest for its support alone on elegance of diction. His whole body was permeated with a consciousness of the righteousness of his cause. No authority was ever cited by him from a superficial reading, but every decision was subjected to the most careful analysis, in order to determine just what was decided in view of the facts of the case as they were before the court, and the language of the court considered with relation to its other pronouncements. His presentation was the result of a preparation which consisted of exploring every possible avenue of approach and discarding every lead that proved to be unsound; and he presented only those facts which a most careful analysis had shown to be unanswerable. He battled under no weight of affectation. Even those striking locks, which grew with his growing frame, seemed necessary to balance his body. His great strength was in his power of characterization. His great jowls and the superfluous flesh that joined his face and head with his body without any apparent neck were hidden by a generous smile that lit up his entire countenance. Unfortunately the text of his argument on that occasion has not been preserved.

The judge, after due deliberation, announced his decision, holding against the charge of conspiracy, but reopening the case in order to allow additional testimony in support of the charge of improvidence of Potter. Thus, so far as Henry Miller was concerned, the trial resulted in a complete vindication.

In order to obtain this additional evidence, Delmas began canvassing those prominent in the night-life of San Francisco, and taking their depositions. This was a little too much for the "German Heirs." They finally got tired of the fight and dismissed their contest, so the case was never finally decided.

Ten years after the death of Charles Lux, his estate was finally settled and the entire matter was compromised by the formation of a corporation to which all of the property was transferred, and of which Henry Miller had complete control, except that he was limited in the acquisition of additional land, and was required to liquidate and sell the property as fast as it could conveniently be done.

But his troubles were not yet over. The ink had hardly become dry on the final decree of the court, when some of the "German Heirs" reappeared, represented by a new attorney-in-fact and by new attorneys-at-law, and brought a suit to set aside the decree on the ground of fraud. This time they took their case into the Federal Court, on account of diversity of citizenship. At that time most of the heirs were with Henry Miller in upholding the settlement, and a new attorney appeared in the picture, representing the Lux estate, William B. Treadwell. When the case came up, there was a notable aggregation of talent at the counsel table, and he presented the argument against the new attack. His method of presentation was quite different from that of Delmas or McEnerney. He did not care much for nice distinctions on conflicting points of view as to law or fact, but his aim in a case was to endeavor to get it into a position where a few clean-cut, practically incontrovertible, contentions could be brought forth which would be determinative of it. His vocabulary was simple. He never used two words where one would suffice. By the time he had stripped the plaintiffs' complaint of its verbiage and brought to the attention of the court the facts that must necessarily exist, because not denied by the complaint, it lay before the court like a skeleton without life or vitality, and when he presented the law applicable to the situation as it was thus pictured, the result was not an argument, but a demonstration. When other counsel supporting the settlement were invited to proceed with the argument, they consulted and merely said, "We are content, your Honor."

The attorneys for the "German Heirs" made a perfunctory argument and the next day were asking for a settlement. They offered to dismiss the case if Henry Miller would buy a portion of their stock. Henry Miller immediately saw his opportunity. He had every intention of buying all of their stock at some time, but at his own price. He knew that a price now agreed upon would be a precedent, and it was always his habit to let people know at what price he was willing to buy, and then they could come to him or not as they saw fit.

A price was agreed upon, the stock changed hands, the suit was dismissed, and for years afterwards whenever the stockholders needed money, he was in the market and gradually picked up the stock at the price fixed.

Henry Miller, surviving partner, became Henry Miller, President, and he began to discharge his duties in regard to the sale of land. His superintendents picked out a piece of land which had never been plowed, but which grew good feed, had it surveyed and subdivided, and offered it for sale. He could afford to put it on the market at a very reasonable price, because it had cost him so little. Soon it was covered by settlers, but in a very short time it was found that the land was shallow, underlain by clay and would not produce. Dissatisfaction arose among the settlers and Henry Miller went down and looked it over. There were some agitators among the settlers who were looking for a fight and were preparing to organize the settlers with that end in view. Henry Miller looked the matter over and said, "This land is no good. I will move the entire colony," and he surveyed an adjoining tract of the finest land available, invited the settlers to choose their own land, brought horses and bodily moved the houses and improvements, and a successful colony was established.

He nursed the colonists along for years, extending their payments almost indefinitely. When he would come down, men and women would cut across fields to intercept him to ask for some help. One would want the loan of a bull, one would want a milk cow. It was one of his rules never to sell an animal with his brand upon it, but he would lend his bulls, even lend his cows, until the colonists were in shape to get their own. "You can have the cow, but you gives me the calf," would be the way he would frequently handle it, where a woman with a lot of children was in need of milk. He would advise them, tell the women to grow hogs, chickens and turkeys, so that there would be no waste. He would buy their hay and in a thousand other ways make suggestions to them so that their farming operations would be a success, and he sold them water for a dollar and a quarter to two dollars and a half an acre, probably the cheapest water in the West. Frequently they were newcomers in the country. Many of them were anxious to grow fruit, but he said, "Too much work, and it takes too long. Grow alfalfa to feed cattle and sell butter and cream and you will have money at once." He proved to be right and built up one of the finest and most successful dairying territories in the West.

Soon the heirs, now minority stockholders, again became uneasy and complained that the land was not being sold fast enough. Henry Miller said,

"You may know more about this than I do, but there is no sense in selling this land anyhow, I have to not only use this land in order to make money for you, but I have to rent three hundred thousand acres more in order to get enough feed for our cattle. We don't want any more quarreling about how fast I can colonize and sell this land, but I'll agree to pay you every year, somehow or other, three per cent on the capital stock of the company, and we will sell enough land to pay it, if necessary."

This was agreed to by the requisite two-thirds of the stockholders, and the necessary amendments to the articles of incorporation were made, when one of the heirs attacked the validity of this on the ground that the capital of the company could not be so distributed. It certainly seemed that there was nothing that Henry Miller could do that would please everybody. If he distributed the capital, it was illegal, if he did not distribute it, it was unfair. This matter was then litigated, but resulted in a decision favorable to Henry Miller and upholding the validity of the amendments. Then came the other provision of the articles that he should not buy land. There did not seem to be any out so far as that was concerned, but land he needed, land he must have, and, therefore, he took his share of the dividends and bought more land in his own name and then leased it to the corporation so as to pay himself five per cent interest on the purchase price; and even the minority stockholders winked at this apparent evasion of the spirit of the settlement.

Years went on. In order to improve the position of the company in its litigation, it was reincorporated under the laws of Nevada. In the meantime Potter had died and likewise his wife. His son had now come of age and came on the scene with new attorneys and they grabbed at this reincorporation as a drowning man would grab at a straw, contending that it was illegal and resulted in a reversion of the property to the various heirs. He refused to take stock in the new company. Henry Miller refused to pay him dividends unless he did take it. Actions and cross-actions were brought; appeals and cross-appeals were taken; decisions favoring one side or the other were rendered. At one stage of the case for a technical violation of a decree all of the directors were adjudged guilty of contempt and ordered imprisoned until they complied with its terms.

But before any final determination was made Henry Miller said, "If these people want a partition of the property, let them have it. I won't get hurt by a partition," and he got one of his friends among the heirs to bring a partition suit. Having thus turned the tables upon them, a settlement was soon arrived at, and this resulted in Henry Miller purchasing all of the interests of the Lux heirs, so that he finally became the owner in fee simple absolute of the entire property. He became in law, as he for a long time had been in fact, Miller & Lux.

The Empire was now complete. Over a million acres of land fully stocked, all owned by Henry Miller.

XIV. HIGH FINANCE

IN THE days of gold the Bank of California was the leading financial institution of the West. Into its coffers came a large part of the gold of the West. The leading financiers of San Francisco controlled it. In the Comstock days it established a branch in Virginia City and the wealth of the Comstock was also thrown into its lap. It was considered as strong as the Rock of Gibraltar, and as stable as the Bank of England. It was the particular duty of Charles Lux to ingratiate the firm with its officials. At times Henry Miller would send him drafts for the purchase of cattle or of land in staggering amounts, and it was the duty of Charles Lux to explain these to the bank and the profits that would result, and keep the firm in good financial standing.

Those were the days of loose banking and the overdraft. Checks and drafts of men of proper credit and standing were cashed without any funds whatever to their credit. Hundreds of thousands of dollars were carried merely as overdrafts, not even represented by the formality of a promissory note. During the periods of moving the crops and

of purchases of land or large numbers of livestock, staggering overdrafts would frequently be
carried by the firm. At other times the money
would roll in in a steady stream and its account
would be overflowing with a large surplus. The
account was considered a valuable one and it was
the particular duty of Charles Lux to have it so
appear. He moved in the same social circle as the
officers of the bank, and the firm never wanted for
credit.

The firm never gave any security for the money
it borrowed. It never placed a mortgage upon its
property, and, if it bought a piece of property, as
it frequently did, subject to a mortgage, the mortgage was at once paid off, even if it caused an
overdraft to do so. A mortgage was deemed beneath the dignity of the firm. "Never run in debt,"
was one of Henry Miller's maxims. These overdrafts were entirely seasonal, and seldom, if ever,
ran over from year to year.

The leading spirit in the bank was William C.
Ralston, a striking character, a man of delightful
presence, public spirited, and enterprising. He was
not only president of the bank, but was connected
with numerous enterprises, both public and private.
His enterprises covered a broad field, extending
even to an experimental tobacco farm on one of the
Miller ranches near Gilroy. He stood high in the
social affairs of the city and had a large country
place at Belmont, some thirty miles to the South.

He was instrumental in getting the city to lay a plank road out through the Mission and onto what is now known as El Camino Real, and was instrumental in importing the eucalyptus tree from Australia into California and planting it on the Peninsula.

He was a lover of fine horses and as Saturday noon approached there might be seen in front of the bank an old fashioned English tallyho with four horses, the driver in uniform, and the footman armed with a trumpet. Into this he and his friends would climb, he would himself take the reins from the driver, and the prancing steeds would go through the streets and out on the Mission Road. He aimed to time the trip so that he would pass in front of the train at the Valencia Street depot and then drive so fast that he would be able again to pass in front of it at Belmont Station, and this he would actually accomplish. Maybe he would stop at Baden and pick up Charles Lux, or at Burlingame and pick up Crocker, so that when he finally arrived he had a large week-end party. Others took to the same sport, and probably he would be followed by Haggin with his Arabian horses. His entertainments were lavish and expensive and were joined in by the best people of the city.

One of his greatest undertakings was the construction of a big hotel, and it was he who laid the foundation for the Palace Hotel.

About this time speculation in the stocks of the Comstock mines was rampant. The vein was lost and found again. The Sutro tunnel was completed and was draining the mines of water. Exaggerated reports were circulated as to the amount of ore in sight. As the extraction of the ore became more and more expensive, more and more stock was put on the market. Soon the prices of the stock were out of all proportion to any possible value of the ore. The bank was backing numerous of these mining companies, when gradually the public began to scent the fact that the veins had been lost and might never again be found. The boom collapsed. The great days of the Comstock were at an end. The day of reckoning was at hand and when the accounts were balanced, the Bank of California was found with fifteen million dollars of liabilities and only thirty thousand dollars in cash. The iron shutters were closed on its doors.

The shock could not have been much greater if the sun had failed to rise in the morning. At first great indignation arose against Ralston. All of the trouble was attributed to his extravagant habits and wild speculations. If he had appeared, it is uncertain what might have been his fate with the infuriated depositors. The next day the sun rose upon his body, washed ashore from the bay.

The foundation of the Palace Hotel was only partly laid and the enterprise came to a standstill. All of the other enterprises which were essential to the growth of the city and state and in which he was the leading spirit fell to the ground. A few days later Senator Sharon and the other principal persons interested in the bank and in the financial affairs of the city, including Henry Miller and Charles Lux, met and faced the situation and determined that William C. Ralston should not have died in vain. They agreed to rehabilitate the bank and contribute sufficient funds to wipe out the indebtedness and again start in business. The slate was washed clean. Each contributed the amount assigned to him, and the last dollar of indebtedness was paid. The bank reopened and until the day of Henry Miller's death his representatives were carting through its doors money from his properties, or borrowing money for their continued operation.

This rehabilitation caused a sudden revulsion of feeling. The hatred that had been aroused against Ralston was turned to pity, then to sorrow, then to admiration. His great accomplishments were recognized and extolled and his last great sacrifice made him the idol of his city and state.

During these years of hectic speculation many attractive opportunities were brought by Ralston to Henry Miller, but never would he permit himself to be drawn into any speculative enterprise. He did not want to be involved in any business he did not understand and did not control. His money was never idle and he needed all of it to run and expand his own business. He cared nothing about making easy money, he enjoyed rather wringing the money from the resisting soil. If anybody wanted to grow tobacco, he was perfectly willing to let him have some of his land to try the experiment, and even when oil was discovered on or about his own land, he always considered it a speculative business, and never spent a dollar drilling for it, but was ready to give oil leases on reasonable terms to any one who wished to drill for it. One of the first known surface outcroppings of oil in the San Joaquin Valley was on his property.

One day Azro N. Lewis, one of the trustees of the estate of his partner's widow, said to him, "Mr. Miller, I think there is a chance for oil on that quarter section up on Kern River above Bakersfield," pointing it out on the map. Henry Miller replied, "I haven't any money to use looking for oil." Dr. Lewis said, "Well, Mr. Miller, I am pretty confident that there is oil there. Would you mind selling me the property?" Henry Miller was very anxious to keep the friendship and coöperation of Dr. Lewis, so he sold him the property at just what it was worth for agricultural purposes, which was little or nothing. About six million dollars of oil was afterwards taken out of this quarter section.

But even this did not necessarily prove that his principle was incorrect, for numerous wells were put down by lessees upon his property and thousands of dollars spent by them, and only a comparatively small amount of oil was ever found. Some of the finest oil fields were within a quarter of a mile of his property, and still no oil was found thereon. But he helped the oil industry in every way. He would lease any property on an eighth royalty. He would sell water to an oil well, when he would not sell it to a cattle man. He said, "They can't put down oil wells without water, so we'll have to give it to them. But they are able to pay a good price for it," and the revenue from this source was very considerable. But if an oil company tried to take his water without paying for it, there was trouble. One company put down a water well a few hundred feet from the river, and in that way pumped water from the river to which he was entitled. The oil company said it did not come from the river. He said, "Well, if it does come from the river, will you pay what it is worth?" This being agreed to, he employed the best geologists from the University of California and Stanford University and proved beyond a question that it did come from the river, and it cost the oil company twenty thousand dollars for the water that they had taken for their steam engine.

One day he thought he had discovered a coal deposit on his land and he said to his foreman, "I am going to get some samples of that coal. It looks like very fine coal to me. You come along and dig it out." Some good samples were cut out and put in a sack and he took them himself to an

assayer's office in the city, and said, "I think I
have some very fine coal on my land. I wants you
to examine it and let me know about it." The
assayer said, "All right, Mr. Miller, you come in
to-morrow evening before you go home and I will
tell you about it." The next evening, he came in
and said, "Did you examine my coal?" The assayer
said, "Yes, Mr. Miller, it is very fine coal, but it
is not hard enough." He was quite pleased and
said, "Well, how long will it take to get hard
enough to use?" and the assayer said, "Well, it is
difficult to figure very accurately on that, but I
would say a minimum of twenty-five hundred
years. Beyond that you can't exactly tell." Henry
Miller said, "Well, I can't wait that long," and
without another word departed.

He was always ready to try anything in connection with his own business. He was one of the first
to introduce the use of alfalfa in California. He
was one of the first to grow rice in California. He
was one of the first to grow cotton in California,
and alfalfa, rice and cotton are now major crops
of the state.

One day he was riding along a road and looking
up a little canyon was surprised to see a lone cow
with two calves. He directed the driver to stop,
climbed out of the cart, walked up the canyon and
found that the calves were obviously twins. Twin
calves are rare, and a cow will never willingly
nurse the calf of another cow. When a cow dies

in giving birth to a calf, the calf, which is called a leppy calf, is fastened by a double leather collar to the calf of a healthy cow, and thus the leppy calf is given an opportunity to nurse while the cow's own calf is so engaged. Soon the mother gets accustomed to the intruder and freely permits it to nurse. This obviously was not such a case. The calves were both young and had no collars. They were obviously twins. One was a heifer and one a bull calf. He went back and said to the foreman, "You mark those calves. It might be we can breed twin calves and that would be a great business. You keep track of them and breed them and we will see." The experiment, however, was unsuccessful.

Dry farming was probably the most experimental and speculative feature of his business. He didn't like it and tried to reduce it to a minimum. If he could induce any one to rent his land for dry farming, he was glad to do it, and would even advance renters considerable sums of money. He always said, "Whenever you rent land for grain, always reserve a right to pasture the stubble. They generally have no use for it, and don't recognize its value, but it is very valuable." One time he reserved the right to pasture the land, but the judge held that the right to pasture the land did not include the right to eat the straw which was scattered over the land by the headers. But on appeal it was urged that the sheep would not be discriminating enough to eat only the stubble that was not cut and therefore it must have been intended to allow the cut straw also to be fed. This argument seemed to appeal to the court, so he got the right to eat the stubble and also the straw that was scattered from the header.

"Always burn the stubble off, if you can't feed it. If you plow the stubble in, you just make a lot of chimneys for the moisture to come out of the ground," Henry Miller would say. His accounts often showed very heavy losses for money advanced to dry farm tenants, but probably the losses were many times made up by the pasture that he received and the share of the good crops that were cut. If his own dry farming crops did not mature, he could always turn in sheep, hogs, horses or cattle, and eat up what there was.

After a particularly dry year many tenants lost their land and besides found themselves in debt to the firm for materials and provisions they had bought at its stores. Charles Lux directed that some three hundred suits be brought against the unfortunate tenants. When Henry Miller learned of this he was furious and dismissed all of the actions. His partner said, "Did they not owe us the money? They were honest debts. Why should we not sue for them?"

Henry Miller said, "I takes the land and they takes the road. That's enough. You can't do this to men in this country when they are unfortunate.

They would burn your haystacks, steal your harness and leave your gates open. You'd lose more money in the long run."

On one occasion there was a series of dry years, resulting in a tremendous loss of cattle all over the State. He survived because he had a large reserve of feed and pasture. The cattle of others were so thin that it was useless to ship them to market and they were permitted to perish on the plains. He then conceived the idea, which he speedily put into execution, of erecting all up and down the valley great vats, and he got permission to slaughter the animals before they perished and to boil out the fat, which was converted into tallow. As the shortage of cattle increased the price of lard, he made a fine profit by this operation.

When the dreadful period was over his herds were greatly depleted. Collections were slow and a general condition of financial depression prevailed. In order to build up his herd, he required large sums of money and more than his own bank could advance in justice to its obligation to its other customers, so he was compelled to seek elsewhere for financial assistance. He approached his own countryman, Claus Spreckels, who had made a great fortune in Hawaiian sugar and other enterprises. He explained the situation to Spreckels, and Spreckels said, "Yes, Mr. Miller, I have the money. What security are you willing to give?" If he had asked Henry Miller to cut off his right hand, he could not have shocked him any more. He said, "Mr. Spreckels, I've been in business in California for forty years and my word has always been good enough security." Spreckels said, "I don't do business that way and my lawyers will have to be satisfied that I am thoroughly protected." Henry Miller said, "This drought has been a great public calamity. It has set back the livestock business for years. I have got to build up the herds of the State and the city must be supplied with meat. You know I will not give security. I've never asked you for help before; I need it now and you are in a position to give it to me, and I have a right to ask it. I consider that you have insulted me. Good morning." "Good morning," said Spreckels.

Henry Miller never forgot and never forgave. Years later his real opportunity came to even scores with Spreckels. Taking advantage of the growing hostility to the Southern Pacific Railroad Company, Spreckels conceived the idea of putting in a competing railroad through the San Joaquin Valley. In doing this, he posed as a public bene- factor relieving the people from the exactions of the "octopus." He prevailed upon many people to grant rights of way free of charge to the new com- pany, and prevailed upon the cities to grant all kinds of favorable franchises to it. Looking over the map of the West side of the San Joaquin Valley, he found that he would have to go through the Miller & Lux land for about a hundred miles. He wanted to go down the West side because the Southern Pacific already had a road down the East side. So he sent his right-of-way man to Henry Miller.

This man was a high pressure salesman and had his lesson well learned. He praised Henry Miller for his great public enterprise, pointed out how this railroad would benefit him and give him a ready means of shipping his cattle to San Francisco, and finally wound up by asking him to give a right of way as other public spirited citizens were doing. Spreckels had anticipated that Henry Miller would insist on a personal visit from him, and he dreaded the time that he would have to enter Henry Miller's office with his hat in his hand to ask this favor. But he was relieved to find that apparently Henry Miller had entirely forgotten the affront to his dignity, because he gratefully accepted the fine words of praise as to his public enterprise, and said certainly he would give a right of way and for them to send in a description and he would have his attorney draw the contract. In fact he seemed to be in a hurry to grant this favor, because he told the right-of-way man that he would be in town for a few days, and, if the description was sent right over, it would get immediate attention.

The description was sent and the contract was drawn, and in the contract he inserted two innocent provisions; one, that if the railroad was not built and operated within a certain length of time, the right of way would revert to him, and, second, that the railroad grade must be commenced within a certain length of time, and that he should be afforded all necessary crossings for his water and be entitled to retain the grade in case the railroad was not completed or was abandoned.

This right of way was located through the low and overflow land of Miller & Lux, and Henry Miller did not tell Spreckels' man that for years he had been endeavoring to get the Southern Pacific to put a railroad down the West side further to the West and on the higher land where there was much more settlement and where the land was better developed by irrigation. Very shortly the railroad grade was hastily thrown up to comply with the terms of the contract. But in the meantime the Southern Pacific had quietly been obtaining a right of way through the very heart of the country and suddenly put on its crew and built a railroad in a location that practically killed the Spreckels road.

The only thing that was left for Spreckels was to pick up and move to the East side of the valley, and this he did, abandoning the right of way and a hundred miles of road grade, which then reverted to Henry Miller and became a highway through his low land and a levee for irrigating some hundred thousand acres of land. This was the cheapest irrigation in the United States. All he had to do was to put a few gates in this grade and the water could be flooded over the land or drained off at his will. This railroad right of way also later served for a pipe line to carry oil from the oil fields to San Francisco Bay, and Henry Miller granted the oil companies the right to maintain oil pipes along it. So without even an ill word he had his revenge.

Under slightly different circumstances his action was quite different. When coming by boat to California, a man of whom he inquired for some information snubbed him. This man was a pompous individual, who later became a prosperous business man in San Francisco, but the time came when, due to one of the fires that destroyed the city, he had to borrow money, and he swallowed his pride and requested a loan of Henry Miller. Henry Miller never loaned money more willingly, nor with greater pleasure. He knew that a refusal would not hurt the man as much as was his pride by being compelled to ask this favor of one whom he had spurned when conditions were reversed.

XV. POLITICS

AMERICAN citizenship and how to obtain it
was one of the first things in which Henry
Miller became interested, and at the earliest opportunity he took the necessary steps for admission
to citizenship. There was considerable red tape necessary, on account of his change of name, but that
was finally straightened out and he received his
certificate, and this certificate he kept all through
his life, taking it religiously with him when he
registered. He always registered as a voter and made
it a point not only to vote but to go over the can-
didates with others so as to vote as intelligently as
possible. But his politics soon became very simple.
He voted for every Republican candidate for President from John C. Frémont to William Howard
Taft. His political ideas were well expressed in
the San Francisco *Argonaut* which he always carefully perused.

In local politics he was extremely tactful. He
did not want any of his own men in politics, and
rather resented it when one of his foremen left him
and was elected sheriff. His theory was that the
best people in the country admired and respected
him, and if they could be elected, he would be in

safe hands, but he feared the demagogue and graft-
er. He urged all of his men to take a friendly interest in public officials, and he always made reasonable contributions to their campaigns. The only
thing that was ever criticized was the fact brought
out during his contest with the "German Heirs"
that he had made certain "policy loans" which had
resulted in losses, and one of those "policy loans,"
which was unsecured, was to an assessor of one of
the counties in which he owned a large amount of
land. He saw nothing wrong in this and said, "I
don't want any favors from the assessor, I just wants
to be treated like every one else. There is no chance
of the assessor assessing my property lower than my
neighbor's, because he could not hold his job if
he did."

His worst brush with politics of the State was
in connection with the great riparian fight, and
there he came in contact with the boss system which
existed in the metropolitan areas and more or less
throughout the State. It was not the situation of
one big organization, but there were numerous
petty bosses controlling certain blocks of votes and
certain localities. They were mostly of a low character, but had an uncanny method of controlling
party primaries, such as they were, and consequently
party conventions. Most of them were venal, not to
say corrupt. The saloons and even the criminal
elements were their handmaidens. His experience
disgusted him with the system.

After that fight was over, and he had selected William F. Herrin as his attorney, he talked this matter over with him many times. Herrin had the same experience and appreciated the weakness and defects of the system. Henry Miller said, "There are so many of these bosses that you no more than get one of them lined up than he sends another one to shake you down. It is bad enough to have to buy them, but the worst of it is that some of them won't stay bought. The national political parties seem to be fine organizations. Couldn't we have something of that kind in the State that would protect people and their property?" Herrin said, "Yes, Mr. Miller, I think that could be done, but it would take lots of money to do it." "Well," said Henry Miller, "Bismarck got rid of all the little kings and princes in Germany, and I would like to get rid of all the little bosses in California."

It was not long before the Southern Pacific Railroad Company took Herrin away from Henry Miller and made him Chief Counsel of that company. The railroad company was the greatest victim of the demagogue. Any yellow dog that wanted to be elected to office generally accomplished it by posing as an enemy of the railroad, and soon the duties of Herrin of a strictly legal nature were expanded so as to include the general political affairs of the company, and he thus had an opportunity to carry into effect the idea which he had expressed in his conversation with Henry Miller.

Herrin proceeded to build up a state political organization. It was easy to obtain the cooperation of others who were interested in protecting their property from the demands of the petty politician. Then there was the great army of railroad employees. Foremen and superintendents were selected who had a genius for political organization, and who could not only organize their employees, but their friends in the various communities. Then there was the ability to issue passes, and it was surprising how many men would almost sell their souls for one of those pieces of pasteboard. It was a form of genteel bribery to which many men were subject, although they would have recoiled from a monetary transaction. Then the man who could transport all of the delegates to a convention free might expect to have some reasonable influence over them after they arrived at the convention auditorium.

But the most effective way of controlling the situation was by controlling the bosses. The business of being a petty boss was not all it was cracked up to be, because frequently he would spend a large amount of money in a campaign and then lose the campaign and his opponents would have the offices for several years and there would be poor pickings. Herrin's idea was to make the business of being a boss a sort of perpetual profession, so there would be some reasonably good pickings no matter how the fight went. So he supplied the sinews of

war for the bosses and the bosses were supposed finally to deliver the votes to him. It did not make any
particular difference which boss won, the only difference was who would deliver the votes to Herrin.

Down to this point the whole procedure was
sordid enough but considered necessary in the conditions that prevailed. But from there on Herrin
handled the thing on a higher plane. It was his
endeavor to put at least the nominal control of the
parties in men of character and standing in the
community, and still in men on whose loyalty he
could rely. It was also his policy to nominate for
office men of high character, good standing, and
fitness for the offices to which they were nominated.
This was the secret of his success and ability to
carry on the program without public revolt.

Then ambition was another motive which
brought men to his organization. It was a common
saying that no one could hope to succeed politically
unless he swore allegiance to the railroad. Others
expressed it more bluntly that any one desiring to
succeed must sacrifice his independence to his ambition. Another thing that helped make the plan
succeed was that the people had seen so many men
elected to office on a platform of hostility to the
railroad and then found them to be corrupt, that
it was rather a proof of standing that a man running
for office was being supported by the railroad.

But the thing that gave the scheme the greatest
impetus was inherent in the purpose of the plan,

which was to protect property, and that could best be done by keeping down the tax rate. So the cardinal principle of Herrin was low taxes. That principle appealed to farmers and property owners throughout the State, and as the bosses were particularly skillful in getting the votes of the laboring men and the disreputable elements in the community, the combination was almost irresistible.

So it happened that in a very short time the office of Herrin became the headquarters of the "invisible government" of the State of California, and the most extraordinary feature of the matter was that this condition continued for a period of over twenty years.

As Henry Miller was one of the biggest tax payers in the state, a low tax rate was almost essential to his existence. When an assessor was elected by the organization, he knew that he was not expected to do anything but be fair to everybody, because the organization owed a duty to many who contributed to its existence and success. He owed his job to no one but "the organization," and was selected on account of his availability, but never losing sight of his honesty and loyalty. Fair treatment was all the big concerns needed and all they could expect.

But in another particular the big concern was able to obtain great economic advantage. That was by means of freight rebates. Henry Miller shipped thousands of livestock over the railroad, to say nothing of all kinds of materials. He could say to the railroad, "If you don't meet my terms, I'll run some boats up the river, or I will drive my cattle to market." If this was not sufficient to justify the favoritism shown, the railroad would say, "It is easier for us to do business in carload lots, or in trainload lots, and if we know that we are going to get the business, we can afford to do it at a cheaper rate." Fortified by these plausible arguments, the practice of giving rebates on trainload lots and on carload lots made Henry Miller hundreds of thousands of dollars. No one profited more than he by rebates and drawbacks, which were in vogue in these years. The railroad was his partner.

Thus did he build his business into the political institutions of the State. Under the system, he saw some of the best lawyers on the courts of the State and his property was safe. Assessors could not over-assess him. Legislatures could not impose excessive taxes upon him. Meat inspectors could not levy tribute upon him. He belonged to the "organization," and the State belonged to the organization too.

XVI. A DAY'S WORK

IT HAD been a hot summer's day in Bakersfield, but that was not unusual, because most summer days are hot in Bakersfield. By the time the sun set the old hotel was almost a furnace. A typical wooden structure of the nineties, it seemed to receive and hold all the heat there was. It had a long and uneventful career until the oil excitement came, and then it was all bustle and business. It was filled every night, and its patrons took what was given them without complaint. Haggin & Tevis owned all the good corners in the town, so no one else could build a hotel anyhow. The building cooled off enough by ten o'clock so that the patrons began to be able to get a little sleep, if without any covers they were lucky enough to be able to curl up near an outside window. Those in the inside rooms were so uncomfortable they could not distinguish between the discomfort of the heat and of bed bugs. But finally all became quiet, save for the footsteps of the night watchman.

He had just now punched his time clock at four o'clock, and a streak of light was appearing in the eastern sky. He heard a slight noise down one

of the corridors and walking in that direction he
met in a darkened hall the figure of Henry Miller.
He was already dressed. It was not unusual for the
watchman to meet him at that time in the morning
and exchange a morning's greeting with him. But
this morning he was surprised, because Henry Miller was carrying a slop bucket and heading toward
the public bath. The watchman stepped aside and
said, "What are you doing with that, Mr. Miller?"

"Just saving the maid a disagreeable task," he
answered, and continued on his way to the public
bath.

A few minutes later he entered the hotel lobby.
There was a sleepy night clerk behind the desk.
Distributed around on chairs and lounges were
several guests who were unable to procure accommodations and who were trying to snatch a few
hours of troubled sleep. Henry Miller went to the
back of the lobby, sat down at a little writing table,
lit the flickering gas light, took out a little pad of
writing material, dipped his pen in the ink, and
began writing in a close hand on both sides of the
paper. The never ceasing scratch of his pen joined
melodiously with the snoring of the traveling salesman. When the roustabout came in to "hose out"
the place, he was still scratching away; when the
boy came in with the morning papers, he had a
neat pile of letters all written, sealed and addressed;
when the cook came through on his way to the
kitchen, he was already on his twentieth letter; and

when the night clerk and day clerk exchanged shifts, his pen was still droning on.

Promptly at six o'clock the waitress opened the dining room door, and at about the same time a buggy with two horses came to the front of the hotel and the driver entered. Henry Miller was just depositing his letters in the mail box. They were to superintendents and foremen all over three states, giving the most minute instructions as to the movement of cattle and management of ranch property. If perchance one of the foremen was new, he would tell him the difficulties and advantages of the particular properties under his control and how he could best operate them. The letters formed an encyclopedia of farming, stock raising, and practical philosophy. The writing was fine and cramped. The orthography was often defective. But the orders were clear, and the criticisms short and to the point. But the contents of these letters deserve a separate chapter.

The driver greeted Henry Miller and they immediately went in to breakfast. The driver said, "Mr. Miller, that oil man working out at Templor wants to see you about getting some water for his rig, and I told him that you would be here this morning."

He had hardly ceased speaking when the oil operator approached the table and greeted Henry Miller. In order to avoid delay, he was invited to sit down to breakfast. He said, "Mr. Miller, I would like to get some water for our wells over at Templor."

Henry Miller said, "How far would you have to carry it?"

"About ten miles," said the oil operator.

"We are awfully short of water," said Henry Miller, "but if you will lay the pipe and put in some troughs for our stock, and put an automatic gauge on the troughs, and keep the troughs filled with water, you can have water for your rig. We are getting as high as twenty cents a barrel for water, but that is a long way to carry it, and you can have it for five cents a barrel."

As soon as the man had gone, Henry Miller said to his foreman, "I've been wanting water out there for a long time for the cattle, but it was too far to take it. This is a good opportunity to get more cattle out there, and we can run two thousand head more with this water. You take it up with him and see if we can't sell him that old pipe we have, and probably we could lay the pipe for him too. You have some idle horses and they might as well be doing something."

Between the courses of a very substantial breakfast, he gave the driver directions as to the places they would visit during the day, and in a few minutes he was seated in the buggy ready to start.

"Take me down to the railroad corrals and let

me see these Arizona steers," said Henry Miller.

A few blocks driving brought them to a large band of cattle held in the railroad corral. The owner was there, and the steers were for sale. Henry Miller drove around the bunch and looked them over carefully. When he got through, he said to the owner, "You must have picked those steers up from different ranches. They show different breeds and irregular size and color. It is hard to estimate their weight. I haven't got time to stay and see them weighed, but I will give you thirty-four thousand eight hundred dollars for the lot."

The owner said, "That price might be all right, but my people would rather know how much a pound they are getting for their stock."

Henry Miller had been figuring on a basis of seven and one-half cents, so he immediately said, "All right, if you want it that way, I will give you seven and a quarter cents for them."

When the cattle were weighed, the owner got about a hundred dollars less than the original offer, but he said, "It was worth a hundred dollars to prove that what I had heard about Henry Miller's ability to estimate the weight of cattle was true. He certainly is a wonder."

As soon as the deal was closed, Henry Miller said, "My foreman will attend to the details, drive on," and soon they were lost in a cloud of dust. A short way down the road he met a man with a bunch of hogs.

"Mr. Miller," said the man, "I have some fine hogs here. Would you like to have them?"

"I have more hogs than I can use. The market is glutted with them."

"You can have them cheap," said the man in a pleading voice. "Six cents?"

"No use," said Henry Miller, and touching his hat said, "drive on."

In a few minutes he said, "Stop and let me out at the telephone in that saloon."

Once inside the telephone booth he got his nearest foreman and told him he could now get the hogs very cheap and to run into the man casually and make a deal. When the man met the foreman, the latter said, "It's no use. I could not pay more than five cents without instructions from Mr. Miller." He finally with apparent reluctance bought them at that price, remarking that Mr. Miller would probably fire him.

It was not long before they arrived at the first of his ranches. During the drive he learned all the driver knew about cattle on the ranch, water conditions, crop conditions, and man power. The driver had hardly stopped before Henry Miller was on the ground. The foreman was there to greet him and the rounds of the ranch commenced. He walked rapidly, the foreman trotting along to keep pace with him.

"There should be a wire netting over that porch to keep the flies out. The grass in front of the house should be trimmed and fed to the chickens. The chicken house should be white-washed to kill the lice. A new cook will be down to-day. When a new cook comes, have him clean the shelves in the kitchen, so he will learn what is there and will not be buying unnecessarily. It don't look to me as if you have enough chickens here to take care of the waste. Those potato peelings are too thick. You can always tell a good housekeeper by looking at the potato peelings. What is that man doing out there in the orchard, picking oranges? Oranges should never be picked, they must be cut. If you pull them off at the stem it leaves a place where the heat gets in and they dry out.

"Why are those pitchforks standing with the prongs on the floor? They should always be standing with the prongs at the top. That will keep the prongs from rusting and deteriorating. I've been telling men that all my life, but they never will do it. But I'm going to keep on telling them anyhow. There is too much straw in that manure pile, your men are too careless in cleaning out the stalls, they throw out too much straw with the manure. It is very wasteful. It spoils good straw and makes poor manure. That hay stack is too close to the barn. If it should get on fire it would endanger the ranch buildings.

"What is that hay rake doing outside of the shed? Always keep your implements under cover. They won't last long if they are out in the heat of the summer any more than if they are out in the rain. What is that small hide doing there? You mustn't kill these small steers for meat on the ranches. Kill the old cows. Are you shipping that bunch of cows? I notice there are quite a number of them forward with calf. They must never be shipped to market in that condition. As I came along I saw a man on a mowing machine with loose sleeves; that is dangerous; they are liable to get caught in the blades. What is this? You charged one of our neighbors for meals he ate here? Never charge our neighbors for meals. You should go out of your way to maintain friendly relations with our neighbors. Friendly neighbors are valuable and it is best when they are under some obligation. Never charge them for meals, but whenever you eat outside always insist on paying for your meal.

"That fire wagon over there is not located right. You should have your fire wagon where you can get at it quickly. Have nothing in front of it. Those grain sacks on that fire wagon are too light to fight fire with. You should have coal sacks. You haven't any barrel of drinking water on the wagon. When men are fighting fire, they must have water to drink. You should have a barrel with a tin cup attached to it. I noticed altogether too much grass along the road as I came in. That is where fire starts, because people are traveling along the road.

You should put some sheep in there and eat it off. Even a shod horse striking rocks or bottles will start a fire in dry grass.

"Those new sheds you are building should be turned around just the other way, so their backs will be toward the general direction of the heaviest wind. The gate is too heavy. Three boards and two wires make a better gate than five boards. If it has five boards, its own weight in a hot climate will draw the nails, and the heavier the gate the shorter time it will last. As I was coming along I saw some men building a fence, and their material was spread all along the line. That is not the way to build a fence. Have your material on a wagon, and drive the posts directly from the wagon. In that way you are above them, and you carry your material with you.

"Your vegetable garden here is not big enough for the number of men you have. Good vegetables make the men more contented and draw a better class of laborers. I see a broken window over there in the men's room stuffed with rags; that is not right. The men's room should be kept up in nice shape. They will do better work if their rooms are clean and comfortable. What is that man doing over there painting that wagon? Those things should be done during the rainy weather when men can't work at anything else. The harness should be repaired, cleaned and oiled at the same time. I noticed you haven't put any lime on the floors of the warehouse to kill the weevils and you haven't smoked the bats out. I am glad to see that you have some cats; they are better than traps.

"You planted that alfalfa right after you plowed the land. You should not do that. You should let a crop of weeds come up first, and then kill them off before you plant your alfalfa. You are irrigating a field of alfalfa out there that has grasshoppers on it. Never irrigate when the pests are around, it only causes them to hatch a second brood. The best way to get rid of grasshoppers is to starve them. Turn the cattle in on the alfalfa and let them eat it down. They don't have to eat it down very close to the stool of the plant because the grasshoppers never do, they only take off the top part. I see you put sheep manure in the orchard. That is an excellent thing to do, but there is no use of leaving it on the surface where the sun will bleach the best properties out of it. Fertilizer should be put on just before a rain, otherwise the sun will bleach it out.

"It doesn't look as if those troughs have been cleaned out lately. There is no good in having clear fresh water polluted by a dirty trough. Water can be none too fresh for stock. It would be better if you turned well water in there, as it is better than the water in the ditches. Cattle should not be fed from a hay stack of old hay in that manner. After hay has stood for several years, a narrow swath should be cut all the way down from the top, so that the hay will be mixed and the cattle won't get good hay one day and bad hay the next.

"Those mangers shouldn't be heaping full; they should be filled about half full and kept that way. The way to tell whether the cattle are getting enough feed is to inspect the mangers every morning and see if they are eaten out clean. If they are eaten out clean, they are not getting enough; if there is anything left over, they are being overfed. That haystack isn't built right. The broader the stack the more it will sag in the center and the more hay will be wasted, because it forms a pocket for the rain to collect and the water gradually seeps through the entire stack. The sides of the stack should be combed with a pitchfork, so as to turn all of the heads downward. This will drain off the water and prevent its trickling down.

"Those hogs shouldn't be permitted to eat those figs off of the ground. The figs should be scalded before feeding or they will scour the hogs badly. Always feed them from a trough. Those trees should not be held with one stake. Always use two. Tie a cloth to the stake and twist it around the tree. In that way the tree is held straight, no matter in what direction the wind blows."

During this flow of criticism, he had gone through the chicken yard, corrals, orchard, barns, kitchen, and bunk house, and examined everything from the top shelf in the kitchen pantry to the ash barrel. The foreman was trotting along, trying to keep up with him, saying, "Yes, Mr. Miller." Finally they came back to the buggy and he got in and said, "Good morning, drive on."

After they got down the road a way the driver said, "Mr. Miller, I never saw that place looking better. That foreman is a good man. Don't you think you were a little severe on him?"

Henry Miller said, "Yes, the place did look fine, but how long would it stay that way if I didn't keep after them?"

Thus they continued the round of the ranches to Wible, Panama, Buena Vista, Chester, Shinn, Old Headquarters, Buttonwillow, Adobe, and Fowler. The foremen were all taken by surprise and knew nothing of his coming. As they approached Buttonwillow, they passed a great herd of elk, the last herd in California. They had jumped the fence and were feeding in the fields.

The driver said, "Mr. Miller, those elk eat an awful lot of feed, break down an awful lot of fences, and cost the company lots of money."

"Yes," said Henry Miller, "but they were here before we were. It's against the law to destroy them and some day we will give them away to public parks." Later this was done and they were shipped all over the United States to various parks and museums.

As they crossed the great levee which formed Buena Vista Reservoir, he said, "This levee never was strong enough, but I'm negotiating with the railroad company, which is going to build a branch line to the oil fields, and it wants to lay its tracks across this levee. If it does that, it will help take care of the levee. With the railroad here, it will be easy to bring material to strengthen the levee. What is that lumber there?"

"That is an old box that we had to take out because it was rotting," said the driver.

"Stop and let me see it." After looking it over he said, "Just what I thought; they should use redwood under ground. It will last forever. Such stupidity costs me lots of money."

Thus they went from ranch to ranch, reaching the Fowler place as the sun was setting. He entered and greeted the foreman's wife by name, went into his bedroom, and she followed him and pulled off the boots from his tired feet. This was one of the pleasant duties of every foreman's wife. She beamed on him as she showed him that clean water, soap and towels were in place and slippers ready for his feet.

After the evening meal he sat for two hours giving the superintendent a world of instructions as to the details of his duties. Seventy-five miles had been traversed during the day.

This completed the day's work. If perchance he had had an engagement the next day, he would have ridden on horseback for three or four hours in the cool of the night in order to keep the appointment. In fact if necessary to keep an appointment he would ride all night. On one occasion he rode sixty miles just to look at two jacks which had been selected by a foreman. After looking them over he said, "Those are fine jacks," and turned around and started back.

XVII. BARBECUES

IT WAS May Day in the San Joaquin Valley. The intense heat of the summer had not yet set in, but the season was already well advanced. The first crop of alfalfa had been removed; the canals were flowing to capacity; the vast plains which had once been parched, dry and forbidding, were now carpeted in green. The rabbits and coyotes had been replaced by cattle standing knee deep in luscious grass. The open plains were now divided by fences. Farm houses and hay stacks were along every road. Towns had grown up.

Along the roads are seen conveyances of all kinds headed toward the growing town of Los Baños, for this is the day that Henry Miller entertains the countryside.

The park which he had given to the town is gayly decorated with bunting. Tables are spread over a large area. The May pole is surrounded by children in white frocks and one is crowned Queen of the May.

Henry Miller sits under a spreading tree; age has bent his back. He has seen one generation pass away and two generations grow up. Now and then one of the old men who helped build the Great

Canal comes up to pay his respects and to remind him of some incident of the dim past. But the great majority of his guests are the children and grand-children of his early associates.

The May Day barbecue had become an institu-tion. To it came public officials from all parts of the valley. The local supervisor added a political touch, and the local editor was there looking for news items. The rich and the poor, the employer and the employee, all rubbed shoulders in truly democratic fashion. The superintendents and fore-men from the ranches came with their wives and children. Hundreds of farmers who had bought their farms from his vast holdings were there. The men and women who irrigated their farms from his canal, purchased their supplies from his stores, and deposited their cream checks in his bank, all crowd-ed around.

At this barbecue all pay homage to the host as they would to a king. He sits dressed as always in dark or black clothes, cut after a rather anti-quated pattern, with a black bow tie, and below a small stud. He is always neat, but eschews all dis-play. He is quick as a flash, sure and rapid in his judgment of men, courteous in manner, quick tem-pered, and inclined to be fiery when opposed. He always addresses his superintendents and foremen as "Mr.," and no one ever addressed him by his first name.

He can without offense make it evident that he

is displeased. He can be sarcastic and can address his men with such admirably framed words, that, on receiving his letters, they are at a loss to know whether they were being praised or blamed. Whichever it is he always succeeds in tying them more firmly in their allegiance to him.

The tempting odor from the sizzling meats whets the appetite, and finally Henry Miller sits at the head of the table and carves the huge roasts that are brought from the fire. Wine is served from his own vineyard, and everything served is produced on his own land.

The only time he ever drank wine himself was at meals and then very sparingly, but he always frequented saloons and urged his men to do so, in order to pick up information about the livestock business because that was where cattle men could be found.

When he was once asked if he did not think he should forbid the sale of liquor in the colonies he established, he said, "If the men are not drinking, they will be doing something worse. You can't control them."

Often after a Sunday men would not return to work. Saloons had a back room where they threw the men after they became dead drunk and had been "rolled." If workmen were scarce, a wagon would be sent Monday morning and the drunks would be thrown into it and returned to the ranch, so that they would be ready to go to work when

they sobered up. This process was often hastened
by throwing buckets of water over them to bring
them out of their stupor.

All the afternoon and well into the night the
local band played and the young people danced,
and thus every year the people showed their appreciation of "the man who knew dirt" and who had
transformed a desert into a prosperous farming
community.

There was another institution and that was the
family barbecue on Sunday. In early days his Sundays and holidays were spent with his family at
Bloomfield Ranch in the Santa Clara Valley. Later
he acquired the Mount Madonna property on the
top of the mountain between the Santa Clara Valley and the ocean. No matter where he was, he
would aim to get home for Sunday.

One Saturday he was traveling through San
Luis Obispo and Santa Barbara Counties. It had
been a hot ride and a dirty one across the Carrisa
plains and then through the Rancho rented from
Senator Perkins. Alkali dust clung to man and
beast when the buckboard finally came into the
charming and aristocratic City of Santa Barbara.

Henry Miller drew up before one of the best
appointed and exclusive hotels of this watering
place, climbed out, approached the desk, and was
about to write that simple name which always put
a thrill in hotel clerks. But Henry Miller was a
stranger to this one who was accustomed to judge

men by their appearance. The clerk looked down upon the dusty figure before him and said, "There is a hotel down the street which is cheaper, in which you will be more comfortable." Most men controlling the millions of Henry Miller would have been inclined to show the clerk his place, report him to the management, or otherwise show displeasure at his discourtesy. But Henry Miller seemed to enjoy the joke, and, to the surprise of his superintendent who stood in the background, thanked the clerk, turned, and walked out without another word. He knew that he could trust his superintendent to get word later to the clerk of his mistake. "If I had raised a row, the clerk would have lost his job, and I guess he needed it more than I needed the room."

He took a late train that night for Gilroy, because he wanted to spend his Sunday at home. He always rode on scrip, which was then in vogue, and after taking it out of his purse he dropped the purse in trying to return it to his pocket. It was later picked up by the station agent who had recognized Henry Miller and found his name in the purse. The agent then wired the conductor, "Uncle Henry lost his purse and is on your train without money. Please pay for his breakfast" and signed it "Aunt Emma." The conductor was puzzled and went through the train to find some one who might be "Uncle Henry," and asked if anyone had lost a purse. It was not until he had

HENRY MILLER AT SIXTY

MR. AND MRS. HENRY MILLER

reached the observation car and saw Henry Miller, who was often affectionately referred to as "Uncle Henry," that the conductor realized he was the object of a joke, so he showed the message to Henry Miller, who said, "Too bad I gets off before breakfast."

Arriving at Gilroy, his team was waiting for him and soon he was at his breakfast table at Bloomfield Farm. His wife was at the other end of the table. Soon his son, Henry Miller, Jr., joined them and was seated, and he was followed by his sisters Nellie and Sarah Alice, who kissed their mother and father and were soon quietly enjoying the breakfast bacon.

The incident at the hotel and of the lost purse were related and his wife said, "You must be careful, Henry, how you lose money, or we shall all be in the poor house."

The children only spoke when they were spoken to.

In later years the family spent its Sundays at the summer home on Mount Madonna. Each member of the immediate family had a separate bungalow. They were simple and comparatively inexpensive. Other relatives and guests lived in tents. There were thirty nieces, nephews, grandnieces and grandnephews, and all of them were assisted in one way or another by Henry Miller. They were invited to spend their Sundays and vacations at Mount Madonna. Later his grandchildren came also. Then superintendents and foremen and their wives came from the hot San Joaquin Valley to enjoy a few days of ocean breezes. Some brought their children. The meat was barbecued out of doors and the table spread under the trees. Sometimes as many as thirty or forty attended these affairs. Everything was simple and democratic.

After the repast he took his guests over his property, pointed out his trees and vines, his water supply, the tall redwoods, and the place where one could stand and see the Pacific Ocean on one side and the Santa Clara Valley on the other. Then the rock quarries from which rock was obtained to build the city hall at Gilroy; then the shady drives down and around the mountain. All of these things he showed with the simple pride of a child. Such was the home life of Henry Miller. Here Henry Miller was at his best. Here among his trees and vines he was the son of Christine Doroth Fischer, the vintner's daughter, mild, affectionate and generous. To-morrow he will again be the son of Christian Johann Kreiser, the butcher, and will be figuring to find some way of producing a steer for a fraction of a cent less than his competitors.

XVIII. EPISTOLARY

HENRY MILLER was a glutton for letter writing. He always carried with him a pad of small sheets of cheap letter paper. When on the road he would write letters for hours before any one was up. He wrote in a small cramped hand. At the office he dictated letters by the hour.

He followed the livestock from the time the bulls, boars and bucks were turned out with the cows, sows and ewes. The most minute directions were given as to the class of stock to be used. Where to pasture, graze, water, ship or feed them. When to buy and when to sell.

How to prepare the land, when to seed it, how to irrigate it, and how to harvest the crop.

How to keep up fences, kill the squirrels, destroy the carcasses of dead animals, remove dead trees, burn cockleburs and tumble-weeds.

How to feed the men, house them, and keep them contented. How to treat tramps, neighbors and visitors. How to run kitchens, grow chickens and turkeys, prevent fires and be economical.

How to deal with the public, the press, public officials, public institutions, and public improvements.

223

How to get rid of tule, white alkali, (sodium sulphate) and how to prevent the accumulation of black alkali (sodium carbonate). How to treat livestock diseases, anthrax, blackleg and cholera. How to make use of cow chips as fuel to run machinery. How to feed beet pulp from the sugar refinery, pomace from the winery, and every imaginable kind of feed for livestock.

One day he would write a foreman, "You should have some cats to destroy the mice in the granary." The next day he would write, "I have directed that two cats be sent for the granary." The following day he would write, "Have the cats arrived for the granary?" The next day he would write, "Do not let the cats get food around the kitchen or they will catch no mice." The next day he would follow these letters by one asking, "Are the cats catching the mice in the granary?" By this time the foreman would think that the mice in that particular granary were the most important things on the mind of Henry Miller, and he would soon report that the mice were all destroyed. Immediately would come back the order, "You don't need more than one cat now, so send the other to the Midway Ranch."

These letters constitute an encyclopedia of farming and cattle raising. Most of them are written to his superintendents and foremen. They would probably prove too technical for the general reader, so we have limited ourselves to a comparatively

few extracts which best illustrate his philosophy.
We submit them without comment:

*

It is not work that ruins so many horses, but in-
competent men handling them.

*

It is not the acreage of pasture that counts, but
the amount of feed on the land.

*

Poor hay for stock is dear as a gift.

*

Unbranded calves on the ranges is bad business,
as it might induce some of our neighbors to be
dishonest.

*

I can stand severe losses where unavoidable, but
losses due to carelessness and inattention are unbearable.

*

Always compare costs with results.

*

Comfort is as necessary as feed for stock.

*

A friendly neighbor is a great asset.

*

It is more lack of will than want of time that
much work on the ranches goes undone.

A man can't do justice to his employer on an empty stomach.

*

A good loyal employee is one that goes out of his way to make a saving and a profit for his employer.

*

The best way to hold good men on a farm is to keep their sleeping quarters clean.

*

No man with backbone is willing to do a woman's work on the farm.

*

It is no disgrace to ask advice from one holding a position beneath you.

*

There is a class of people not made to be prosperous. The minute they have a jingle in their pocket or a dollar's credit they are ruined and lose their bearings.

*

There is always hope for a drunkard, but none for a lazy, slovenly man.

*

"Letter writing cuts no figure [in employing a sheep man]. That should not stand in the way. He could come up and have his letter dictated, or could have them done at some of the places along the road.

"Do you think our sheep that have teeth could eat the pine melons by splitting them in two with a spade, if they could be bought for what they are worth?

*

"I expect that the old straw settings are scattered out, also the hay stack bottoms, so that the stock will eat some of it, and the balance will do for manure, which can be plowed under.

*

"I am also pleased to know that the sidewalk is a success, and people will appreciate it, and that the hotel is run satisfactorily. The streets and gutters should be kept in credible order. Not often in a new town are the streets fixed so that they are passable.

*

"I should think it would be cheaper and better to use boards for shelter for horses than a tent.

*

"When men have large families, if the wife and children become dissatisfied, then the man is not satisfied.

*

"Let Gonzales have half of what he owes the merchants, taking his notes for the same, and charging interest on the loan. He should not spend the money before he earns it. When a man once gets in that habit he never gets out of it. Most of his children could earn something, if put to work.

*

"The Frenchman who has been farming our land for years must do better work, clean up the place, haul out manure, make the place look respectable, and our orchard man should go down and show him how to cut all the dying limbs off the trees. If he wants to cultivate the orchard, I have no objection. The yard is also too large.

*

"This man attending to the butchering must be a scallawag, otherwise he would take the hides off just as carefully if he did not get a ten dollar advance.

*

"Do not allow our men to again get the habit of using the quantity of meat which they did formerly. At the very outside, they should have but one and one-half pounds; no pork, no veal, but beef, and once in a week a variety of sausage. We will send some liver pudding, headcheese and tripe after this.

*

"Her husband is worthless, but she writes me that she is now away from him with her children and wants us to give her some oats. I wrote her that we want security for the same, in the way of having somebody vouch for the payments, but if she cannot get any one to do that, and she may lose the crops, let her have the oats, and if she does not pay

I will stand the loss. Let her know soon, so as not
to keep her in suspense.

*

"I hope you have time to see that the butchers
take the hides off of the animals without cutting or
scouring them, and see that they are properly
salted, so that a part will not spoil, as has been the
case.

*

"I have been considering the letter which you
wrote to the firm regarding your objection to
having the school children making too free with
the occupying of the buildings. I admit it is annoy-
ing, and when you moved your family there arrangements should have been made right then to
prohibit it, or caution the teachers that the children
should take no privileges whatever. But, as it has
been allowed thus far, if you were not to allow the
children to use the buildings it would probably
create some feeling. Therefore, I hope you can endure it for a short time, and a change for the better
can be brought about. As I stated to you, as soon as
you become acquainted with the people and know
the good from the bad, and what it requires to have
them friendly toward the firm, I will certainly be
only too glad to have you assume charge of the
property connected with the town. You should not
lose sight of the fact that the people as a whole are
against us, and nothing is gained by having their
ill will. You will find it very agreeable to have the

people's good will and learn their ways, so that their interests will be the same as ours.

*

"Have the cattle branded, but I do not want them thrown down on hard ground and have their hips broken, or otherwise bruised.

*

"He reported to me that the cattle broke out five times, and there was not an animal but steers, and nothing to eat up the waste hay, although you were instructed to leave a bunch of stock cattle there, to which the bad hay could be hauled out, and there must be some feed outside of the field which could be made use of. It seems you have not carried out my orders. I am very sorry to have to call your attention to these facts which could have been avoided.

*

"Those steers should have had more cows with them, and the corrals should have been washed. There are always some cattle that will run together and if they are parted they are bound to try to get back, and on the whole I consider our feeding there a very unfortunate affair.

*

"In regard to posts, if you do not need a whole car load, the freight rate is very high. I think willow limbs would answer, and fire them at the bottom so that they will not grow, and they would last three or four years.

"Why not put in about twenty-five cows in each corral; such cows as would do to fatten. I think that would make the steers more quiet, and there should be no dogs around the corral. When the cattle once break out, it is the hardest kind of work to try to keep them in.

*

"As to the hospital, I am pleased that you [the local supervisor] express yourself as being interested in bringing about the change for the better. So far as any authority we have been assuming is concerned, we will be only too glad to turn it over to you. We will be prepared to do our part to assist in making the hospital what it is intended to be used for.

*

"Do not fail to give satisfaction to the settlers who want water. The matter of extending the new canal will be taken in hand and every effort made so as to come to some understanding with the people.

*

"There are also more trees around the house than are necessary. I consider there is too much shade from the trees to have the place healthy.

*

"When cattle are once allowed to commence wasting hay, they never stop. They do not gain anything by allowing them to waste it. Then you may keep some of the cattle for the purpose of eating up some of the waste hay.

*

"Avoid surplus writing, and do not send telegrams if there is time to write. Be explicit, and state for once and all if only four hundred cattle can be fed on the ranches. I want this information.

*

"I am in receipt of your letter in regard to your boy mutilating the tree. There is nothing further to be said on the matter, only that in the future you will try to keep him at home.

*

"My sister will call upon you, and if she considers that you are in actual need, she will assist you.

*

"Why not publish in the papers that we have a first class barber shop with baths, and that everything is kept in proper order, and that the shop was built with the intention of keeping it so it will give satisfaction to people.

*

"There is no doubt but that the people of the town have been conspiring so that the shop could not be rented. It does not speak well for the people.

*

"Try to solicit as much business as possible in connection with the bank, and where men are saving and thrifty, we would make them liberal advances without asking too much security, but of that you must be the judge. Some people we can accommodate on their simple notes.

*

"Regarding the hotel, I was dissatisfied with the first meal I had there, and it looks to me very odd that he should use condensed milk in a country where milk is produced in such quantities.

*

"I hope you have arranged matters for our mutual benefit, and not pasture more stock on our neighbors than they pasture on us. That is a rule which we always want carried out.

*

"I deem it necessary to find out whether you are really in need of assistance, as on many occasions matters have been misrepresented to me. On receipt of a report from my man stating that you are worthy, I will assist you, but not otherwise.

*

"When you asked me last year for the loan of a horse to attend the rodeo, I told you you could have it for one month. You have kept the horse ever since, and I want you to send it immediately to Peach Tree, or I will put you to some trouble. I like to accommodate you, but you do not seem worthy of it. You cannot keep your word. I want that horse put back where you got him from at once, and I do not want you to fail to do so.

"Do not allow the cattle to get into the habit of wasting hay. They would do just as well being allowed to eat the bottom, chaff, and so forth. The bottom can be loosened up, and what is mixed with dirt taken out and given to the stock cattle, by taking some old sacks, splitting them, then stitching them together, making a kind of cloth in which the stuff can be taken out to the cattle and put on the most suitable ground, so the cattle will waste nothing.

*

"When the cattle are all parted out to ship, then you can go amongst them and reject such as are not desirable, and put nothing in the cars which will likely get down and we lose them. If there is an animal of that kind, trade it with the Indians, or kill it at home and sell part to the Indians, or use it at home.

*

"I received yours regarding my nephew. When I was his age I worked for about eight dollars per month, and from early until late at night. Of course, times have changed, so have young men's expectations. There are a great many educated young men idle in San Francisco who would be only too glad to work for small wages. I will allow him forty dollars per month, with board and lodging, and give him a suit of clothes for Christmas. There have been some faults in his typewriting. On one occasion, when instructed to mention thirty dollars he put in thirty-five, and the consequence was that we could not make the trade which was quite a loss to us. In his letters he is flighty and does not take the pains that a person of more mature years would. You will have to talk with him.

*

"I also want to point out to you [a foreman] that you must not overdo yourself. You need rest and to take care of your personal comforts, nor do I wish your wife to make a slave of herself.

*

"I hope the enterprise [furnishing magazines by American Woman's League] will be well managed, and in the end be a credit to the ladies who have started it, and also to the town.

*

"I appreciate how kindly you feel toward the young generation that need guidance and advice, but my experience so far has shown me that that class of people need more than ordinary care and training, otherwise all the labor spent on them for years would be lost, and it would cost a small fortune to take care of them. Every county in the State where there are Spanish families, or families of Spanish descent, should have a school of that kind, or put them in a separate class by themselves and have them taught. I have taken a number of our vaqueros' children and had them educated, and the labor and expense were lost.

"I have authorized Mr. Smith to donate for us twenty dollars toward tag day, and I want the Italian children to get a portion of it, so as to make a showing in their report for the district.

*

"In regard to making the loan, I do not think it would be good business for us to do so. If it should be a matter of accommodation, and the loan is secured, I will make it to him, but the people do not appreciate accommodation. They soon forget it.

*

"When a bull is cross, it is a sure indication that he is not doing well, and if sent to the city would most likely be condemned.

*

"If that horse of the foreman's wife is fit for nothing but to eat grass, kill it for the hogs and give the old lady a horse which will suit and not likely run away.

*

"Regarding the fountain, no action will be taken either for or against this matter until I look into the matter myself, and if the fountain will be an ornament to the place, I will arrange to see that there is sufficient water furnished without charge, but, if otherwise, I do not want it there at all. As far as my personal interest is concerned, I will fully do my part, and no doubt, the ladies [of the Women's Club] will, but I am sorry to say that the gentlemen are lacking in ambition and taste.

*

"When there is a requisition for meat, he should name the number of men he has, and he should not figure over one and one-half pounds to the man, not including articles of which one pound ought to answer for two—sausage, headcheese and tripe, instead of bacon, dry salted pork must be used; no smoked meats, but it should be heavy meat and should be thoroughly salted. No thin meat is profitable. The heaviest part of the pork is the most profitable for us to use.

*

"I hope you keep in touch with the market as to prices of lumber. We do not want to overcharge people, nor do we want to be too exacting in regard to their paying for the lumber when they receive it. We want to show some liberality.

*

"As no one else seems to take any interest, I hope you will see to the potholes in the street where the water will likely stand, and the holes get deeper. Once in a while put your men to work and keep the place in order. Also have the gutters cleared of standing water. Some people never practice neatness, but in time they will get used to it and take kindly to it. In the meantime, we will have to do it ourselves.

*

"We do not want to have sheep for show, nor

are they to have too much feed. All of our sheep-
herders have the idea that we have so much feed
that we can not get rid of it, and they allow the
sheep to waste about as much as they eat.

*

"I do not want you to take too much on your-
selves. You should have put up with the shortcomings of that man who was there. He had the
makings of a good man. I saw him at work and he
was an expert at the work he was doing.

*

"I hope you will make use of my grandson and
put him on his mettle and give him some respon-
sibility and instructions and see that he carries
them out. It would please his father and be very
gratifying to me if he be given an opportunity so
as to show what is in him. The most important
thing is to keep him busy.

*

"The death of your cattle man is a great loss to
me. Who knows the range as well as he did? Who
can we get that will keep the people's stock from
eating us out? We should have a man who knows
our exact boundaries and what free range we are
entitled to. I hope you have given this attention.
I wrote to his wife and extended to her my sympathy, and I also stated that I would pay his wages
up to the day he died, deducting nothing for the
time he lost, also that we would pay part of the

funeral expenses, if you see fit. I paid something like four hundred dollars for him at the time of his first sickness.

*

"I want turkeys given to the people who have been friendly to us, where it is a matter of policy, also to give a turkey to each of the oil stations, and one to the assessor, and to any one else to whom you think it is policy to send one, and to whom we have given turkeys before.

*

"There should be a couple of loads of very coarse straw hauled up to the breeding places, to put in the hog pens before the hogs have pigs. That would be better than hay as there is no dirt in it.

*

"The man down at headquarters tells me that our poultry there has decreased to about forty of the commonest kind, for which I am very sorry. How often have I called your attention to having competent men look after them? That old man puttering around the yard should have taken care of the pigs and the fowl, and some one else could have attended to the mail. This is certainly no credit to us. We should have hundreds of chickens, and have the chicken house in first class order, and the roosters changed and a good breed of chickens raised. We could have an incubator. All this has been mentioned to you, but for want of time, you could not attend to it. Your foreman has not any domestic habits; it is not in his line. Neither has his wife. I asked her to go and see how the poultry was doing, and she said, 'well,' and now we have the information that it is not so. What you need most is a sort of foreman who will stay with the men and see that they work and also work himself.

*

"If any machinery is actually needed, do not stop for orders, but order at once such as is most useful and modern and will require the least amount of repairs.

*

"The men watching the ewes in all the fields where the ewes are lambing have time to pull up the cockleburs and put them in piles so that they can be burned up some evening. In that way they can clean up the field instead of standing around idle. If you tell the sheep boss how necessary it is to have this done, he will see that the men do it, but they will never do it without being told.

*

"Give to the editors of both papers nice turkeys for Thanksgiving, also to such other friends of the firm as are favorably inclined toward us, also some of your friends.

*

"The man you have has plenty of time to clean up the garden and keep out such vegetables as are surplus, and put up some fall vegetables. If you let up on him, by and by he will want to do as little as possible.

*

"I want that man at the River Ranch to go around and fix up the fences and pick up things; burn up the carcasses, pick up the bones, bring them home. He should do enough to pay for his board. In fact, we do not get any good out of the man we have there.

*

"A carcass should not remain out without being found, if a man is careful. Some men are worth a great deal more than others. Some men go around but do not want to see things. They are indolent; do not care, and when they cut a hide they cut it all to pieces and make it worthless, or when they bring it home they do not take care of it.

*

"You may notify your three cattle men that they may each get a suit of clothes as a Christmas present from the firm.

*

"I wish to state that you may go on either side of the river and get some downed wood. If there are some trees which are dead, or which have large bodies with limbs projecting out, covering a great deal more than is necessary, and part of the limbs are decayed, you will cut such limbs off of the main body of the trees. When you go after the wood, do not have any dog following.

*

"Now is the pinch, and I hope you will do your very best and show your loyalty to the firm.

*

"Please go and see how those people are fixed, and if you [his sister-in-law] think they are worthy of assistance, give them what they need most. I am sending you a letter from a Mexican woman. Please buy something for her so as to make her comfortable during the winter. I hope you patronize all the merchants and bought such presents as will give the best satisfaction.

*

"In regard to the cattle coming from the north, we can not make them any better. You must kill them and make the best of them. This is the result of not having expert men buying cattle for us. He means well enough, but he cannot distinguish between a prime bullock and a half fat bullock.

"I will write you particulars in regard to buying things for the people. You will consider the condition of the people and treat them accordingly. Where the people are in actual need, you will be liberal.

*

"If a man is sensible he will not run his horse to death to get back a calf that runs away, but will let it come back of its own accord. Knowing these things is what makes a good cattle man.

*

"A man slovenly in his surroundings is the same way in his work.

*

"As soon as a hide is taken off a carcass it should be rubbed all over with salt and hung up. That will prevent its shriveling.

*

"The only objections I have to putting a price on your cattle is that it is like putting the cattle up at auction. If you would put a price on them we would then have a chance to either accept your offer or reject it.

*

"If the horses have sore or blistered backs, I want their backs taken care of, and I do not want them ridden. From time to time you will examine the men's saddles and blankets. See that the men have good saddles and blankets and not get the horses' backs sore, and not ride them one foot out of the road unless it is absolutely necessary. As you know, there are some men who ride their horses twice the distance during the day than is actually necessary.

*

"I will let you have the oats if you can get a good endorser to your note for the amount. If you have left your husband, I suppose it is only temporarily, as a husband who has been supported by his wife is hard to drive away.

*

"I want no sausage maker who can not make sausage that is up to standard. It should be such as the people will like. You could taste the sausage yourself, and by this time you should be an expert and know precisely what sausage will take best with the people and be most profitable for us.

*

"As to the stock you buy from the people, pay a fair price for what is good, and such stock that other people will not buy you can not buy too cheap. Let the people take care of their little starved calves, instead of us buying them and having to nurse them.

*

"In regard to the deed to the Dos Palos Park, you will find out from the people to whom the land should be deeded. It is to be given to the whole community without regard to class or politics.

*

"Find out about the Catholic Church. We will treat them the same as we treat the other religious orders. The land is to be located where it will not likely depreciate the value of the land adjoining. People do not like to buy property near a church. We will give them two twenty-five foot lots for the Church and parsonage.

"I have nothing against this man only I think he will not work. He has a hard working wife, which is generally the case with a lazy man. I saw him looking at the sky when he could have been at work which he hired some one else for, but he may be a better man than I think. We should keep no favorites.

*

"I want you to give this man Jones a chance. I am in honor bound to give him employment, because I have kept him waiting for such a length of time, and I could not break my promise.

*

"Have such men on the outside camp as do their work faithfully, and earn their wages, and their families are not extravagant, and their wives do the cooking, as long as there is not a great crowd of men, and keep the houses in order. The man must be handy, willing and progressive.

*

"I have seen men trimming trees which were dead. They did not take pains enough to notice.

*

"Have all the dead limbs taken off of the trees in the orchard, and all the ones which are nearly dead dug out and a stake put in where the old tree stood, so as not to put the new tree in the old ground.

*

"Regarding the men who stole the pigs, I do not want to prosecute them. If the District Attorney cannot convict them, we will do nothing, because if it were found out that we were the prosecuting parties, in the end I would get the blame. I expect you to see the importance of this.

*

"A good resolute man will encourage the men under him to work and make a showing while a drone will not work himself, and will keep others from working.

*

"We do not want to hire a man with a slovenly helpless family of children. The woman must be able to take care of the house and see that the victuals are put on the table in good shape, and make herself useful.

*

"In regard to your request, you will have to grant me time so I can see you [an editor] in person, when I will explain to you why we do not want to put ourselves before the public, but will enable you to write up such articles as are for the general good of the country, and the progress it has made since the time when we first started in to make any improvements.

*

"I hear that our supervisor has been defeated, and his successor will probably give us a fair deal. I hope nothing has been said to cause him to feel that we have been working against his election. I am told your foreman voted against our supervisor. I can hardly believe that, but I shall find out; I wrote him explicitly that we not only wanted his assistance, but also that of his men who were registered, and have them vote for our man.

*

"I was informed that you were under the influence of stimulants when you called there, and I would not give you employment under any consideration, until you can clear yourself of that charge.

*

"It appears to me that the cause of that tank falling down was that it was empty and the bottom rusted out. If it had been full of water, that would not have happened.

*

"I am told that the man at the Midway is addicted to drink. Now, is it possible that you have not found that out, or do you allow it? We want to do nobody an injustice, but we want no low class men in our employ, who set a poor example to the other men. We want men in charge of our properties who will stand up, and can be respected by those under them. I hope you will not lose sight of this. No matter how good a worker such a man is, sooner or later he will cause trouble. There are plenty of men who make a good appearance, and demand respect. That is the kind we want. We do not want any man with large families and slovenly wives.

"I wish to call your attention to the fact that the people who have been using water should be ready to use it, and I wish you would see that they get it in such quantities as they are actually in need of, and use it with economy. Do not allow any to go to waste, and do not give them the chance to say that we have been using the water and depriving them of it when they wanted it. Regarding the measurement of water, the people should know that they are being justly dealt with.

*

"If you think it is policy, and the people of the town will also contribute toward the erection of the club house for the women, you may pay one hundred dollars toward it.

*

"Regarding the man Jones, you will pay him. This is like giving the money away, but I would rather stand the loss than have any ill feeling. Was he of any service to us, or was he only a boarder?

*

"This man ought to be with us somewhat longer before we give him a machine. This going over the ground so quickly gets people in the habit of not remaining long enough at the various places. I think by going in a team, he would feel more like stopping for a length of time to look around and post himself, and see what is going on. I would call your attention to the fact that you are going too much for the good of your health. There are many trips you could avoid, attending to them by correspondence, and when you go to the various places stop long enough to see what is going on.

*

"There is no occasion for you to spend any time or labor to find out what the exact damage from the flood amounts to. We will discover that soon enough.

*

"As to dealing with the users of water, you have my consent to do what is fair, but we will not recognize furnishing water to people where the land is a bed of gravel and has heretofore produced nothing. They should be obliged to pay an additional amount to what other people are paying for land which is subject to irrigation, where the water will sink out of sight. It is for you to deal with the people at all times so as to retain their friendship, that is, the ones who are willing to act fair. As to those who think they can force us to do what they want, and are not willing to be satisfied, we will not allow them to impose upon us.

*

"Explain to the editor of the paper our standing with the people, and once in a while give him some advertising so that he will have a chance to make something which will have its good effect.

*

"Buy the renters' grain and pay them a fair price.

"I hope you will not overburden yourself with too much care.

*

"It has always been my aim to encourage the men by promoting them when possible.

*

"I hope you will not undertake more work than you can attend to. Sometimes you load too much upon yourself, and cannot comply with your promises. You should not have a lot of worthless men who take advantage of you.

*

"I thought that man was getting fifty dollars a month, and now I understand we are paying him sixty-five. We want to get rid of him as soon as possible.

*

"In some of the places the pump men should cook their own victuals. They will not starve. There are plenty of men who would be only too glad to get the job.

*

"Sheep skins should be dried on the ground, and, as soon as they are dried should be piled away and not allowed to be out in the sun so that the skin is burned up and of no account.

*

"I have read a letter regarding our horse stock, which is clear evidence that the stock has been very badly neglected. This puts me in a very bad light. I never thought we would have to have outsiders point out our shortcomings.

*

"We should have some advertising in the local papers. Their good will is worth having.

*

"I hope you will have the good will of the people so that business will increase.

*

"Can you put any vim into the man in charge of that new headgate? I have been told he is very slow with the work. He is capable of doing good work, but he needs some one to urge him.

*

"I note what you say about the man attending to the hogs. That he proved himself very capable in attending to the cattle that were choked up by the beets. We will give him a nice suit of clothes for Christmas.

*

"When you go to the various places, give the men advice and a word of credit if they deserve it.

*

"During the last three years, we have lost a fortune by fire. There is no use thinking that they are of incendiary origin. It is nothing more than tramps sleeping in the hay stacks or barns and smoking. Nearly all men of that order smoke and carry matches in their pockets. You should have your foreman or watchman go around each night before retiring. He should take a good lantern and see if there is anyone stopping around the barn, outbuildings or hay stacks. In a great many cases that is how a fire gets out. Of course there are many instances in which hay gets afire by combustion. I do not think that any one would willfully start a fire. I hope you will carry out my orders and see that our property is protected.

*

"I would advise you not to have the old foreman put away, so as to feel that he is humbled, but give him a small crew of men and put him where he is comfortable.

*

"Use juniper wood for smoking out bacon and ham, as it gives it a peculiarly fine taste.

*

"On all the land I own, I have done more than all the balance of the neighbors in destroying squirrels. I have saved neither time nor money, and if you [Squirrel Inspector] take pains to ask men, even those not favorably inclined toward us, if they will tell the truth, they will uphold me in this.

*

"There is no use of buying hay for cattle along the road unless you have water. If they have water, a mouthful of hay is all they need.

"I have just been informed that there are three watering places on that land you wrote me about. I never knew of but one. If I had, I would have purchased the land, or made some exchange. I am told that part of the land has been overflowed by the creek, which is quite a surprise to me. Put in a levee at once, so that we can use all the water. If we allow them to use the water for a certain number of years, they will lay claim to it, and, as we have plenty of land on which to use the water, I hope you will make every possible effort to use it on your own land.

*

"If the people should want to hunt for a day or two, they should be allowed to go in and not be disturbed, and I hope you will use your best judgment so as to have no ill feeling between the public and the parties who are paying for the privileges. There is room for everybody.

*

"This unfortunate murder at the ranch ought to give us warning. No one should be allowed to use liquor, or bring it to the ranch from town.

*

"Do not take any chances of getting hurt, especially when you are loading or corraling cattle. Do not ride a horse that is unsafe.

*

"You can very soon see which men do the feed-

ing as it should be done, then, to those men give
some authority.

*

"There is no use giving a person a turkey and
expecting him to appreciate it unless it is in fine
condition.

*

"At the bar there should be such stimulants to
be sold as come under the law, so as not to compel
the men to be entirely shut off from having some
place to spend their money, or having to go elsewhere, or buy liquor by the bottle.

*

"Do not let the men ride colts which they are
breaking into town, under any conditions.

*

"I saw a good many apples piled up. If it would
pay to haul them to the Chinaman, do so. They
are worth very little for housekeeping.

*

"On most of the cattle which you have purchased
for us, we have met with losses. It seems you were
looking more for the commission than to see that
stock was such that the firm would be able to
make something on. I am very sorry to make these
remarks. I have not mentioned this to you before,
but I feel now that you should be informed of the
fact. It is our aim to be on friendly terms with
everybody, and especially with men in our line of

business with whom we come in contact. If you had studied our interests, and done us justice, you could have gone and done any amount of business with us. It is either for want of justice, or want of will, that you bought such cattle for us as were not fit to go on the market.

*

"Your assistant has been with us long enough now to show if he is progressive and looks after things himself. If you have to be calling to his attention all of the details, then it would be better to have some one else in his place. I appreciate good service, and a man should be ambitious and see things without being told. The work should drive him, and he should be up and doing, and not have to wait and have everything pointed out to him.

*

"It is nonsense to keep up stock in the summer and let them starve in the winter.

*

"Potatoes should be boiled with their skins on.

*

"Do not wean a very poor colt from a very poor mare, but feed the mare and the colt.

*

"If the Boy Scouts need any assistance so as to fit them to become properly drilled, I will assist them.

"I am told the housekeeper is a capable woman, and she must be sustained; if she comes to you and tells you there is any trouble and some man does not treat her with courtesy, I want you to have it rectified.

*

"I do not want any of the poor people in town omitted. If we have any grievance against some of them, that does not cut any figure at Christmas time.

*

"As long as Pachuca Higuerra [an old pensioner] is able to ride a horse and be about, I expect him to go out with the dogs and see if he cannot kill a coyote once in a while.

*

"You must have meat which will give satisfaction to the men, and have no meat used which is not in proper sanitary condition.

*

"Saddle horses not ridden are a poor property.

*

"You should never have attempted to start a dairy. However, as I know you did it with the best motives, there is nothing further to be said.

*

"If a man is poor and you sell him an animal for a little less than it actually is worth, then it has its good results. I would rather waive getting the very last cent, that is, we do not want to sell a man a horse and give him a bad deal. If it is found out that the horse is not what we expected him to be, and shows a blemish after the sale is made, we will take the horse back, or make some reduction.

*

"In opening stacks of hay, open them on the south end.

*

"There are some mares that can be worked up to within a month of the time that they have their colt, while others can not be worked that long. When a mare gets beyond a certain age, she has not the strength to suckle the colt and do some work besides.

*

"It is a standing order that every man that comes to the ranch or to the camp should not be sent away hungry, and they should be fed so that they will appreciate it.

*

"When you have men who are not willing to carry out your orders, you must not keep them. You can make a good man by keeping him strictly under orders.

*

"Four bulls to one hundred cows is ample on level ground. In the mountains, in broken, or in wooded country there should be more.

"You will not let your men know what number of cattle we have. You should hold your own counsel.

*

"It seems to be a great effort for you to write a letter. I expect to hear from you.

*

"It is of the utmost importance that when we send to the city for men we stand in good repute with the Italian public in general. In that way, good men will be sent to you.

*

"We will take that land on the south side of the river, if it is necessary to keep out the kind of people we do not like to have among our stock.

*

"The old Californians will remember that these thickets on the south side of the river were considered a shelter for outlaws and thieves, and that kind of men would not help the country, only give it a bad name.

*

"We found a man at the H. land when you and I once went there, when a dead steer was lying in sight, and the old scoundrel stood there sunning himself. There is no charity in supporting people who are too lazy to make their own living. You do not want a man on the ranch who will commence sweeping when you happen to come along.

"If you have a mechanic whose wife does not expect to do any work, and is only a boarder, I do not want her to cause any trouble or extra work for the cook. She should have no business in the kitchen or store room. When a man is unfortunate enough to have a bad wife, she is likely to cause trouble.

*

"As I pointed out to you often, the hospital, or the poor house, is the place for those old men whose lives have been a failure and they finally fetch up with us.

*

"I should be pleased to have a personal letter from you written on the typewriter. By this time you should certainly have accustomed yourself to dictating to the stenographer, which is a great deal easier than writing by hand.

*

"Read this letter carefully and do not consider that it is written to find fault, but I feel I have a right to express my opinion and point out to you the shortcomings, and where improvements can be made, and you will see that they are carried out.

*

"We do not want to hire any man having one leg or one arm. There seems to be a blight on them. They are sore against the world, and are vicious and make trouble. Of course, there are some ex-

ceptions, but very few. Better give them something
so as to enable them to move along. No man should
be turned away hungry.

*

"The milk should be boiled for the coffee. Those
who generally have their mouths burned by stimulants are the ones who do not want milk in their
coffee. I think the sugar should also be put into
the coffee for the men. Some of them use so much
sugar that it leaves a syrup in the bottom of the cup.

*

"When the time comes to send your children to
school, I will arrange to see that you get a light
rig and a gentle horse, and some one can take the
children to school.

*

"If any of the people want fruit and cannot pay
for it, give it to them rather than have it go to waste.

*

"We now have between two hundred and three
hundred elk, which we have grown from thirteen
head, which we had thirty of forty years ago. What
they eat costs us a thousand dollars a year, and we
do not want to kill them. Take it up with the
authorities and see if they can not send them to
the National Park.

*

"You can make a good man out of a tramp, and
on the other hand a good man can become a tramp.

You should have a man of prime age to attend to the cattle under your direction, and not depend on an old man whose time for good service has passed.

*

"We are feeding too many people with our cattle. The feet of the cattle were evidence of the fact that the people were killing young calves instead of older cattle.

*

"You should have the papers print a good article once in a while in our favor, and it would have its good effect. I consider money paid out in that way would be well spent.

*

"It is also essential to have the people's good will. They will keep the bad element from killing our cattle in such numbers as they have been doing.

*

"Hire men who are from good families and have some honesty about them, and appreciate good treatment.

*

"We had a man there for years who ran the ranch for about half of what it costs now, but, unfortunately, he got among the Indians and used stimulants, either one of which vices would be enough to ruin him.

*

"The cook should be instructed to save the drippings from the meat, where there is so much used, instead of buying lard.

*

"The man you have knows everything in regard to the cattle, but his mind does not work right, and he will not give you a decided answer. He agrees with you in everything you propose, no matter how disastrous it might turn out.

*

"The heads should be used by cooking them in a kettle, so the skull and bones can be pulled out and leave the meat in a solid lump. Then it can be trimmed and sent around to the various camps and used cold, or for stew or hash.

*

"So many of our men hire men with families. We have no objection to a family in which the children are large enough to make themselves useful, to help their mother, and do some outside chores, but we do not want them put on the payroll unless they do enough work to entitle them to it. Most men do not figure the expense of boarding the children, and where the wife is not willing to do any work, that is quite an item. The best way is to have an understanding beforehand as to what is expected of them, and what the children are to do. You will allow no company unless permission is gotten from you or the superintendent, but it must be understood how long the company is to

remain, otherwise there is no telling how long they
will expect to.

*

"I looked into the dairy and saw some bulls
which were bought at one hundred dollars each,
which is like throwing the money away. They are
out of shape and show no quality. This pedigree
business is only a deception. Pedigrees and fine care
must go together to make cattle show up well.
Of course, there are some exceptions. This idea of
having a man especially engaged to test cows for
the butter fat does not strike me favorably. It is an
expense which does not bring enough results.

*

"It is of utmost importance to see that the ship-
per who comes from the city does his part, and
does not sit on the fence watching the others do
the work.

*

"When a man gets off his horse he should loosen
the cinch, move the blanket, and allow the horse's
back to cool.

*

"When a man buys a carcass for feed that is un-
satisfactory, and he has just ground for complaint, we ought to make it up to him. A little liberality shown sometimes goes a long way. We want
to do business in such a manner that we must show
progress instead of decline.

"You should not have your horses standing on hard planks. Cattle should be put in cars at least a half hour before the train starts, so they will settle down and be quiet.

*

"The casings of the sausage are too thin. The proper size should be used, for after the sausages are fried, there is nothing left of them if unsuitable casing is used.

*

"Every effort should be made so as to have our goods as good as can be found in the market.

*

"Our drivers should be accommodating.

*

"Do not allow the rabbits to eat the bark off of the trees. On Sundays the men on the ranch can be given a gun to go out and shoot rabbbits. A man will do it for the asking.

*

"I would be pleased to hear from you occasionally, but as it seems that you do not feel that you have the time, or are not inclined to comply with my wishes, you need not do so.

*

"I do not want the practice continued of hiring a lot of worthless men who have been in our employ once or twice and have been discharged, when they return, or are taken on temporarily, or for pity. If they need a pair of shoes or trousers, see that they get them. Allow them to remain over night, and then take the road in the morning.

*

"We want to be friendly with the new neighbors and to accommodate them whenever we can. We do not want a lot of worthless dogs on the place.

*

"In shipping cattle, you should put some sand in the cars instead of alkali dirt, so that the cattle will not slip and fall down.

*

"Whatever you do, I hope will be done in such a manner as to show that you have some grit and determination, which, unfortunately, you do not exhibit. If you will consider in what way you can please us, it will go a long way, but you lack either the strength or the determination. If land is not grazed closely enough, it impedes the growth of the new grass to a great extent.

*

"If a man can keep a herd of Herefords, he can take out the thoroughbreds and only use them for two crosses, as the third cross will show a decline in shape, and they will run back and become ordinary.

*

"Once when I pointed out your shortcomings, you answered that if you could do as well as I could you would not be in our employ, which was entirely out of place.

*

"We want to be on friendly terms with those people who are going on the land, by selling merchandise to them and being accommodating whenever they will appreciate it. Where the people have families, we will be willing to let them have a cow, but they must take care of her and see that she is properly fed, and have a small pasture fenced in, so as to hold the cow. We want to lend no horses, but sell them to the people on time. Have security for the payments, but give them ample time with moderately good security. Keep your own counsel and do not allow yourself to be questioned. Get in conversation with men who have been all over the country, and they can give you some information which it would be to your advantage to have. Ofttimes you will come across men who will get all the information they can out of you, so you must be on your guard.

*

"There is a part of Arizona and a part of New Mexico where the cattle eat a great deal of feed which is partly covered with sand. They also eat a lot of prickly pears, and their tongues get in such condition that they cannot digest the food so as to get the benefit of it, and, therefore, they never get in any more than ordinary condition.

"If a horse has a sore on his back, it should be allowed to get well before the saddle is put on again.

*

"A horse that stumbles can be ridden by a man who has been warned as to it, but do not give him to a man who works with stock and may likely get a fall."

XIX. TRAGEDIES

Sarah Alice Miller

ONE morning at the breakfast table, Henry Miller turned to his twelve year old daughter Sarah Alice and said, "Are you taking good care of your horse, Dan?"

She said, "Yes, Father, but he was pretty tired last night. We had a fine ride to Soap Lake and back."

She did not tell him how she and her sister Nellie had run a race from Soap Lake to Gilroy. They had only slowed down as they passed through Gilroy, and many an admiring glance was turned toward them as their horses trotted through the town. Their cheeks were flushed. The horses were the blacker and smoother because of the perspiration which bathed their bodies. The heart of many a young man beat faster as the girls gave a recognizing smile.

One of the natives said to a stranger, "Those are Henry Miller's daughters. They are chips off the old block. Those horses are thoroughbreds and so are they."

They rested their horses under two wonderful walnut trees which grew before a little place rented by Henry Miller. The far spreading branches of the trees furnished a shade under which Henry Miller always rested his horses as he drove to the station. The walnut trees still remain along the side of the road. They ultimately grew twice as high as the telephone poles. When an electric power line was put along the road, the company wanted to cut a space through these trees for the wires, but Henry Miller asked them to spare the trees, so on each side of the trees high towers were erected to carry the wires over them and the trees still stand.

Sarah Alice said, "I wish I could have a younger horse, because Nellie's horse outran mine yesterday."

Her father said, "Be careful of your horse and save him, and maybe I will get you a better one on your next birthday. You must be careful."

That night he left for San Francisco and immediately after breakfast the next morning the girls were again on their horses. They clattered over the bridge and down the road and were soon lost in the dust kicked up by their horses. In those years the roads were dusty, but between the graveled road and the fence was a path used by pedestrians, cattle and horsemen. It was narrow and tramped hard. The girls rode in single file and their aunt rode nearby in a carriage. The horses were fresh and were extending themselves and pulling on the bits. The girls wore no hats and their hair streamed back with the wind. Nellie was leading, followed by Sarah Alice. Suddenly in the narrow path, the horse of Sarah Alice stumbled, she was thrown on her head on the hard road, and instantly killed.

The horse stopped and ran back to the barnyard and into the stable. The hostler was stupefied and threw himself on the horse and raced down the road. Soon the news spread to the house; all was confusion. Horses were hitched to a wagon and raced down the road and soon brought back the limp body of Sarah Alice Miller.

Henry Miller had himself once been thrown from a horse on his head and had been unconscious for a long time, so hope lingered for a time. But the truth was made evident by the doctor who soon arrived, and the pride of Henry Miller's life was laid to rest under the cypress trees which already shaded the grave of his first wife.

The shock of this event was so severe that Henry Miller himself suffered a nervous breakdown, which necessitated a complete rest. This was obtained by a trip to Europe and to the land of his birth.

Henry Nickel

The second grandson of Henry Miller, Henry Nickel, was staying at Mann Lake, in the Oregon Country, learning the cattle business.

One cold, stormy, wintry day, John Devine sat at the Alvord Ranch looking out upon the Alvord Desert, covered with snow and sleet driven before the gale. He was surprised to see a horseman wandering aimlessly across the desert, also driven before the blizzard. He at first could hardly believe that any human being would venture upon the desert on such a day, but he trained his glasses upon the little speck and assured himself that it was indeed a man mounted on a horse, and as the sun set the little speck was enveloped in the driving snow and sleet and lost to view.

"Who could it be?" mused John Devine. "Is it possible that is the grandson of Henry Miller who has been sent up here to learn cattle raising in Oregon? If it is, he has lots to learn because no man can survive in such a storm, and he is the last hope of Henry Miller for an heir bearing even a part of his name."

The next day the storm had abated and the man who carried the mail from White Horse to Mann Lake broke through the trail, and at the lower end of the desert, still within sight of the Alvord Ranch, he found the frozen body of Henry Miller's grandson, Henry Nickel. He had not known the way, and the horse would not buck the storm, but allowed itself to be driven the way of least resistance until its rider finally froze in the saddle, fell off, and perished.

George W. Nickel

Two other tragedies came into the life of Henry Miller. His own son was a cripple and died in middle life.

His first grandson, George W. Nickel, was running one of his ranches in the San Joaquin Valley. His grandfather had written him, "Get out among the people and be friendly with them, and they will bless you for it." This he did and became exceedingly popular.

But one day a half crazed man with some imagined grievance against the company met him as he got out of his car to open a gate to drive on to the road. The man approached near enough to almost touch him, and without warning pulled a revolver and shot him in the breast. The bullet went through his body and out of his back. But he was quick enough to grab the man's gun and run his finger under the hammer and thus prevent a second shot.

The tragedy was telephoned to San Francisco and Henry Miller's doctor got in touch with the local doctor and advised him not to probe for the bullet, but to put the wounded man on a train and send him at once to San Francisco. In a few minutes the railroad furnished a special train which broke all records and brought him to the city. The failure of the X-ray to locate the bullet in the body puzzled the doctors for some time, as they had not as yet turned him over. But finally they turned him over and found that the bullet had emerged through the back. The wound healed and did not prove fatal.

Bandits

Besides these tragic events, Henry Miller had many experiences in which he narrowly escaped tragic consequences. The following may be related:

One day Henry Miller was going over the Pacheco Pass road with a considerable sum of money in his saddle bags, as he was intending to purchase some cattle, and thought he could make a better deal by paying cash. Suddenly he was confronted by a bandit, Chavez. Henry Miller always traveled through the roughest country, and passed among the roughest men, without any fire arms either on his person or in his saddle bags, and, he, therefore, looked complacently into the muzzle of the pistol of the bandit and permitted his money to be taken. He finally smiled and said, "I have a long trip to-day, and will need a little money for my food," so the bandit bowed and handed him back twenty dollars. Henry Miller ceremoniously thanked him and passed on.

Some time later Henry Miller was seated in a saloon at Gilroy. There was a large number of people in and around the saloon and drinking at the bar, when a rough bunch of riders entered, booted and spurred, and proceeded to take drinks at the bar. The minute one of them spoke Henry Miller became alert, for he recognized the voice. After a minute's thought he placed him as the bandit who had relieved him of his money on the Pacheco Pass Road.

He rose, walked across the room and touched the man on the elbow, and, as the man turned, ready for a fight if necessary, Henry Miller greeted him, handed him twenty dollars, and said, "There is the twenty dollars you so kindly loaned me," and bowed and went out before the astonished Chavez could realize that he was receiving back the twenty dollars he had so graciously left with Henry Miller that day on the Pacheco Pass Road. This ability to remember voices as well as faces was characteristic of Henry Miller. He never forgot a face, a name, or a voice.

Cattle Rustlers

On another occasion while riding, he suddenly came upon the outlaw, García, and his band, skinning an animal. He rode up to them and said, "Whose animal are you skinning?" They answered, "Miller's." He said, "All right boys, whenever you need an animal of mine to eat, take it, but be sure and hang the hide on the limb of a tree, and tell my men where they can find it, and if you don't need all of the meat, but only want the best juicy steaks, tell some of the Mexicans around the country where they can find it, so that the beef won't be wasted," and with this he bowed, bade them good day, and went on his way.

Later on this gang became more bold, and one night ran off a large band of Henry Miller's cattle. A foreman immediately notified the sheriff and stated whom he suspected, and, as a result, some of García's men were arrested.

A short time later, Henry Miller was again passing on horseback over the lonely Pacheco Pass Road, when he was met by García and his band. They immediately surrounded him and began to make suggestive signs regarding their lariats and the limb of a great oak tree, and it looked as if the career of Henry Miller was about to terminate. Henry Miller said, "What is the matter?" They said, "You told the sheriff we took your cattle." He replied, "No, I never did. My foreman told the sheriff, and, anyhow, I didn't say you could drive off all my cattle, but simply said if you needed some beef to eat I was glad to let you take it."

This explanation was not at all satisfactory, but one of the leaders in the gang saw the fairness of his position and prevailed upon the others to let him go, and he said "good day," and passed on his way unmolested. Thereafter, when this man grew old, Henry Miller supplied him with food for the rest of his life, and, finally after he died, erected a headstone over his grave as a suitable mark of his appreciation for the bandit who had been fair enough to see the validity of his argument, and to save him from an ignominious death.

Kidnapers

As Henry Miller was one day traveling through Kern County, he came to a forlorn place and found a Mexican woman who had been terribly beaten by her worthless husband. He had come home drunk and almost killed her, and had then ridden away with his disreputable crew. She was without food or medical attention, so Henry Miller sent a doctor, nurse, and provisions, and had his superintendent look after her until she recovered. He soon forgot the incident, but the Mexican woman did not forget.

Years went by and the woman fell into evil ways, and fell in with evil characters. A vaquero began to consort with her and she gained his confidence. When half drunk he confided to her that he and his companions had concocted a plan to kidnap Henry Miller, carry him away to the mountains in a remote part of Kern County, and hold him for ransom.

After her drunken companion had fallen asleep, she quietly slipped out of the room, saddled a horse and rode to the Buttonwillow Ranch. She moved carefully like a shadow around the barn and outhouses and on to the porch, and quietly tapped on the superintendent's window. He came to the window and saw this frightened Mexican woman crouched with her fingers at her lips. She whispered the story to him, and finally said, "He keel me if he know," and silently disappeared into the night, mounted her horse, rode home, and crawled into bed, while her drunken companion still slept.

The superintendent spilled the story to a friend who was correspondent for the San Francisco *Call,* and that enterprising journal played up the story, giving the names of the supposed kidnapers, with pictures of Henry Miller and vivid descriptions of the forbidden territory into which they planned to take the Cattle King.

One of the men named employed an attorney who had recently settled in Bakersfield after a meteoric career in the state legislature, and brought an action against the publisher of the newspaper to recover damages for libel.

The publisher was defended by Samuel M. Shortridge, later United States Senator for California, and John E. Richards, later Associate Justice of the Supreme Court of California.

They found themselves in a difficult position, since the man who sued was not the one who had told the story to the woman, and her testimony was, therefore, not admissible against him.

The best the newspaper could do was to plead
her testimony to show its good faith and in miti-
gation of damages, hoping that the evidence being
in, the jury might not be too particular in applying
it.

Witnesses were brought from far and near to
try and connect the plaintiff with the conspiracy.
He and the others were trailed all over the country.
One of them had come from Texas and had
changed his name. The lives of these men and
their general reputation became the subject of the
trial. What was lacking in evidence was supplied
by imagination and innuendo.

One day the attorneys for the newspaper heard
of a man who they thought could testify to seeing
the three men together. He worked for Henry
Miller, so they asked him to assist in getting the
man to court the next day. Thinking the man was
working at Buttonwillow, he wrote a short letter
to his superintendent to get the man and have him
in court the next morning. The man was in fact
fifty miles further away. When the messenger rode
into Buttonwillow with this letter, the superintendent, accustomed to obey without question,
called two riders and told them the man wanted
was with the sheep somewhere near Carrisa and
to ride until they came up with him. They rode
until midnight, changing horses at every opportunity, finally closed in on the man, pulled him
out of bed, put him on a horse and rode him all

night to Bakersfield. He was a sheepherder and
not accustomed to riding, and when he arrived he
was so stiff that he had to be supported by two
men in and out of the courtroom.

The publisher claimed the credit of having discovered the plot and saved the community from
an awful crime, and being convinced itself of the
guilt of the men, and the truth of the testimony of
the woman, the newspaper attempted to supply the
lack of evidence with argument and inference.

It attempted to introduce all kinds of evidence,
which was clearly inadmissible, and let the plaintiff have the odium of keeping it out. Day after
day Shortridge would stretch himself out to his full
length, and, with his index finger pointed in its
most menacing fashion, would hold forth on the
freedom of the press and kindred subjects,—as to
which it was no effort for him to be eloquent, en-
tertaining, and voluble. His whole object was to
ridicule the plaintiff and his claim for damages,
and when Shortridge would tire, Richards would
jump into the breach and swamp the attorney for
the plaintiff with a flow of classical references
and Biblical quotations which were given an added
emphasis by his clerical appearance.

The serious features of the trial were overshad-
owed by the highly farcical ending. Under the
law, at that time, the winning party had to pay
the jury fees, and when a verdict was brought in
by a jury and handed to the judge, he would look

it over and then look down and say to the attorney for one of the parties, "You may pay the jury fees," and everybody knew that his client had won the case.

Like everything else, this case finally approached its last stage. The court fixed the time for argument, and then said, "Counsel, of course, will each be prepared to pay the fees of the jurors."

Shortridge voiced a sweeping affirmative, and the plaintiff's attorney, in a halting manner, did likewise, but when he got out of court he realized that these fees had now run into a large sum of money and his client had little, and he had less. He had taken the case on a contingent basis, and his credit was already sorely overdrawn, but he spent the night seeing some of his friends and explaining to them that he would only have to pay the fees if he won the case. But even this was hardly sufficient to induce any one to advance money for such a cause. He finally, however, negotiated a hard bargain with an individual who promised to put up the money, but said that he would hold on to it until he found out who had won the case. This was satisfactory, and the next morning he was on hand with his bag of gold. In due time, the jury came in and handed its verdict to the clerk, who in turn handed it to the judge. The judge solemnly examined it and then looked down at the attorney for the plaintiff and said, "You may pay the jury fees."

His friend handed him the bag of coin and he marched up and gave it to the clerk. It had been taken from a saloon till and was in rather small denominations, and the clerk insisted on counting the money. This was done and found to be correct. The judge then handed the verdict to the clerk, and the clerk read:

"We, the jury, in the above entitled action, find a verdict for the plaintiff and assess his damages in the sum of one dollar."

Since the plaintiff under the law was only entitled to recover his costs when he obtained a verdict in excess of three hundred dollars, the chagrin on the face of the money lender can well be imagined. So far as the attorney for the plaintiff was concerned, he left the courtroom, and packed up his belongings and left the county.

XX. ABATTOIRS

THE problem of obtaining a permanent site for a slaughter house in San Francisco early attracted the attention of Henry Miller. The Pueblo of San Francisco under Mexican law was entitled to one square league of land, and for this it received a patent from the United States. This was mapped, liberal land reserved for streets, squares, schools, parks and so forth, and the balance granted by the legislature to those in possession between the first day of January and the twentieth day of June, 1855.

Henry Miller found a piece of land which seemed at that time far enough out for his purpose, although it was situated in what in later years became Chinatown. It was only a short time before the growing city made it imperative that he move from that location, but in keeping with the policy which he then formed and followed through life, he retained the property and immediately rented it for other purposes. It is interesting to note that as years went on it became valuable as a part of the Chinese Colony and brought him in good and substantial rent. He built and rebuilt on it, in keeping with the growth of the city.

The improvements were finally destroyed in the great fire of 1906 and he again built a substantial building upon it. But Chinatown did not come back as fast as had been expected, but scattered to the other side of the Bay. As a result the neighborhood changed and instead of Chinese tenants he could rent it only to people who intended to run something in the nature of a lodging house, and this he did. But soon he would find that a disreputable house was being conducted and immediately he would throw the tenant out, because he would not rent property for that purpose. This continued for some time, until in desperation he departed from his fundamental principle of always buying and never selling, and this was one of the few pieces of property that he sold.

He next found a location which he thought was surely far enough out to be suitable for the butchering business. It was a hundred vara lot, that is 275 feet by 275 feet, a fifty vara lot being 137 feet 6 inches square. It was located on the northeast corner of Howard and Fifth Streets. He bought it for a few dollars and retained it until the time of his death.

The subsequent history of this lot is quite interesting. It was not long before the growth of the city again made it necessary that his slaughter house be moved and this was done. But he followed the same practice of retaining this property. So he rented it to a primitive subdivider of the period, who ran an alley-way through the property so that more houses could be built on it. This alley was in the form of a *cul de sac,* but was in line with a regularly laid out street through the adjoining block. It was paved, sidewalks laid, and street lamps installed, and it so remained until the day of the fire in 1906, when all of the buildings were burned In the meantime, this alley had been put on the city map as a public street. When the land came back to Henry Miller after the fire, all title papers having been destroyed by the fire, it became necessary to establish the title of record.

He said to his lawyer, "This is one of the largest lots in the business district of the city. It is valuable. I don't want it divided. I had nothing to do with putting that street there." The City claimed it as a street, but old timers were dug up to testify that the "street" was paved by the lessee and that even the sidewalks were laid and the lights put up by him, and Henry Miller testified he had never authorized the tenant to dedicate it. As a result it was held not to be a street and was finally closed. This property served as a temporary office for the company after the great fire in 1906 and remained in the ownership of Henry Miller until the time of his death.

When the growth of the city made it imperative that the slaughter house should be removed from that location, Henry Miller called together all the men engaged in slaughtering in San Fran-

cisco and suggested that they get together and
select a permanent site which would be dedicated
to that purpose, and where they would not be disturbed. It was finally decided that it should be
over salt water, so that they would have a place for
ready disposal of offal. The State owned the tide
lands and he suggested that the slaughter houses
should be built over salt water on those lands.

This was finally agreed to and an application
was made to the legislature of the State to set aside
and grant to the butchers a permanent Butchers'
Reservation with a guaranty that butchering might
be there carried on for a period of ninety-nine years.
Such a bill was prepared and put through the Legislature, and a large tract of land was set aside by
the Legislature especially for butchering purposes,
and was subdivided into lots and sold for that purpose. Immediately Henry Miller contracted for the
erection of a wharf or platform big enough to accommodate not only his own wants, but the wants
of all other butchers in San Francisco. This was
constructed upon piles over the water and covered
many lots which had been purchased by the various butchers. Upon this wharf or platform each
butcher built his own slaughter house.

This platform and the slaughter houses built
on it remained from that time until the great fire
and earthquake in 1906. By that time the buildings, which were entirely of wood, had become
old and quite dilapidated. The piles remained for

the reason that the large amount of offal that was deposited in the bay under them was of such nature as to prevent the teredo from carrying on its deadly work, since the teredo only thrives in pure salt water. Still the piles had also deteriorated and the result was that the wharf was by that time quite weak. The earthquake totally destroyed it.

The embers of the destroyed city had hardly cooled before Henry Miller had plans for the construction of a new slaughter house, but that was to be now called an abattoir,—this more euphonious term hardly being appropriate to the character of construction in the early seventies. He had no time to waste for surveys or plans but immediately began the work of clearing the property and laying the foundation for the new structure, which finally cost him over half a million dollars.

When the building was well along in course of construction, his next door neighbor had a survey made and found that the building was seven and one-half feet over on his property. With his old neighbor, a difficulty of this kind would have been speedily straightened out, but his old neighbor had died, and the property had fallen into the hands of collateral heirs, and their demands were considered so unreasonable that they could not be met. The result was suits and cross-suits.

Henry Miller said that the building was exactly where the old building was, and therefore it must be in the right place. His memory was so good that he could point out things on the ground to establish the correctness of his contention. But that was not enough, because under the law of California no title could be acquired by adverse possession, unless the person in possession paid the taxes on the property, and he never had paid the taxes on this overlapping seven and one-half feet. But there was one loophole, because prior to 1878 this requirement of the law did not exist and therefore if it could be shown that he was in possession of the seven and one-half feet five years before 1878, he could maintain his title.

He then remembered the contractor who built the platform, and even found the old contract for driving the piles and building the platform, notwithstanding the destructive fire of 1906. He even remembered an old surveyor who had once been city surveyor and who had made surveys of the property. This man was finally located and it developed that when he left the office of the city surveyor he had taken with him most of his notes, which he kept and used in his private practice. There was one pile out in the bay that was not removed when the property was cleared after the fire, and an old survey was found which located the old wharf with reference to this pile, and showed that it was in fact seven and one-half feet over the line.

In addition to this he remembered that the insurance company had made a survey of the property and he had many arguments with them as to the high rate of insurance. The insurance company's books were examined and it was found that they had kept plats showing the location of all buildings, but unfortunately after the fire new plats, showing the situation of the new structures, had been pasted on top of the old. But the insurance company permitted these new plats to be moistened and removed, and thus the old plats became visible and demonstrated that the old building had been in fact seven and one-half feet over the line.

When the case came to trial, the opposition thought it impossible for anybody to establish the necessary facts, but Henry Miller was there with his memory, with his old contract, with his old survey, and with the insurance books, and by these methods his right to the seven and one-half feet was established, and his half million dollar abattoir was safe.

The action of Henry Miller in getting all of the butchering interests located at this one point proved to be a fine piece of statesmanship. He came to be recognized as the leader of the butchering interests. The butchers became closely associated. The prices of meat were practically fixed by him. It was his custom to credit his ranches with a certain price for the livestock delivered at the butcher shop each day. He furnished to the newspapers the quotation on livestock, and, as he could credit the ranches with any amount he saw fit, the quotations were simply statements of his ideas as to the value of livestock on any particular day.

Careful coöperation was carried on for years between the butchers in order to avoid excessive slaughtering and unreasonable prices. During all of those years, there was not only no prosecution for violation of the Sherman Anti-Trust Law, but there was never any question raised as to the subject. This was not due to the fact that there was no combination or no restraint of trade, but it was due to the fact that by forty years he anticipated the decision of the Supreme Court of the United States that the test was not whether there was a combination, or whether there was a restraint of trade, but whether the combination and restraint were reasonable.

Frequently his competitors urged him to raise prices and pointed out that higher prices could be obtained, but he always said, "We wants the people to eat meat, we wants to encourage them to buy meat, we wants to make it cheap so they can buy it," and no amount of urging could induce him to charge a price which would cause a protest or reduce the quantity of meat sold. The result was that for years good meat and cheap meat prevailed in San Francisco and that condition prevailed up to the time of his death.

The settlement in regard to the seven and one-half feet did not dispose of all the trouble with regard to the abattoir site. It developed that when the platform was built, it occupied two blocks as they were delineated upon the map of the tract. The result was that his property appeared on the map to be bisected by a street, but as time went on he had connected the buildings on one side of the street with those on the other side, so that he occupied the area delineated as a street. When it came to reëstablishing title after the great fire, it was discovered that there was no record title whatever to this so-called street, although it had been occupied for over thirty years. The city laid claim to it. After a trial it was held that it had never been in fact used as a public street, the offer to dedicate it had never been accepted by the city, and he had acquired title to it by adverse possession, and his title to the property was finally established.

His wisdom in the selection of the site was proved by the event. It is reached by every transcontinental railroad. It is located within three miles of the business center of the city, and still it has continued to exist until the present time without any serious complaint. This was due largely to the unlimited amount of water available to wash out the offal and prevent the place from becoming a nuisance.

Here it was that he worked out plans by which everything was utilized except the squeal of the animal. The fat was saved from the entrails, the hair was saved from the hide and used to hold plaster, the hides were tanned, the hoofs, horns and shin bones were converted into buttons, the wool was pulled, blood and meat scraps were made into chicken feed, fat was made into lard, and corned beef and sausage took up the unsalable portions of the meat.

Above all, cleanliness was the first and last rule. Most any time of the day or night he might appear on the scene, and woe betide any one who had been derelict in keeping the place clean. A block never went unscraped, a floor never went unwashed, a wall never went unpainted. No matter how careful the workmen might be, he was always able to show some possibility of improvement and insisted on a high standard of cleanliness. He constantly had new schemes for labor saving. The animal went up on its own power and came down through the various stages by the power of gravity until it was finally hung in the cooler.

XXI. THE KING AND HIS
COURT

T HE "court" of the Cattle King was always
on "circuit" and generally in "camp." Even
while traveling through the country he was giving the superintendent, foreman, or cattle man
with whom he was riding information, advice and
instructions. At night they would gather around
him and listen to his criticisms and orders. Letters
would be presented to him and answered with a
word. Important transactions were concluded by
the word "yes" or "no."

Let us follow the court from Silvies Valley in
Oregon, through Nevada and California.

One day late in the fall, Henry Miller might
have been seen mounting his horse at the Trout
Creek Ranch in Silvies Valley. The temperature
had already begun to fall to the freezing point.
The cattle had already begun to straggle in from
the hills. He rode out among them, focusing his
eyes on certain points at which he could determine
at a glance whether they were fat.

As he moved out on to higher ground, he could
look up the Valley and see his fields on both sides

of Silvies River, which was hidden in a dense
growth of willows, completely covering it as it
flowed through the Valley. At intervals tributary
streams entered it from the mountains and they
too were indicated only by irregular lines of willows. Thus he could trace the course of Cotton-
wood Creek, Camp Creek, Bridge Creek, Poison
Creek, Jump Creek, Flat Creek, Trout Creek,
Spring Creek, Hall Creek and Payne Creek.

The bottom land was fenced, and the returning
cattle were trying to break in to reach the feed.
Through the fields were stacks of hay, but a large
part of the fields had not been cut. "This country
is too cold for cattle in the winter and you have
not enough hay to keep them in condition," said
Henry Miller. "Separate the young stock and take
it below, keeping only the old cows. You can do
better here wintering horses." So the work of branding the young stock and cutting out the steers from
the cows went merrily on.

A high piece of land was selected, and there
sat Henry Miller watching the horsemen skillfully
letting the cows into the fields, and as skillfully
cutting out the calves. He sat motionless on a finely
set up animal, with a warm coat about him, and
looked the part of a general as he watched his
men outwit the "enemy."

While one set of riders was making this general
segregation, another was separating the branded and
unbranded stock. One by one the unbranded ani-

mals were lassoed from two directions and thrown. "Do not throw them too hard and bruise them," Henry Miller would say.

The glow of a fire of coals could be seen in the center with men arranging the branding irons so they would heat. No sooner was the animal thrown than one man cut the ear and another planted the branding iron on the left hip. The sizzling of the burning hair could be heard, blended with the cry of the animal as its flesh was seared, and the pungent odor of burning hair and flesh was mingled with the smoke from the fire. In a moment the ropes were removed and the animal, smarting and indignant, ran into the corral prepared for it.

Soon the unweaned calves found themselves separated from the cows, and the cows found themselves separated from their calves. Their answering cries rent the air and both got as near together as the intervening fence would permit. As the number separated increased, the bellowing became louder and less distinguishable, the deep bass of the cows blending with the plaintive notes of the calves, until they finally became one great diapason, and this continued for hours.

The neighbors were there to help separate their stock from the stock of the company, big grizzled good-natured men who rode up and greeted Henry Miller. He might not have been there for several

years, but he would instantly recognize them and
call them by name.

"Good morning, Mr. Camblin," he would say
to a little man whom every one else addressed as
Dan.

"How are you, Mr. Craddock? Can you get
Mrs. Craddock to cook me some more beans?"
would be the smiling way he would tell the man
they all called "John" that he remembered his
hospitality.

"Good morning, Mr. Byers. That is a fine dam
you put in the river, but if you don't mind, please
let a little water come down for the cattle at Trout
Creek." "Well, I was here first," said Byers.
"Well, I will be here long after you are gone,"
said Henry Miller. "Does that mean you want to
buy me out?" said Byers. "You already owe me
more than your place is worth, but the two places
are better together, so I'll give you two thousand
dollars for what you have left." "Sold," said Byers,
and the matter was ended.

Sometimes there would arise some friendly dispute about the ownership of a calf. The men would
call each other "endearing" names, and a stranger
would expect a combat at any moment, but it would
all be in good natured fun.

"I saw that calf with the white spot over the
right eye with my cow up on Spring Creek," said
Craddock, "and I don't let any cattle stealing son-

of-a-sea-cook take it away from me." "No cow of yours could have a good looking calf like that," said Hopper, the foreman of the Miller property. The calf was lassoed and turned into the field with the cows, and in a minute it was sucking a cow bearing the "S Wrench" brand. "The drinks are on me," said Craddock, but they were a long way from that institution where cow punchers love to get together, known as a "saloon," so they were soon back on the job.

As soon as the steers were gathered and the calves were weaned, the drive began to Harney Valley. As they went down along the outside of the fence, the cows were still watching, but the pain of separation had already abated, and the calves had begun to enjoy being "on their own" and seemed to enjoy the new adventure. Fond farewells were rudely interrupted by the riders, and soon the animals were proceeding with almost military precision through the country. They passed through the timber and down the canyons, finding an abundance of feed and water on the way. They moved slowly so as not to lose their fat. Henry Miller said, "I'm never more happy than when I'm riding behind a bunch of fat cattle."

The cold weather of the mountains made the cattle hardy and healthy, and the Government Forest Reserve had furnished an abundance of feed, so they were fat. The country was damp from the dew of the cool nights, so the drive was not dusty and the animals were clean and their hides a beautiful red.

As they dropped down into Harney Valley, the weather became warmer. The cattle of that region had not yet returned from the ranges, but no sooner had the bunch of cattle been put in the fields for a few days' rest and to cut out the steers for the next drive, than the cattle from the mountain began to drift down to Harney Valley ranches. Soon every road and every lane was full of them trying to get into the fields. Instinctively, every animal returned to the place where it was born. Riders were opening gates and letting them in and cutting out animals belonging to others.

Soon Henry Miller was in the principality owned by him in Harney Valley. "These calves will do well here," he said. "The heavy grass and tule will protect them, and you won't have to feed them long unless it is a hard winter."

In the evening his superintendent, John Gilcrest, and his foremen from the various ranches, would gather in the company's office at the Island Ranch: Charlie Cronin, who spoke clearly and quickly and knew the whole country like a book; Ben Newman, heavy and slow, and with a dark complexion which flushed dangerously when his anger was aroused. He was once on the witness stand, testifying against a picturesque figure in the place where the trial was held. His adversary was also heavy and dark with great eyelashes, and the two sat facing each other. Newman had testified that he found a channel which his neighbor was enjoined from interfering with blocked by the dead bodies of his neighbor's cattle. He was being subjected to a searching cross-examination by his adversary's attorney, who seemed to doubt the testimony as to the cattle belonging to his client. Without batting an eye, Newman grasped the arms of the chair in which he was sitting, and looking his enemy straight in the eye, said, "I don't know whether they were his cattle, all I know is that they were marked with his brand." The possible but totally unwarranted imputation of this as meaning that his brand might be on the cattle of others was so clear that for a moment every one held his breath, until the attorney beat a graceful retreat and directed the examination along other lines.

"How are you getting on improving the property, Mr. Gilcrest?" asked Henry Miller. A great map was on the table before him, and he put his finger on the piece of land farthest up the river, and Gilcrest said, "That's the Savage place. I've put in grain because the flour mill is just below." "How is the mill getting along?" asked Henry Miller. "I think we should take a little stock in it to keep it going. This is not a grain country. Too much frost."

Gilcrest proceeded, "I have drained the Warm Springs School Section so the water from the spring will spread out better."

"Watch that spring," said Henry Miller. "It's fine water and just outside of town. It will be valuable some day." The water has since been used to form a mill pond for a lumber mill, and the land is the terminal of a railroad built to bring the timber out of the Silvies Valley region.

"I have made new channels for the river through the Potter Swamp, as you told me," continued Gilcrest, "and now we get some good hay from it."

"That's down by the place we bought from Goodman," said Henry Miller. "We paid him a good price. I hear his son is Sheriff now. He should be friendly to us and get some cattle thieves."

"I have tried to get some water over the Hudspeth School Section, but it is too high to do much with," continued the superintendent. "Do not waste any money on it. It is next to town and some day will be valuable. Use it for gathering cattle in the meantime," said Henry Miller.

Gilcrest continued, "I have helped Mr. Hanley extend his ditch so we can get water on the Ben Brown place." "You must work in harmony with Mr. Hanley," said Henry Miller. "He's our most important neighbor, and buy as much as you can from Brown's store. They are good people."

"I tried to reclaim the Bugler and Porter places, but Mr. Hanley would not let me deepen the river along there because he wants it to overflow his land," said the superintendent.

"Well," said Henry Miller, "build a levee so

as to control it on our side, and some day Mr. Hanley will be glad to have a good channel for the river. Do not quarrel with him." Gilcrest said nothing, as he had already come to the breaking point with his powerful neighbor.

"We have put in a lot of grain on the Mace place, and it is doing very well," continued the superintendent. "That's where all those settlers were, Mace, Ambrosig, Woodruff, Woodfin, Meadows, Terrell, Weeks, Mason and Roberts." "That's good land, but don't spend too much money growing grain. It's better to buy it from others who don't know better than to grow it in this country. The frosts are too severe," said Henry Miller.

They were now down at the "Red S" field and Henry Miller's face began to brighten. Gilcrest continued, "We have put dams in Chapman Slough and in the west fork of the river, and improved the old Elk, Poujade and Foley dams, and run a big ditch around Wright's point, as you told me, and spread the water over lots of new land."

"Always keep up those old dams Mr. Foley and Mr. Poujade put in. They will prove our early water rights," said Henry Miller. Years later this proved to be true, and they figured prominently in many legal battles over the water.

Gilcrest continued, "When you go out there and see all the water and grass around the base of Wright's Point you will almost think that the tes-

timony of that man in the land contest was true."
"How's that?" asked Henry Miller. "There was
a contest between a settler and a swamp land
claimant," continued the superintendent, "and a
witness testified in the land office that he sat on
Wright's Point and fished off of it in the water
at its base. This was too incredible, so the settler
got the land. We have swamped it now." "If he
did that," said Henry Miller, "he must have had
some rattlesnake poison, because I never saw so
many rattlesnakes as I saw on Wright's Point."

This reminded Foley of a story, and he said,
"That is about as bad as the story of the man who
testified in a swamp land contest that he knew the
land was swamp because he had traveled all over
it in a boat. It later developed that his testimony
was literally true, but that the boat in which he
sat was upon a wagon drawn over dry ground by
horses." This story later gained wide circulation,
and, being enlarged upon, was changed so as to
make it appear that Henry Miller had himself acquired swamp lands by those means. Of course,
there was no foundation for the story, but it stuck
just the same.

Gilcrest then continued, "I have cut the School
Teacher's Ditch through that high piece of land,
and it irrigated a lot of land just as you said."

Henry Miller smiled, but this time not at the
thought of green grass, but at the incident that gave
the ditch its name. It seemed a tall Yankee school

teacher had taken the school in the vicinity and on
Sunday had dressed up and started in a buggy to
call on a girl living on a distant homestead. The
men around the ranch made much fun of him in
his strange clothes, and told him about a short cut
to the girl's house. They said there was a ditch
but it was shallow and he could easily cross it.
Being in a hurry to reach the object of his infatua-
tion, he gladly accepted the advice and set out.
The ditch was, in fact, very deep, and the buggy
was overturned, the school teacher nearly drowned,
and his clothes ruined. The horse ran away and
the school teacher was compelled to walk back to
the ranch house. The ditch was thereafter called
the "School Teacher's Ditch."

"Tell me, Mr. Cronin," said Henry Miller,
"how you dug this ditch we call the Cronin Ditch."

"Well, that was funny," said Cronin. "Mr.
Devine wanted to prove he had reclaimed the land
so he brought down some big timber from Silvies
Valley, and brought some rails from the railroad,
and with them built what we called a go-devil. It
was 'V' shaped, and about twenty feet wide at the
back. The railroad rails held it together and the
point was covered with iron brought to a sharp
edge. In the fall we plowed the line of the ditch,
hitched thirty-two mules to this go-devil and
made the ditch. Fortunately the next year was dry,
and the ditch carried all the water, and you could
go all over the land, so Devine had affidavits made

that the land had been reclaimed by the ditch. The next year the land was all flooded again."

"I have preserved and improved those ditches as you told me," said Mr. Gilcrest, "and last year we wintered 5,700 head of cattle on the 'Red S' field without feeding any hay at all."

"That is the way to grow cattle," said Henry Miller, "but keep improving that land so the grass won't be too rank. Rank grass has no nutriment. Big haystacks do not make big beef, unless the hay has nutriment."

By sun up the next morning, Henry Miller and his superintendent were on their way to the Malheur. They drove through the flat country to the north of Malheur Lake and then pulled up "Nigger" hill, where the road was through solid rock and the horses slipped on the smooth surface. Soon they were in the hilly country where the Malheur had its origin. From stream to stream and valley to valley they rode, stopping at each ranch. At each the foreman was put to the test by a searching examination. Coming to Pine Creek, Henry Miller walked along the ditches and said, "Mr. Griffin, extend these ditches and irrigate more land." "Yes, they should be extended, Mr. Miller, but there is a settler down there," said the foreman. "Buy him out," said Henry Miller.

Coming to Kimball Flat he remarked when he saw the alfalfa, "Mr. Drake, that is the finest alfalfa I have ever seen." Drake was pleased and took him to the site of the old mill and showed him how the ditch could be carried high up on the side of a hill and through a tunnel to irrigate the Drewsey flat. "It's a fine piece of land, Mr. Drake, but it's too expensive to build ditches on rocky hillsides and through tunnels. It would never pay," said Henry Miller.

Then down to Warm Springs Ranch. "How is the ditch work going, Mr. Jourdan?" asked Henry Miller. "Come up on the hill back of the house and you can see," replied the foreman. Climbing a slight eminence, the little valley on each side of the Malheur River could be viewed, and along the side of the valley the dust conld be seen rising from the plows and scrapers which were excavating the ditch. "Where is that dam site where the government engineers propose building a dam to make this valley a reservoir?" asked Henry Miller.

"See that narrow gorge at the lower end of this valley?" asked the foreman. "There is a fine dam site there and the whole ranch can be made a reservoir. The Government proposes irrigating all the country around Vale."

Henry Miller looked the scene over and said, "Well, they will find a fine farm here when they come. Hurry with the ditches and get the land into grain and later into alfalfa. It is heavy land and must be plowed at just the right time. Any one who builds that reservoir will go broke."

Years after the Warm Springs Ranch had ditches

on both sides of the river and the dry land had been turned into beautiful fields of alfalfa, when the farmers at Vale formed an irrigation district and sought to build the Warm Springs Reservoir. The dam site was just below the Miller land and when they began to build they said that they would not close the dam but would leave the middle section open until they had paid for the ranch.

It was soon found that they were building clear across the canyon, so an injunction suit was instituted and the court compelled the district to deposit two hundred thousand dollars to secure the landowners.

Finally the ranch was condemned and the reservoir built. After it was built it was held that the district only obtained an easement, and Henry Miller still owned the land and could graze his cattle on it after the water was drawn out of the reservoir, so he got the value of the land and kept the land also.

The district was a failure, as he had predicted. Most of the farmers went broke and the district defaulted on its bonds, so Henry Miller saw the men who built the Nevada Ditch, and fought him for the waters of the Malheur, ruined by this illadvised project.

When the party approached the Agency Ranch, Henry Miller again rested at the top of the mountain and viewed the valley. It presented a new picture. The entire valley was now irrigated and developed. The agency buildings were now used as ranch headquarters. When he met the foreman, he said, "Mr. Wright, we made no mistake when we got this place. I see a little piece across the creek which is not irrigated. Build a flume and irrigate it. Do not lose an acre of it. This would be a good place for a garden to grow things for the ranches. The men need fresh vegetables. Put in a good garden."

Coming to the Chidsey field, he suddenly said to the driver, "Stop." He got out and examined some grass and said, "Mr. Sturtevant, that is Kentucky blue grass. Where did it come from?" The foreman answered, "That is funny, Mr. Miller. The Indian agent brought that out and planted it as a lawn around the buildings at Agency Valley, and the seeds drop into the river and flow down to all the ranches along the river. It is an awful nuisance." Henry Miller said, "Fix things so that it will not go to seed up there, or the alfalfa fields will be ruined. See that it is cut and given to the chickens."

Thus he went from ranch to ranch, Indian Creek and Otis Creek, and finally came through the chalk hills and flats to the Harper Ranch. "What's the prospect, Mr. Fenton, of the railroad coming in here?" "There is lots of talk of it," said Fenton, "but the government engineers also want this ranch as a reservoir site to store water for the land around Vale and Ontario."

"The government don't seem to be interested in the cattle business," said Henry Miller. "They have the Snake River at Ontario, and the people around Vale seem to be trying to destroy these cattle ranches in the mountains. If they would let us use the water we would be reservoiring it in the ground and they would get it later. Encourage the railroad to come in and that will end the reservoir project."

Things actually worked out that way years later, when the railroad was extended through the valley.

From here they rode across the Malheur River and continued south to Mann Lake. "Mr. Clark, are you using all the water of these creeks?" "Every drop," answered Clark. "Well, you must look out," said Henry Miller, "because there is a lot of good land in this valley, and it will be taken up if there is any water."

"We have a ditch which picks up the water of all the creeks and brings it to the Mann Lake Ranch," said Clark.

Years later, two men threatened with tuberculosis left Chicago and found their way in a cart to the Mann Lake Valley. One was an engineer and the other a lawyer. It was late in the fall and the creeks were dry, but they saw the towering peaks of Steen's Mountain and the streams coming down to the valley, and they saw the good land to which Henry Miller had referred. It was level and the soil was evidently the result of deposits washed down from the mountain and forming alluvial fans at its base. Big sagebrush covered it, the surest sign of good soil.

These men halted and soon got a large number of people to come west and settle on this land. They formed a water company with an imposing name and sold stock in it.

They filed appropriations of the water of all the streams irrigating the Mann Lake Ranch and the Alvord Ranch. Soon their little cabins could be seen in every gulch. They all had children and soon had a school house, where one of the party taught. When the irrigation season came around, they awoke to the fact that the greater part of the water ran off of the other side of the mountain into the Donner and Blitzen Rivers, leaving only enough on their side to supply the old ranches.

The engineer was not discouraged but endeavored to turn the water through a divide back to their side, but the ranchers around Harney Lake enjoined such a reversal of nature.

Then "the company" obtained an injunction to prevent them from taking the water needed for the Mann Lake Ranch. The attorney came out from Chicago to try the case. The testimony was taken out of court and to convenience the parties who were poor, a little house of two rooms belonging to the company situated on the edge of the Alvord Desert was converted into a courtroom.

The room was about twelve feet square, and

along a rude table the reporter, three attorneys for the company and two for the settlers gathered for days. Along the walls the women sat, generally with babies in their arms, while the waiting witnesses hovered around the door.

The Chicago attorney always wanted the window closed and the engineer wanted it open, so he retired into the adjoining kitchen and, perched upon a stool, drew maps, charts and profiles, colored cultivated areas, figured coefficients of roughness and computed stream discharges.

Various members of the party had attempted to measure the turbulent streams as they threw themselves down the narrow gorges and over the bowlders and rocks and became lost in the great deposits of gravel. Floating pieces of sagebrush were used to get velocity, and most astonishing results were obtained as to the amount of available water.

Day after day the parties gathered with cold lunches and listened to the pathetic picture of these misguided people trying to find more water than the pioneer ranchers had ever discovered. At noon they dared not wander far from the house, because the surrounding fields were infested with rattlesnakes, and the wind from the Alvord Desert blew like a hurricane. The atmosphere in the little "courtroom" often became unbearable and short recesses were necessary in order to fumigate it.

The living quarters at the ranches were inadequate to care for the unusual gathering, and some of the engineers and witnesses had to sleep in the hay. By the time the case was over the attorneys could not bear the sight of a hard boiled egg.

The court gave the bulk of the water to the company and the settlers gradually pulled up and moved away, all fine people, misled by misguided speculators. To make sure of its position, the company appealed, claiming still more water. It then claimed that the court should have referred the case to the State Water Board, so the Supreme Court sent the case back to be decided by that board. In the meantime the war had come on and the last of the settlers moved away, so the "company" was left in undisturbed possession. Thus did the warning of Henry Miller serve to protect his interests.

When he left Mann Lake, he crossed the Alvord Desert and entered the narrow gorge which led to the White Horse Ranch. The road through this gorge was composed of sand of such texture that no automobile could get traction to run over it, but this was before the days of automobiles, so Henry Miller's horses soon brought him to the fields of luscious clover, which presented a strange contrast to the desert through which he had just passed.

As he sat that evening talking to his foreman, he suddenly put his finger on the map and said, "Mr. Cronin, our engineer says our stables are on land of the road company."

"So I understand," said Cronin, "and a large part of our meadows too."

"I don't think the road company knows where its land is, but if it ever claims it, we can take the water down to Coyote Meadows, and without the water their land will be no good," said Henry Miller.

Years later the road company, which owned every alternate section for miles, conceived a scheme of disposing of its lands by a colossal lottery. The land was all divided on paper into twenty acre lots. Rights to purchase lots were sold all over the Union to people who never saw them, under an arrangement that each group would have a representative who would be present at the drawing and choose lots for them. As a result, one might get twenty acres on a rocky hillside or on the Alvord Desert, and another a fine piece of land along a stream for the same price. A woman in Woolworth's in Chicago might find herself the owner of twenty acres in a country where a farm of that size was worthless.

It resulted that the meadow which Henry Miller had occupied for years became owned in twenty-acre lots by people scattered from Maine to Los Angeles. None of them ever showed up to claim the land, and gradually they let the taxes go delinquent, and the company bought it in. To this day the winners of the lottery probably never knew that they owned the stables which John Devine had built to house the race horses in which his partner delighted.

While Henry Miller was moving through Oregon into Nevada the gathering of the cattle for the drives to market continued. The gathering of the cattle on the Island Ranch was stupendous compared with the scene in Silvies Valley. The cattle came in from thousands of square miles of range, cows with calves, bulls, and steers of all ages. The moaning of the cows and calves when separated rose in great volume and continued far into the night.

The old cows were turned into the fields of grass, willows and tule to shift for themselves. During the cold winter they would struggle for existence, breaking through the ice on the river to get water to drink, tramping up the snow on the ground to reach the grass below, and sleeping in beds made by themselves in the protection of the tules. On some cold day or colder night a calf would come and the mother would lick it with her tongue and protect it from the blizzard with her body, until it could get upon its feet and escape from freezing.

As the winter progressed and the snow, ice and sleet became too severe the cattle were rounded up and fed from the stack. The temperature was often as low as twenty degrees below zero, and the hay stacks dwindled as the cold weather continued, and the fear grew that the cattle might perish. The feed beneath the snow could not be reached. The weak cows and calves died, and when the winter was over the remaining cows were more like skeletons than living animals, but they were still alive and capable of producing another bunch of steers to be driven to the market.

With several thousand in each drive, the great drives commenced in the fall down through Oregon and Nevada. Men went ahead to prepare food and water, and the drive moved with the precision of an army. Experience had taught them the time required to move from place to place.

"Never hurry the stock," said Henry Miller, "or the fat will all be lost on the way."

Finally they would come out on the seemingly endless plains of Nevada. The alkali dust would rise to choke man and beast. You could see them strung out over the sagebrush plains with the dust rising above them, as they slowly moved through the heat of the day. For over one hundred miles they traveled through a continuous stretch of sagebrush plain, then dropped down into Paradise Valley where hay could always be found, then tramped through the sand blown country north of Winnemucca. Here the sand was so bad that the only way a road could be maintained was to cut sagebrush and put it on top of the sand, and still the sand rose until fences were obliterated and even telephone poles were completely covered. For long distances the sagebrush had been cut to maintain the road.

It was through this country that the animals

were carefully coaxed until they finally arrived at Winnemucca Field and the railroad. The field was along the Humboldt River and was the first green field for miles. It was cut up with sloughs. One day a drive was completed and the cattle brought to the railroad that paralleled the field. As the animals were crossing the track, a train came down and the engineer gave three blasts of the engine whistle. The cattle had never before seen a railroad or heard a locomotive. They stampeded into the field and kept on running for several hours, never stopping when they came to the sloughs, and many of them were drowned. This incident was unusual. Generally the cattle arrived in fine condition.

Leaving Winnemucca Henry Miller would take the train to Mason Valley. "Mr. Radaman," he would say, "are the cattle still in Bridgeport Valley?" "Yes, sir," answered the foreman, a tall, thin man with one eye covered by a leather flap, "but they must leave in a few days before the snow falls." "To-morrow we will go up and see them," answered Henry Miller.

"I see you still employ those worthless Piutes," continued Henry Miller. "There are too many squaws around the ranch. They are poison."

Radaman shifted uncomfortably and took a side glance at his employer out of his remaining eye and answered, "They are all we can get to do heavy work like putting dams in the river."

"Are you still putting brush dams in the river

every year?" asked Henry Miller. "I will have our engineer come up and put in a wooden weir."

"It will be the first one in this river," said Radaman.

Radaman now climbed out of the cart and opened the gate into the first field.

"What are you using this field for?" asked Henry Miller.

"We are breeding the mares here," said Radaman. Looking across the field Henry Miller soon observed a bunch of mares and a stallion circling around them.

"You should never drive a horse into a field where a stallion is with the mares," said Miller. No sooner did the stallion see the horse attached to the cart than he made a circle around the mares and made a dash for the horse, reared up on his hind legs, showed his teeth, and tried to strike the horse with his hoofs, and he was with great difficulty driven away by Radaman's whip.

"That stallion might have killed us. That was very stupid," said Henry Miller. He was provoked and gave Radaman a hard day.

"What is that I smell? Stop," said Henry Miller, and crawled out of the cart and into the brush along the river. "Just as I thought. A dead cow, not even skinned.

"The foxtail was not burned along that levee but was allowed to go to seed. You will soon be irrigating foxtail instead of alfalfa.

"That bull is in poor shape and color. Send him to the market with the next shipment."

Thus he continued for hours until Radaman was about exhausted.

"To-morrow we will start early for Bridgeport," said Henry Miller, as he finally climbed the stairs of the old Mason mansion to bed.

Long before sun up he was again behind the horses driving up the Walker River through Mason and Smith Valleys, and was soon in the canyon of Walker River and the Bridgeport Valley. A great round valley six thousand feet in elevation, with mountains around it rising over ten thousand feet. The snow already covered the high elevations but the grass in the floor of the valley was only brown from the early frosts.

The cattle had wallowed in the luxurious grasses and pastured the fields for several months, and were beautiful to behold. The cold nights kept the fields free of dust, the hides of the steers glistened, and the fat actually rolled on their sides. Henry Miller drove among them and every care left his face as he estimated their weight and figured what they would produce on the block.

"Start the drive at once," he said, "and get them to California. Eighty percent of them are already fat."

He returned by way of Carson Valley. As he drove over the divide and came out on an elevation above the valley, the sun was almost setting behind the Sierra Nevada which rose abruptly above the valley. The grass was still green and patches of water could be seen here and there, and long lines of water in the ditches. As the slanting rays of the setting sun touched these waters they were turned to burnished gold. The pools of water resembled great caldrons of gold and the ditches golden chains joining them together. Even through the grass the sun caught the water, making a network of gold. The scene was prophetic of the golden harvest from the cattle which were following him. Gradually the sun passed behind the timber and soon behind the mountains, as Henry Miller rolled into the little town of Minden where he took the train to California.

His cattle were following him from every direction. They came up like armies and moved with the precision of military maneuvers. As a general might bring up his reserves, so Henry Miller maneuvered his cattle to fill the demand of the consuming public and outwit his competitors. The cattle came from the Malheur and Harney Valley to Winnemucca and the Central Pacific railroad, from the Quin River country to the Western Pacific railroad, from the Black Rock country to the Nevada, California and Oregon railroad, and from Bridgeport and Mason Valleys to the Tonopah branch of the Southern Pacific railroad.

When they reached California the cars containing the "fat" cattle were taken to San Francisco, those containing the "feeders" were switched to the feed yards at Los Baños, Gilroy, and other feed yards, and the "stock" cattle were delivered to the ranges.

Two thousand miles had been traveled by the Cattle King in reviewing the "army" in charge of his Cattle Kingdom.

XXII. HOBOES

I T WAS a rainy morning a few days before
Christmas. It had been an early and a hard
winter. At the breakfast table Mrs. Miller said,
"Henry, do you want to make any changes in your
Christmas gifts this year?" She had in her hands a
rather formidable list of several pages.

He smiled and took the list and ran over the
names of the numerous nephews, nieces and dependent and faithful servants. As he went through
it he made his comments upon it:

"They have another baby. We had better increase that.

"They've been getting a good salary from the
firm this year. They don't need so much, the company will take care of them.

"His wife has been sick, we had better give them
a little extra.

"That man ought to go to work. There is no use
in trying to do anything for them, but I suppose
we had better leave it as it is," and so on through
the list.

"I'd like to give a little something to that Lu-
theran minister that was here. He seems to be hav-

ing a hard time keeping the Church going. And the priest down at Gilroy seems to be doing very good work with the men; give him something too."

That afternoon the bookkeeper came timidly into his office with a formidable document in his hand and said, "Mr. Miller, do you want to make any changes in the Christmas turkeys this year?"

He said, "It's been pretty hard to raise the turkeys this year, but we still have a pretty good crop. We are getting the wives of the foremen to take an interest in growing turkeys and they are getting good results. The prices are going to be high this year. Let me see your list." He took the list of those to whom it was customary to send turkeys on Christmas,—all fattened, cleaned, dressed, and delivered. The list included all the employees in the San Francisco office, all superintendents and foremen in the country, a large number of public officials, newspaper men, and leading citizens of the various communities in which he was interested, pensioners and old faithful workers, and deserving widows of deceased faithful servants. This formidable list did not include the vast army of laborers, because they received their turkey dinner at the ranch houses.

He went carefully over the entire list, making here and there an omission or addition on account of change of conditions with which he was familiar. He handed the list back to the bookkeeper, and seeing that the bookkeeper seemed to hesitate, he said, "Have you the list of those given a bonus last year?"

"Yes, I have, Mr. Miller."

"Well, it won't be necessary to go over that. You can prepare checks for ten per cent of the entire payroll for the month as Christmas presents for our men, but don't send any checks to any one who has worked for us less than a year. We must encourage our men to stay with us and make it worth their while. Men who are always looking for a new job are of no value."

For several hours he sat patiently while the bookkeeper read the expense items in the various ranch accounts. As each ranch was reached he visualized everything connected with it, and was quick to catch every unnecessary expenditure and to see every possibility of economy in operation. If a foreman was making too frequent trips to town, he would catch it. If he stayed too long, he noted it. If he bought what he should have grown or made, he complained of it. If he had too many men working, or was employing relatives unnecessarily, he put his finger on it. A padded payroll could not get by. He would sense a fictitious name immediately. But this seldom happened because he made few mistakes in choosing men.

Finally Henry Miller emerged from his office with his coat and hat. As he passed the cashier's window, he looked in, smiled and said, "A few quarters, please," and the cashier handed him eight quarters, which he deposited in his vest pocket, saying, "I guess that will be enough to get me across the sidewalk."

The office of the company was on California Street, on a slight grade, and in a rather quiet locality. As the rainy afternoon wore on, some unfortunates began to wander casually into the block. One took up a position by the market across the street, another hid himself in an alley, another stood nonchalantly observing workmen constructing a building. The one across the street kept his eyes glued on Henry Miller's windows. Shortly another approached the hobo in the alley, who said, "Hello, Bo, where did you drop in from?"

"Hopped off a freight from New Orleans this morning," said the newcomer.

"Ever here before?"

"Nope. This is the first time. What are all the boes doing around here? Waiting for hand-outs?"

"Hand-outs nothing. We're waiting for Santa Claus. Ain't ye never heard of Henry Miller?"

"No."

"Well, he stops across the street. He's good to the hoboes. He's generally down the country, but he's in town to-day. He's good for a quarter any time."

About this time the lookout made a motion signifying that Henry Miller had left his desk, and all of the boes gradually headed for the office entrance and lined themselves up in the order of their arrival along the wall of the building. By this time it was raining quite heavily. His hack stood at the curb. As his shuffling steps were heard, the men became more restless, and, as he emerged from the doorway, the foremost one, hat in hand, stepped forward and said, "Let me hold your um-umbrella, Mr. Miller." As he opened the umbrella over Henry Miller, the others, hats in hand, deployed across the sidewalk, and as he crossed he handed each a quarter, which was received with a murmured, "Thank you, Mr. Miller," and "God bless you, Mr. Miller." He finally made the hack, handed his last quarter to the bo carrying the umbrella, and said to the driver, "Drive on."

The hoboes of Henry Miller's day were quite a different variety from the I. W. W. agitators, the youthful wanderers who came on the scene after the World War, or the hitch-hikers of the present day. They were mostly old, decrepit, and unkempt. They were the first tourists to learn the value of California's winter climate. As the snow and ice began to grip the east and middle west, they planned their itinerary so as to be in California. They tramped the roads and railroad ties, dodged watch dogs, cut wood for a hand-out, and slept in hay stacks and barns. They were one of the farmers' pests. Some set dogs on them. Some made them chop wood for a meal. They were supposed to have a sign language and to mark places, so that other tramps would know whether they were good for a hand-out. They would sleep in the hay and frequently burn hay stacks. Petty thefts were laid at their door. They were the terror of children going to school and of housewives alone on the farm. They were beset with the idea that society owed them a living, and they intended to make society pay, and generally succeeded.

Early in his career, Henry Miller established a policy with respect to tramps. He came to a ranch one day and saw what was obviously a tramp chopping wood. He said to the foreman, "Who is that chopping wood?"

"Oh," said the foreman, "that's just a tramp. I'm having him chop wood for his dinner."

Henry Miller said, "Never do that. If a man is so unfortunate as to beg for food, give it to him and win his gratitude. Never make him work for it and get his hatred."

Another time when going through a ranch he saw a tramp sleeping in a hay stack. He said to the foreman, "Don't let the tramps sleep in the hay stacks. Let them know that they can always have one night's lodging in the barn. If they fall asleep in the hay stack, they may stay there several days, break it all down, probably get to smoking and set it on fire. If you give them a bed in the barn they will appreciate it, stay just one night, won't use any matches, and then be on their way. Never let them stay more than one night."

One day he came to a ranch house and found two more men in the dining room than showed on the payroll. He said to the foreman, "How's this? You've got more men in the dining room than are on the payroll."

The foreman said, "Two of them are tramps."

Henry Miller said, "Don't let the tramps eat with the men. The first thing you know, you will have the men saying they are treated like tramps. Let the men eat first and the tramps afterwards."

One day Henry Miller was taken to task by the cook, who said, "Mr. Miller, I came here to cook for the men. I don't like washing dishes for tramps."

Henry Miller said, "All right, we'll have the tramps eat after the men off of the same plates. They will clean them for you."

The cook thought this was a good joke and did not press his point further, so these became the rules for the hobo hotels on the Henry Miller ranches:

1. Never refuse a tramp a meal, but never give him more than one meal. A tramp should be a tramp and keep on tramping.

2. Never refuse a tramp a night's lodging. Warn him not to use any matches, and let him sleep in the barn, but never let him stay more than one night.

3. Never make a tramp work for his meal. He won't thank you, if you do. Anyhow he is too weak to work before a meal and too lazy to work after a meal.

4. Never let the tramps eat with the men. Make them wait until the men are through, and then make them eat off of the same plates. The cook should not be made to do extra work for tramps.

Under these humanitarian rules, which soon came to be well understood, the Miller ranches became a Mecca for the tramps. Some wit christened them the "Dirty Plate Route," but the plates were not really dirty and the tramps got the same food as the men.

Often after a hot day you could see a tramp coming out from under a bridge, another from under a stop gate, another from a clump of willows, another from behind the barn, and all of them would gradually work their way toward the dining room door. Sometimes as many as eight or ten would be on hand at a single meal. Sometimes the foreman would have to stand by the door with a club to keep them out until the men were served. But generally they understood the rules, one meal, one night, and no more.

As the line of march extended for several hundred miles through the Miller ranches, the extent of this drain on the company's finances can well be appreciated. Still Henry Miller figured that he was in money by the policy. A disgruntled tramp could leave gates open, burn hay stacks, and set fire to standing grain. Instead of insuring his hay, grain and barns, he used the premiums to feed the tramps. The result was that they never left the gates open, or burned his hay, barns or grain.

It also removed all personal danger from the tramps. They did not bother the wives of the foremen, nor was there any danger that they would commit acts of violence against Henry Miller or his men. He often said, "If I took everything I could get, it wouldn't be safe for me to go through the country." As it was, the hat of every tramp came off as he went by.

There was another kind of trespasser that made him more trouble. His properties were always open to the fisherman and the hunter. The swamps on his properties contained thousands of ducks and geese. They were the hunter's paradise. But soon came the "market hunter." He was frequently lawless and destructive. He would break locks and leave gates open, shoot without regard to the presence of cattle, stalk behind old stags, use high powered and forbidden firearms, and his occupation as a market hunter was frequently a blind for his real occupation of cattle rustler.

In order to make ponds for ducks, these men would interfere with the water, dams, levees, opening and closing gates to suit their own purpose, and throw hot shells out of their guns into dry feed. Their depredations became so serious that it looked as if it would be necessary to forbid hunting altogether, but finally a compromise was arrived at, and all of the good hunting grounds were leased to responsible duck clubs, which could be relied upon to obey the law and protect the property from the market hunters. These hunting club privileges were much sought after by Henry Miller's neighbors and the opportunities afforded were greatly appreciated. Finally the legislature came to the rescue by passing a law forbidding the hunting of ducks for the market and thus the "market hunter" passed out of the picture.

The seven plagues with which Henry Miller had to contend were hoboes, floods, droughts, animal diseases, earthquakes, fire and cattle rustlers. He survived them all, but the cattle rustler was the worst. As Henry Miller rode along and saw a lone cow bellowing for her calf, he knew an unbranded calf had been stolen. When he came to a railroad station and found a dozen veal calves being shipped by men who owned no land, he knew his calves had been slaughtered. When he branded his calves in Oregon and turned them out on the range, and a third were missing in the fall roundup, he knew that the whole countryside had been feeding on his stock. When he saw a raw brand on a steer in the form of a window sash, he knew it had been put over his "Double H" brand.

Detectives, vigilant riders, and special prosecutors seemed helpless to stem the tide of thievery. Even if his stock was discovered in the possession of another, some plausible explanation could be found.

Even if a detective caught the man in the act of slaughtering the animal, the detective and not the defendant would be tried, and the jury would acquit.

So long as there was no evidence that the defendant took the stock of any one but Henry Miller, convictions were seldom procured. In fact to take his cattle was not deemed a crime.

To stop this drain on his resources was impossible. He reduced it by owning everything and having few neighbors; by good fences and vigilant fence riders; by coöperation with his neighbors in riding the ranges and exchanging information as to the location of any straying stock; and by careful branding, rounding up, and counting of the stock

Even if he could not convict, constant prosecutions broke and discouraged the rustlers.

The loss was thus reduced to a minimum and considered an expense incident to a cheap method of raising cattle.

XXIII. FLOODS

THE miracle of the rivers of California was a subject of annual recurring solicitude to Henry Miller. From the snow peaks of the Sierra Nevada were numerous streams coming down to the floor of the San Joaquin Valley. There they joined the San Joaquin River, which carried the waters through the valley to the ocean.

After the heat of the summer drew the moisture from the soil and melted snows in the high mountains, these great rivers shrank until they became small streams or well nigh disappeared, and then, as the rainy season came on, the mountains were held in the grip of winter, and the snow and ice were packed in the great crevasses of the mountains.

During the greater part of the winter the mountains held on to the moisture and only small quantities of water flowed in these great rivers. Constant reports were obtained of the fall of the rain and snow and the depth of snow accumulated in the mountains.

Then as the winter gradually passed and the warm weather came on, the mountains began to release the waters stored in the soil and in the snow and ice that filled every gorge, and the streams began to rise and distribute themselves over the vast acreage of Henry Miller. Finally as the spring advanced and the heat scorched relentlessly upon mountains and plains, the great flood of the river would come down, overflowing the banks and flowing over wider and wider areas.

The arrangement of the land to receive the benefit of this water was intricate and ingenious. Land lying so low under natural conditions that it was practically in perpetual inundation was protected by levees so as to receive the flood for shorter periods, and then drained so that the sun could reach the soil and produce grasses. The great acreage of tules and cattails was thus dried out and burned over, and then flooded for a shorter period and crops of rich grasses produced. Higher lands were flooded by levees carrying the water out of the low lands and forcing it over the higher areas. During these great floods, cattle were moved with great care from the low lands to the high lands, and a complete plan was laid out for the control of the water and the movement of the cattle during the annually recurring floods.

But the most careful preparations could not take care of years of greatest floods. One year the reports of the weather bureau continued through the winter to record unheard of quantities of rain and snow. The reports showed mountains of snow. Long continued cold weather held this snow gripped in the arms of the mountains. The rivers were low and the cattle covered the plains.

Then early in March, the report came of a sudden change of temperature in the mountain region. Instead of snow and ice, came prolonged warm rains, and with heavy precipitation of rain came the "breakup." When word of this condition came to Henry Miller he immediately realized what was going to happen. The only hope was from the fact that it would take at least two days for the tremendous amount of water released in the mountains to reach its peak in the floor of the valley, and it was a race of horse flesh against water. All night he rode toward the San Joaquin Valley. When he arrived at the first ranch he called for a change of horses and ordered all men to saddle their horses and follow him, and on he went to the next ranch, and thus on and on through the valley, gathering an army of riders.

The rivers were already rising to near the breaking point. Horses, plows and scrapers were ordered out to protect the levees. Carpenters were put to work strengthening the weirs. Still the water rose and lapped the banks and the levee tops. The branch sloughs were carrying all the water they would hold. Hundreds of horsemen were beating cattle out of the brush and driving them to the higher land. Droves of cattle were made to swim the channels. Many of them sank in the soft ground and were pulled out with ropes and horses. Calves were loaded on to great wagons and carried to safety.

All day and all night the fight went on. The frightened steers, refusing to enter the great torrents which filled the sloughs, had to be driven. Time and again the riders had to swim their horses across the channels, urging the cattle on their way. Time and again the lariats flew till the last steer struggling in the mire was brought to dry land. Time and again the horses, bracing themselves to pull the helpless cows, could not get a foothold on the wet earth and were themselves dragged into the torrent.

Hour after hour the fight went on. The cattle were headed for the hills and were tramping trails for others to follow. The wailing of the cows and calves which were separated added a mournful note to the wind and rain. Temporary bridges were thrown up to help the cattle out. Hundreds of men filled sacks with sand to strengthen the levees and prevent a general inundation. Horse after horse became exhausted, and the rider would pull the saddle and bridle, start him in the right direction, saddle another and go on with the great fight.

During this terrible day and night, messages were being received as to the rise of the river above, and finally word came that it had risen several feet above the highest known high water mark, and then it was clear that it was only a question of time when all banks and levees would be overflowed, and the retreat was sounded.

The men were called in and came driving before them the last of the straggling cattle, and behind them was heard the roar of the river as it went over the levees and filled the country in their wake. By the time the last of them had emerged from the lowlands the entire valley was one mass of water, carrying out levees, tearing up land, floating off fences, barns, chicken houses, and even dwellings. Chickens and turkeys could be seen clinging to pieces of floating lumber, and straggling livestock could be seen struggling vainly against the current.

In this deluge it rained almost continuously for thirty days. "The San Joaquin Valley was an inland sea. Steamboats sent out to relieve flood sufferers left the channels of the river and sailed over inundated ranches, past floating houses and wrecks of barns, through vast flotsam, made up of farm products, the carcasses of horses, cattle and sheep, all floating down the mighty currents of the swollen rivers to the sea." For days the flood went on and did its damage, and at the same time deposited over the land a fertility which guaranteed a most abundant crop.

But Henry Miller had successfully retreated before the enemy and his cattle were safely upon the high lands, ready, when the water should subside, to return and fatten on the grasses which would inevitably follow. The high water marks established on the sycamore trees as a result of this flood became the elevations to which future levees were constructed.

The marvel of nature's storage in the mountains of this vast quantity of water during the winter period, and the release of it during the heat of summer, to moisten and irrigate the land, was studied and still more extensive improvements were made to take advantage of the vagaries of nature. Often Henry Miller would say, "I wish I could have in July, August and September, when the temperature is one hundred and ten degrees, the water that flows into the ocean during the flood."

One day a man called upon him and introduced himself as John F. Eastwood. He was an engineer and had a roll of maps. He told Henry Miller that he had devised a plan for holding the water in the mountains until the dry season. He opened his maps and pointed out the places in the high mountains where reservoirs could be constructed. He indicated little blue lakes which could be converted into great bodies of water. He showed their capacity to hold eight hundred and fifty thousand acre feet of water. He showed that from the highest of these reservoirs there was a fall of five thousand feet. He showed how the water could be led through tunnels and dropped through many power houses back to the river channel. He pointed out the millions of kilowatts of electrical energy that could be produced by this water. He showed that the water would all come back to the river and could be used for irrigation in the dry season. He pointed out the acreage of dry land in the valley upon which it could be used. He said that he was interesting financiers in the project of carrying this power to Los Angeles and Southern California, but he wanted to be sure that the development would not be objected to by Henry Miller.

The great utility of the project immediately appealed to Henry Miller. He visualized the opportunity of regulating the floods and producing water to irrigate his land during the dry season, but he did not intend to permit the Los Angeles financiers to pay the expense of getting the power to Los Angeles by selling the water, which belonged to him, for irrigation. So he said, "Mr. Eastwood, this flood water is the life of my ranches. It makes the hay for my cattle, it is worth millions of dollars to me. But get your people in touch with my lawyers and we will see if we can work something out," and so negotiations were opened.

Attorneys argued and engineers made plans. To the Los Angeles financiers, Henry Miller said, "That flood water is like the blood in my body; I can't live without it."

To his own attorneys and engineers, he said, "The flood water is valuable, but the water during the dry season is more valuable. Times are changing. We cannot let the water always run to the ocean.

We must work with these people. If we could get the stored water for irrigation, we could afford to let them use it for power."

When this suggestion was finally made to the Los Angeles financiers, it was a bitter pill to them. They had figured on selling the water for the irrigation of land and had figured on making a handsome profit, which would go a long way toward paying the expense of the development of the power. They saw handsome profits slipping away, but they were men of vision, and knew the value of this power to the rapidly growing territory of Southern California. Its population was growing by leaps and bounds; factories and manufacturing concerns of all kinds were being established; thousands of acres of arid land where awaiting a cheap power to lift the water from underground sources to make it fertile; electric railroads were needed for quick transportation; and a ship channel was being built from the ocean as a harbor for Los Angeles. They had faith in the future and finally said, "Don't let us stop to discuss further the legal question as to whether we have the right to take this water. Miller always wins in the courts. We will store the water for power, leaving him the stored water for irrigation, after we have used it for power," and so the treaty of peace between the great agriculturalist and the power interests was signed.

The water was to be stored, carried through

watertight conduits, and used for power, but all
of it was to be returned to the streams so it would
be available for irrigation, particularly in those
times of the year when the river was low. Immediately the great project started. A railroad was
built from the valley into the mountains at a cost
of a million dollars, merely for the purpose of
carrying material to build the gigantic structures.
Huge dams of concrete were built to hold back
the waters in the canyons. A tunnel thirteen miles
in length was bored through solid granite, big
enough to accommodate a railroad, and through
this great bore the water was carried from reservoir to reservoir and dropped from power house
to power house, and the power taken off on to
transmission lines over two hundred miles in length,
carrying the "juice" to the sunny south. Two
hundred million dollars were spent on the project
by Henry E. Huntington and his associates and
their successors, Southern California Edison Company and San Joaquin Light and Power Corporation. Wells were drilled everywhere into the underground water, and electrically operated pumps
installed to bring the water to the farms; factories
and manufacturing plants were hooked up with
power; electrically operated street and interurban
railroads were constructed in every direction, and
the building up of a community of millions of
people in the semi-arid region of Southern California

went merrily on. Later the plant was also hooked up with the transmission line to San Francisco.

A few more ditches and levees were constructed to irrigate the lands which were affected by the reduction of the flood, and then in the late summer, when the rivers naturally would be practically dry, Henry Miller had a great stream of living water flowing out of these reservoirs, through the power plants, and down the river channel, from which he diverted it to irrigate thousands of acres of his land.

A new era had arrived. Nature's reservoirs were no longer sufficient to keep pace with the growth of population and the improvement in mechanical arts. He saw it was necessary to do something more than merely take advantage of nature. It was necessary to improve on nature; it was necessary to build; it was necessary to keep pace with the developments of the time; it was necessary that this great power of electricity should be indirectly turned to the irrigation of his land. The man who had grown from natural overflow to brush dams, from brush dams to wooden weirs, and from wooden weirs to concrete, was able to go one step further and hook up his destiny with electric energy.

XXIV. DROUGHTS

CALIFORNIA has every conceivable climate. The mountain region is almost perpetual snow, the northern coast and timber region is supplied by abundant rainfall, the south is dry, arid and desert, and Central California, where Henry Miller held sway, has a light rainfall and its great valleys are semi-arid. In wet years, grass was plentiful and even grain could be grown without irrigation, but in dry years no grain could be grown and feed was scarce.

Henry Miller every year had baffling weather conditions to contend with, but the years of real drought indeed challenged his resourcefulness. The first of these droughts was during the time of the Spanish *rancheros*. Their *ranchos* were located largely in the southern part of the State and the coast counties. They were already suffering from the competition of native cattle grown by Henry Miller and other American cattle men. The demand for their Mexican cattle had fallen off, but their extravagant mode of living continued. Their *ranchos* were incumbered by mortgages. Their cattle were ill-bred and poorly fed. Their *ranchos* were not irrigated. They had no surplus supply of food stored away for such an emergency as droughts.

The winter passed with little rain. The streams dried up early in the spring and the hills were barren of grass. The cattle tramped back and forth over the plains nibbling every bit of grass till the very earth was exposed, and the winds blew the dust over the plains, making existence still harder. Even brush and trees were felled in order that the leaves might be eaten by the stock. Cattle tramped around the few cultivated fields, vineyards and orchards, trying to break in and eat the green leaves. Watering holes failed and deeper holes had to be dug to find water to drink. Pumps were put down and old broken down horses or mules were made to run in a circle all day to pump water for the thirsty animals. In the first drought over one hundred thousand head of cattle perished in the southern coast counties. The result was the almost total extinction of the Spanish *rancheros*. Their mortgages were foreclosed and the Spanish cattle barons passed out of the picture.

In one year of drought, over one million head of cattle perished in the state. Every *cienga* became a veritable Golgotha, or a place of skulls. The bleached bodies of cattle were upon every plain. Everywhere the buzzards might be seen gorging themselves upon the carcasses.

Hay sold as high as one hundred and fifty dollars a ton.

Cattle were driven to the mountains, but per-

ished on the way. They could not be taken to
Nevada or Oregon because conditions there were
almost as bad.

Hundreds of ranchers were ruined and fore-
closures and insolvencies were the order of the day.

This emergency was a supreme trial for Henry
Miller. How did he weather it? How did he turn
it to his advantage? In the first place, the passing
of the Spanish cattle barons left him supreme in
the field, and left their *ranchos* to be sold under
the hammer and to fall under his dominion.
Dozens of *ranchos* with delightful Spanish names
thus became ripe for his rule.

The destruction of the poor bred Mexican cattle
left room for the development of the native American stock which he was breeding. The Durham,
Hereford and Devon were being blended by him
into a perfect type of steer which soon became
synonymous with his name and brand.

He had been growing feed by irrigation. He
had been, like Joseph in Egypt, storing away feed
for just such an emergency. His stock were more
hardy and better able to survive.

He could move his cattle from place to place,
from county to county, or from state to state.

He worked day and night carrying feed to
cattle and carrying cattle to feed.

But even when his cattle could not be saved they
were not entirely lost. All over the plains he had
his vats. The animals were slaughtered on the

plains, skinned and the fats extracted, and the balance made into chicken feed. In this manner he utilized not only his own stock but the stock of his neighbors who had no means of salvaging it. The fat alone netted him thousands of dollars in tallow.

The losses were staggering, but the prices of meat were high in view of the shortage. When all was over, most of his competitors were bankrupt, while his resources enabled him to purchase their ranches for a song and to restock them. Droughts not only did not ruin him, but were turned to his advantage. In five years following the drought of 1888 he made a profit of eight million dollars.

XXV. IRRIGATION
DISTRICTS

FOR the small farmer, irrigation districts are essential; for the large landowner and cattle man they were deemed a menace. They compelled development in advance of their wants and improvements not deemed feasible. They transferred control from the large landowner to the populace. They invaded the liberty of action on which the land barons prospered. They gave Henry Miller more trouble than droughts, floods and pests.

As soon as the great canal had been constructed, the Legislature passed an ambitious law forming the West Side Irrigation District, containing several million acres of land. It was a product of the Granger Movement. Every legislative expedient was used in vain to defend it. The best Henry Miller could do was to have a provision inserted that at the first election the electors should vote on the question of a tax and that if they voted "no," no further proceeding under the act should be taken. This failed, for the people voted "yes." This was followed by a great celebration attended by the Governor of the State, but the celebration was suddenly interrupted by an injunction based on the unconstitutionality of the act and all proceedings under it were enjoined.

The next Legislature passed another act forming a like district. The extent of it may be imagined from the fact that the description of its boundaries alone comprised forty-six pages of the statute. The heart was cut out of the act by an amendment which Henry Miller had inserted excluding the territory under his great canal. This was accomplished by sending a delegation of farmers to the Legislature who showed the wonderful irrigation system they had, and which they did not want to lose. Henry Miller then said, "We'll give the people such good service they will not want any district," and for forty years he succeeded in that endeavor.

But ten years later the matter was again made acute by the passage of a general law permitting local communities to form irrigation districts. Of the first forty districts formed under the act, all but six were failures. This was in marked contrast with the success of districts formed in later years.

Under this act the Madera Irrigation District was formed, including a large amount of land of Henry Miller. While there was good land in the district, the land of Henry Miller was mostly hardpan and hog wallow. The expense of the project was very high. It also threatened to invade his water rights lower down on the river. He and other landowners contested the validity of the act in the courts. The matter reached the Supreme Court of the United States. He and other landowners employed Joseph H. Choate to present the argument before that court. It was argued that "the scheme may in some cases result in an abundant supply of water. In all cases it will result in an abundant supply of bonds, assessments, liens and sales for non-payment. The provision is for the creation of a nondescript quasi or semi-quasi public corporation for the purpose of managing the irrigation of private property. The Board of Directors of this corporation may not and probably will not include a single landholder."

The fundamental contention made was that the mere promotion of the interest of individuals, although it might result incidentally in the advancement of the public welfare, is in its essential character a private and not a public object, and, therefore, could not be made the subject of a tax.

This argument fell before the more advanced view of the court as to the right of the legislature to legislate for the public welfare, and the act was upheld.

In the meantime Henry Miller had been carrying on a campaign of education. Repeated tax levies by the district without any water had disheartened the landowners. The expense of the project was played up. The difficulties of getting the water from the riparian owners were stressed, and then came a series of bad years and at the psychological moment a proposition to dissolve the district was submitted and carried.

Twenty years later the district was again formed. Henry Miller was pictured as a hog, claiming all the waters of the river, and bonds were voted for the project, but again consistent education of the people convinced them that the project was not feasible; so nothing was done. The substantial landowners could always be relied upon to accept the view of Henry Miller. He would say, "There is too much good land to develop, and too much already developed to justify spending money to irrigate poor land. The time is not yet ripe. When more people come to the state expensive irrigation will be all right."

Nevada also had the irrigation district craze. Many of the landowners were opposed to the proposed district, so Henry Miller stayed in the background. The election for the formation of the district was called and the day before the election a "miner" came into Yerrington riding a burro with pots, pans, pick and ore sack dangling at the sides. The entire outfit was dusty and exhausted. The "miner" rolled off the burro and staggered into a saloon. After refreshing himself he confided to the barkeeper that he had made a "strike." A few more glasses and he became confidential and told the location of the gulch. Soon the news got out, and in a few hours the town was emptied of a large part of the voting population, all going to grab a claim. The next day the election was held and the landowners defeated the proposition. When the floating population came back hunting the "miner," he had been paid off and disappeared, and they realized they had been hoaxed.

Oregon also had its irrigation districts. A promoter came to Harney Valley and calmly divided the Valley into five parts and proposed to form five irrigation districts. Into each of these districts a portion of Henry Miller's land was to be placed. A goodly area of "dry" land was added so as to control the districts. The day of hearing before the county court was fixed in the dead of winter, in fact for the day before New Year's. The temperature was sixteen degrees below zero. The roads were almost impassable, but Miller's men managed to reach the place of hearing. The petition had to be signed by a majority of the landowners. It developed that a homesteader had died before patent leaving a wife and eight children, and if they were all counted the petition lacked a majority. It was held that title vested in all of them and they were all landowners and therefore the petition was thrown out.

But the promoter came back with another petition involving other land and this time the matter had to go to the Supreme Court and the petition was annulled because the affidavit of publication of notice was not made by the proper party.

Another petition was defeated because the hearing was before the entire county court instead of the county judge.

Finally to prevent the "dry" lands from forming-ing districts to obtain irrigation at the expense of the "wet" land, the owners of the wet lands themselves formed a district as a backfire. This effectually blocked the promoter, as the landowners who had valuable lands could be relied upon not to take any radical action.

Thus for years Henry Miller kept control of his own lands and water rights as against the growing demands for public ownership.

XXVI. EARTHQUAKE
AND FIRE

TWICE in the early days Henry Miller saw
San Francisco ravaged by fire and the greater
part of it destroyed. His slaughter houses were
wiped out, but the next day he was found in temporary quarters doing business as usual. He went
through the earthquake of 1868 and was at the
time riding horseback; just after he had passed
under a great oak tree, it was thrown to the ground
by the shock.

Notwithstanding the greatest care in plowing
around fields he also had his share of grain fires.
As the grain ripened the heat of the sun was frequently so intense that by merely shining on a
piece of broken glass or bottle the grain would be
ignited. Every ranch was equipped with all possible means of meeting such an emergency.
Wagons were on hand equipped with barrels of
water and stacked with heavy sacks, ready to be
taken at a moment's notice to extinguish any fire
that appeared.

But through it all he never carried any insurance on his agricultural properties. They were so
widely distributed that no conceivable loss from

fire could materially affect his fortune, and the money saved in insurance premiums he deemed quite sufficient to make up any possible losses.

The eighteenth of April, 1906, found Henry Miller still living in the house which he acquired in early days. It was situated on Rincon Hill which had once been the fashionable center of San Francisco. He was now a widower, his wife having died the previous year. His only son Henry Miller, Jr., was a cripple, and his only daughter was keeping her own establishment.

At thirteen minutes after five o'clock in the morning he was awakened by an earthquake shock which time and again gripped his home and seemed to threaten to shake it to pieces. Chandeliers, chimneys, cornices, bric-a-brac and bookcases began to fall in a confused mass in every direction. When the shock was finally over and he managed to get out of bed and reach a window, a strange sight appeared. In every direction chimneys had fallen through the roofs of neighboring buildings. Great cornices had been shaken off of houses. People scantily clad were rushing out of every door. In the distance he could see the dome of the city hall with all of the masonry shaken down and the steel frame standing like a skeleton. Shortly here and there smoke arose, and soon flames could be seen, and in a few moments the sound of the fire apparatus, still drawn by horses, could be heard.

Having dressed he went out on the street, walked down the hill, and started toward the business district. No street cars were running, and here and there a night car still stood deserted on the track. People were upon the streets gesticulating and looking at their ruined homes. He came to Howard Street and saw that a band of cattle had been brought in by boat during the night, and was being driven out Howard Street. Many of them had been killed, and the balance were running wildly around the streets, out of control.

Soon he came to the fire and found the fire apparatus connected with hydrants, but the men standing helplessly by without any water with which to fight the fire.

As he approached the business district, the crowd increased and he heard the sound of cavalry, and soon the soldiers appeared and threw a line around the business district, preventing him from reaching his office.

Two of his office force, David Brown and C. Z. Merritt, were more successful. Immediately upon realizing the great catastrophe that had happened, they rushed for the office and managed to reach it before they were interfered with by the military or the police. They found it in a condition of great confusion. The office contained a steel safe and a concrete vault. They were uncertain as to which was the more secure, but finally decided in favor of the steel safe. They opened both the safe and the vault, and put the more valuable papers in the steel safe, and everything else that could possibly be gathered up they carted down stairs and put in the vault. As they went on with their work, lesser shocks of earthquake continued to disturb them. Glancing out of the windows they could see the flames approaching and covering a wider and wider circle around them, but they continued with their work until every book and paper was safely stowed away. Such was the result of long training and faithful service.

By the time Henry Miller got back to his home the flames were approaching it from every direction. He managed to get a horse and wagon from a neighboring vegetable store; his crippled son was put in and they made their way down to the Third Street Depot, hoping there might be a train to take them to his daughter's home. Trudging alongside of the wagon might have been seen the portly male nurse carrying a heavy valueless piece of bronze statuary which he was very proud of having rescued. By the time he had carried it several blocks he wished he had selected something a little lighter.

The gardener came into the house at the last moment and spied a large canvas picturing the Santa Clara Mission. He immediately crossed himself and tore it from the wall and took it down into the garden where he dug a trench and buried it. After the fire it was found and dug up, and still graces the walls of the family home. These were the only two things saved.

Before they went many blocks they looked back and saw the flames creeping up and over the house which was soon in ashes. Finding no train, they continued on over the Third Street bridge and out to butcher town, where they found a room in an old butcher's hotel. From there for three days they could see the flames again burning the city and could hear the boom of dynamite destroying buildings before the advancing flames.

Then they looked upon the slaughter houses which had been operated ever since the early seventies. They had all been built upon platforms constructed upon piles over the waters of the Bay. During the many years they had been used, the piles had become aged and weakened, and the earthquake had shaken the entire structure as a terrier would shake a rat, and it had collapsed and presented an inextricable mass of timbers. Before the day was over he made arrangements to have his slaughtering done at the only slaughter house which was not destroyed, the modern abattoir built by the Swift interests at South San Francisco. The day after the fire was extinguished he was doing business as usual.

It was days later before the safe and vault could be opened. They had to be sealed with plaster and allowed to cool off gradually. If the air were permitted to enter, everything in the safe would be immediately ignited. They finally cooled off and the steel safe was opened, and it was found that it had become so intensely hot that all of the papers and books had been scorched, but were still legible and usable. When they opened the old concrete vault, they had little hope that they would find anything in it, but they found that it had fared better than the safe and the papers in it were in no way injured or even scorched.

In a few days after the earthquake, he had carpenters back on the site where he had his butcher shop some forty years before. The buildings on this property had also been burned, and on it he hastily constructed a wooden structure which served as office headquarters until the down town buildings were rebuilt.

Then came the question of insurance. Many of the insurance policies contained a provision exempting the insurance companies from liability for loss occasioned directly or indirectly from earthquake. Most of the American insurance companies, however, paid their losses without question, but the German companies refused payment, and Henry Miller's house happened to be insured by a German company. Suits were instituted and the property owners attempted to establish that these fires were not caused by the earthquake, but were brought about by some subsequent carelessness in starting fires. Evidence was found that some man somewhere started to fry some ham and eggs and on account of injuries to the flue, or something of that kind, started a fire. In the subsequent jury trials they attempted to trace every loss to some such fire. It was called the "ham and egg fire." The juries were almost always sympathetic with the landowners, and almost invariably brought verdicts against the insurance company, and such was the outcome with regard to the home of Henry Miller.

The earthquake and fire spelled a new era in the industry, the era of automobiles and auto trucks, modern offices, modern abattoirs, and modern homes. Age and infirmity did not stop him and the process of readjustment to meet this new condition began at once and continued with unabated vigor until he saw his new home in the now fashionable portion of the city, his offices in a modern building, and his abattoir built upon modern principles and supplied with autos and auto trucks.

XXVII. HIS LAST CANAL

HENRY MILLER never saw his last canal. One day near the end of his active business career, he came into his attorney's office with a little sketch and said, "I wants to dig a canal from the San Joaquin River to the Fresno River in Madera County. Mr. Clare has made a survey and can take it out at Gravelly Ford. It is hardpan underneath, but we can probably wash most of the top soil out with the water during the flood, and it won't cost very much." His attorney looked it over and said, "That land, Mr. Miller, is not riparian, and I am afraid some of the riparian owners below will object." "Well, times are changing," said Henry Miller, "and if we don't take this water somebody else will. We'll have to find a way," and with that he said, "Good morning," and withdrew.

It was not long before earth was flying over the line of the canal thirty miles long. His attorney began to find some way to take this water. It was soon found that the canal ran through two sections of land belonging to the Talbots, the same family that had been in the project of building the great canal on the west side. They had always remained as minority stockholders and were thought to be

357

friendly, so negotiations were taken up with them to get a right of way through their land. They temporized and delayed, but in the meantime the work went on until a large part of the canal had been excavated through their land and over a hundred thousand dollars expended.

Then they began to imitate Henry Miller's tactics in connection with the construction of the great canal and tried to obtain most advantageous contracts. They first demanded water for the irrigation of their land, then they offered to exchange their land at the rate of one section of their land for two sections of the Miller land. These demands were considered exorbitant and negotiations continued almost indefinitely.

In the meantime, the Miller interests had got an act through the Legislature declaring irrigation to be a public use and permitting condemnation in aid of it. Some amendments were tacked to the bill which weakened it, but it was still thought that it might be sufficient to justify condemnation in aid of irrigation, although the irrigation was entirely on the land of one individual.

Armed with this act, the negotiations were brought to an abrupt termination and the parties were notified that Henry Miller would pay the value of the right of way and nothing more. Henry Miller's attorneys, being somewhat doubtful about this new act of the Legislature, filed two separate suits, one to condemn the right of way under the act, and the other to enjoin interference with the right of way on the theory that by their delay the Talbots had granted a license to construct the canal and were limited to recovering damages.

Then the fight was on. The Talbot people filed a cross-action, but, not being satisfied with that, they went out on the right of way and put up signs reading:

"Danger! This Land is Mined with Dynamite!"

When the men started to work the next morning with the excavator and sixteen horses, they were confronted with men armed with rifles. They only laughed and went on with the work. But when they came to these signs they were puzzled. That was a kind of warfare they did not understand. They knew that none of Talbot's men would shoot. That would be too near to murder. But if they drove on to the mined ground, would that be suicide? They discussed it for quite a while and finally came to the conclusion that, since they would not be present at the inquest to determine that abstract question, caution was the greater part of valor. So they pulled their horses out and went around the point marked as being mined, and started in again digging the canal at the other end.

This was a contingency the other side had not foreseen, and having no more dynamite (if they ever did actually plant any dynamite), and knowing that it was now useless merely to change the location of the signs, they withdrew from the conflict and allowed the contest to proceed in the courts. There a paradoxical situation arose. Both parties lost and won both of the suits, but Henry Miller got the right of way. That happened in this way:

In the trial court Henry Miller won the condemnation case, it being held that the statute was constitutional, but lost the equity case, it being held that there was no license. In the appellate court, Henry Miller lost the condemnation case, it being held that the act was not applicable, but won the equity case, it being held that there was a license. Consequently, by paying the few dollars that the right of way was worth, he obtained the canal.

The attorney for the Talbots in that case was a tall, thin, sweet faced man named Colonel John Webster Dorsey. He was a product of Nevada. He also represented the purchaser of the Rickey property, and it was due to his good sense and judgment that a settlement between Henry Miller and the Rickey interests had been arrived at in Nevada. He was a lovable soul who was able to fish and hunt at the age of seventy-seven. As I am writing these words, I can see out of my window a mortuary chapel. It is a rare bright day, the longest day in the year, and unusually warm for San Francisco, and in that chapel they have just said the last kind words over the body of that kindly lawyer. Neither the heat of litigation nor the warlike gestures of the parties could serve to remove the kindly smile from his face, nor make the sun to set upon his anger.

XXVIII. RETROSPECT

THE sketches of incidents in the life of Henry Miller contained in this book may enable the reader to appraise correctly his character. After his death, a book entitled "My Life on the Range" was published by John Clay. In it Clay sketches his own experience in the livestock industry throughout the western states, and makes this appraisement of Henry Miller:

"Nothing in my experience that I have seen before or since equalled the matchless energies displayed on these San Joaquin ranches. It was no discovery to find out that the great motive power, the irresistible force in this ranch life and management was Henry Miller, a nervous little German who possessed some fairy's wand, for he transformed whatever he touched into gold. He was selfish, grasping, indomitable, thrifty, with a wondrous brain that schemed and twisted and generally routed his opponent. Yet he was a philosopher, a student of the Bible, because he drew illustrations from the life of Solomon and others. In his business he was decisive and you knew where you were at. In my experience his word was good when given. Aside from his own genius his great asset was in choosing men. He had an army of them and they were splendidly drilled, loyal and intense workers. His magnetism permeated the valley, affecting not only his own ranches but it kept the neighbors keyed up.

"In the above short sketch I have tried to place before my eastern readers (the California people know the story) a great personality who but recently passed away. To know him was an inspiration; to trade with him was an education, and the very atmosphere was electrified by his presence. He had many of the characteristics of the late Nelson Morris, but there was a finer grain in his nature, at least to his employees, who from the Mexican vaquero to the boss of the ranch worshipped him and would fight for his honor, for they considered it their own. The love of your fellow man is the best monument that you can leave behind. This in the balmy days of the eighties when I used to meet Henry Miller and watch his organization was the atmosphere in which we lived. Like the golden apple of the Hesperides, it falls at your feet, but many successful men fail to pick it up."

What was the secret of his success? Undoubtedly unusual mental endowments, tireless industry, attention to details, the conditions of the times in which he lived, and his ability to choose men.

Henry Miller was a general. In middle life he was said to resemble strongly in appearance General U. S. Grant, but he was an old style general who rode at the front of his troops. No mountain was too cold, no plain too hot, no road too dusty, no corral too disagreeable for Henry Miller.

No general ever succeeded without able subordinates, and Henry Miller was no exception to this rule. His activity and attention to details was only an example to his men. His ability to choose men, train men, and make men loyal was his greatest asset.

He always recognized his good fortune in the choice of a wife. She was his ideal of what a wife should be: industrious and interested in her husband's affairs. He never objected to employing a man because he would have to feed the man's wife, if she was industrious, but he had little use for idle women around a ranch house.

His choice of a partner could not have been more happy. As a commander of equal rank, Charles Lux supplemented Henry Miller and supplied some of the characteristics necessary to his success.

Continuing the military analogy, we have already shown possibly too prominently his ability in choosing the adjutants who constituted his legal staff.

His ranch and cattle men generally grew up in his service. Many of them remained with him until they died; others became wealthy and retired, or went into an independent business; others were honored with public office. There is no record of any of his trusted men going wrong.

In Nevada "Hoc" Mason was a tall, dignified man, with fine flowing whiskers. He was honored by his neighbors by being elected to the State Senate.

Overfelt in Oregon was himself a man of individuality and high standing.

In the Kern country, he had S. W. Wible, who staged the fight against Haggin & Tevis, and later James Ogden who became an oil producer and was honored by being elected City Manager of the City of Bakersfield.

His "land department" consisted of one man, first, John H. Bolton; and later, David Brown. These men had a complete record of every piece of land which was entered with the same care as items in a cash account. Instead of having this work done by an army of clerks, he had one man who knew all about the land, and saw to it that the title was clear and the taxes paid.

In the San Joaquin Valley, he had J. W. Schmitz, a man of strict ideas and a driver of men, who later amassed a fortune in farming operations on his own account.

J. Q. Drummond, a tall sycamore, was canal superintendent for twenty-five years, and lived to be ninety.

Charles Warfield was lovable and left to become sheriff of his county. Henry Miller never forgave this desertion.

Stockton was a great talker, and after leaving the employment of Henry Miller, became an independent farmer and never ceased to sing the praises of his employer.

H. G. Tanner had a reputation of getting more hours of labor out of his men than any other superintendent. One evening he employed a man, who ate supper and retired. Hearing the rising bell in the dead of night (about 4 a.m.), he arose and went into the dining room and remarked that it was a fine place to work, and the first place where two suppers were served.

Wade White followed the cattle and generally slept out of doors. One night he was sleeping under a tree when a rattlesnake got on to the bed. Sensing its presence, to which he had become as sensitive as a horse, he threw his blanket over it and stamped it to death. This he said was one advantage of sleeping in his boots. His son "Billy" White followed in his footsteps and later became sheriff of his county.

D. W. Wallis was big and bronzed like an Indian. He loved fine horses and always attracted attention because of the finely groomed horses he drove.

"Red" Safstrom was as fiery as his hair was red.

E. F. Ogle was small in stature but a tireless worker.

D. O. Leonard was almost aristocratic in appearance, with a fine cropped beard. After leaving the employ he made a fortune as a money lender and became a leader in his community.

The abattoir was under the supervision of "Charlie" Reddy, a magnetic personality, held in high regard by all the officials and politicians of the city.

C. M. Barney managed his home ranch and had to keep things straight between Henry Miller personally, the firm, and the estate of his partner. They had offices in the same building, and if

Henry Miller got an idea while Barney was outside, he could write a letter and lay it on Barney's
desk.

Albert Long was a nephew and had charge of
actually buying cattle. In the evening, Henry
Miller would lie on a lounge in the office, exhausted from a hard day's work, surrounded by
his superintendent and others. He would abuse
Albert Long like a pickpocket for some error in
buying or failing to buy cattle, still he would show
his fondness for him by kissing him good night.

The engineers of Henry Miller were rough and
ready men who both planned and constructed his
works. They spent little time with plans and reports. They knew what was needed and went ahead
and did it.

Frank P. McCray was the most conspicuous.
He built Buena Vista Lake Reservoir and the weir
across the San Joaquin River. Frank Clare was
one of his aides. Once Clare was an expert witness in court. Henry Miller's attorney suggested
that he would make a better appearance if he did
not chew gum on the witness stand, so he threw
away the gum, but so strong was the habit that
when he got on the stand he chewed toothpicks
and every one was apprehensive lest he swallow
one and choke to death. Still the trial judge in de-
ciding the case followed his testimony more than
that of any other witness.

John Gilcrest was in charge of a larger territory

than any other one man, having all the holdings in Nevada and Oregon under his general supervision. He was trained as a surveyor and land cruiser. He was tall and slim and stood very straight. He rode in a cart for hundreds of miles, sitting erect without resting on the "lazy-back." Under him were many foremen; Charles Cronin, who started as a boy working for John Devine; J. C. Foley, who later became a successful farmer and was chosen as County Water Superintendent; Lamb who became sheriff of Humboldt County; "Cam" Kilburn, who could testify to everything that happened in the country during half a century; and many others.

It was once necessary to prove appropriations of water made in the early eighties on the Miller ranches. The foremen had scattered through Washington, Oregon, Idaho, Nevada, California and Arizona. They were all found and went voluntarily to Oregon to testify for the company. Every one of them had become a successful business man. Such was the loyalty of the employees of Henry Miller.

His accounts and cash were made under the supervision of C. Z. Merritt. He established a code of honesty that permeated every department.

His purchasing agent was a nervous Irishman named John Dillon. He must have purchased millions of dollars of supplies but no one ever paid him a bonus of any kind.

His head cattle buyer was E. J. Rodolph, who worked for him from the time he was a boy. He was honored by being selected as Secretary of the Cattlemen's Association. He was a great duck hunter and golfer and followed those amusements until he was well over seventy. During the time when market hunters were such a pest, Rodolph's son was a game warden. One day Rodolph was in the valley and saw his son ride off on his horse. Rodolph had a field glass, and as the boy rode across the country, which was quite flat, he followed him with the glass. He saw him overtake a hunter driving a wagon. His son apparently halted the driver and proceeded to look into the wagon for contraband ducks, when the driver drew a pistol and shot, killing him instantly.

These are only a few of the principal men who aided Henry Miller. He outlived most of his contemporaries and we are now drawing near the end of his career.

Toward the end of 1910, Henry Miller paid his last visit to any of his ranches and to his office. For a year he had been confined to his home with a rheumatic condition of his feet. The visit to his ranches was confined to those around Gilroy, which were his favorites and constituted the country home of himself and family, and were readily reached by automobile from San Francisco. For the last time he drove around his herd of fat cattle. For the last time he saw the little plot of cypress trees which marked the resting place of his wife, son and youngest daughter. For the last time he visited Mount Madonna, from which he could see on one side the proud sweep of the Santa Clara Valley and on the other the Pajaro Valley and the Pacific Ocean. For the last time he saw the spot on the top of the mountain where he had directed his mortal remains should lie.

He visited many of his old friends and his car drew up before the modest cottages of many of his pensioners and faithful employees.

He drew his will, in which he remembered every relative he had, the poor of the city of Brackenheim, where he was born, and his old employees and pensioners.

His last visit to his office shortly followed. Certain persons holding high positions in the financial affairs of the city had requested an interview, and he came down town for that purpose. When they called, they reminded him that the Panama Canal was soon to be completed, and that, due to its great importance to the Pacific Coast, the event should be celebrated in a fitting manner in San Francisco, and they proposed an International Exposition.

He had read with interest the progress of the canal, and had compared the method of construction used by General Goethals, with the wealth of the United States behind him, with the means he had been compelled to use in constructing waterways. The canal passed through the same general territory he had traversed when he came to California. The importance of transportation of the crops of California was already deeply impressed on his mind. He knew the yet undeveloped land of the state and the possibilities from cheap transportation of men from Europe and of freight to Europe. He eagerly grasped the suggestion, and before the conference broke up each of the persons had signed an initial subscription of twenty-five thousand dollars toward the Exposition and thus the initial "Magical Million" was raised for the project.

This was followed by a public meeting in the Chamber of Commerce at which millions were subscribed. Then followed the donation by the city of San Francisco of five million dollars, and by the State of California of a like sum. The project was hailed with delight and enthusiasm by the people of the city and state, and an act was introduced in Congress inviting the nations of the world to participate in the Exposition. Then the city of New Orleans put forth the claim that she should be the hostess of the nations of the world on this occasion.

A spirited contest between the East and the West followed. The powerful interests of the Middle West from New Orleans to the Great Lakes supported New Orleans. The railroads in that section were vitally interested in the cause of New

Orleans, and she, being so much nearer the center of population, was able to make a strong argument in her favor and to obtain the support of many influential politicians. Each city maintained powerful lobbies in Washington and indulged in every legitimate method of winning the necessary Congressional support.

When New Orleans seemed to have the case all but won, President Taft gave utterance to that now famous remark, "San Francisco knows how," and came out strongly for the city by the Golden Gate. His influence gave a political touch to the situation,—the North against the South, a Republican stronghold against a Democratic City,—and the politicians began to ask what votes they might expect to get from Louisiana in a National Election. When the votes were counted, California won the day (and at the next election went Democratic).

Then followed the selection of the site and the construction of the Exposition buildings. The Government extended invitations to the nations of the world to participate, and the Exposition sent representatives to foreign countries to make arrangements for such participation. The invitation was not accepted with the alacrity which was expected; the cause was not understood; for a time the public was kept in the dark as to the situation, and preparations for the International Exposition continued without abatement. But finally the harsh truth was recognized. Europe failed to participate. France alone of the large countries, after long delay, did have an exhibit.

Still the cause was unknown until the events immediately preceding the World War led to the conclusion that the great powers foresaw that conflict and were preparing for it, and so this great event, which should have more closely bound the nations of the world, was celebrated during a carnival of blood.

Notwithstanding this calamity, the Exposition continued and was a complete success, financially and otherwise.

When the War began every one recognized that the admonition of President Wilson to *think* in terms of neutrality was futile. The over-running of Belgium aroused a general feeling of opposition to the German cause. The fine response of England and her determination to enter the War aroused the admiration of many Americans, and the feeling existed in no small part of the country that the United States should follow suit.

Henry Miller sympathized with the German people, but not with the cause of the German rulers. His grandson, J. Leroy Nickel, Jr., was in Yale, and carried away by the enthusiasm of his surroundings, flashed the word home that he was going to volunteer as a private in the French Army. This he did, driving a truck with ammunition to the front, and he continued in active service in the

French Army until the American Expeditionary Forces arrived in France, and then continued with the American Forces until the end of the War.

When America finally entered the conflict, his other grandson, George W. Nickel, and his grandson-in-law, George M. Bowles, entered the officers' training camp. His daughter engaged in war work, and his corporation, now in the control of his son-in-law, J. Leroy Nickel, devoted its funds liberally to the prosecution of the war. In other words, Henry Miller and his family had become in thought and in action one hundred per cent American.

Henry Miller did not live to see the triumph of the American arms, the overthrow of the German military rule from which he had fled, and the establishment of the German Republic.

As the great Exposition drew to a close and the "lights went out," he sat in his wheel chair, still neatly dressed, a robe tightly wrapped about his limbs, facing the window to the west and toward the setting sun. As he dozed, he saw spread before him the million acres of land he had acquired through the states of California, Nevada and Oregon. He saw the hot plains, the green fields, and the thousands of miles of canals he had constructed. He saw the colonies and towns that had sprung up on the lands he had brought from aridity into production. He saw the cattle barons he had supplanted, the floods he had conquered, the droughts he had survived.

He saw the banks, stores and lumber yards, scattered throughout his territory. He saw the oil derricks on his lands, and the pipe lines carrying oil to his city. He saw the great levees, dams and reservoirs which he had constructed to hold and control the forces of nature. He saw the alfalfa, rice, and cotton which he had introduced on a large scale into the industries of his state. He saw his million head of livestock, the breeds of which he had developed and improved. But he saw no son to perpetuate his name and work.

Finally he again saw the mighty herd of cattle slowly moving across the plains, and he smiled as he saw the fat on their sides, their white faces, the favorite color of their hides, and the "Double H" brand neatly placed on the left hip. He saw them gradually vanish over the distant horizon, and saw them swallowed in the rays of the setting sun. And on that fourteenth day of October, nineteen hundred and sixteen, his soul, too, passed to the great beyond.